ACADEMIC LIBRARY
MANAGEMENT
ISSUES AND PRACTICES

MOHAMMED M. AMAN

Global Information Co., Inc.

Mequon, Wisconsin, USA

Published and distributed by Global Information Company, Inc.
10936 N. Port Washington Road # 107, Mequon, WI 53092-5031 USA
globalinformationco@gmail.com

Library of Congress Catalog Card Number: 1450718671

First published in 2010 by Global Information Co., Inc.

Printed and bound in the United States of America.

The paper used in this book complies with the minimum requirements of the American National Standard for Information Sciences-Permanence of Paper for Printed Library Materials, ANSI Z39.48-1992.

Library of Congress Cataloging in Publication Data

Aman, Mohammed M., 1940-
    Academic library management : issues and practices / Mohammed M. Aman.
    xiv, 225 p. ; 26 cm.
    Includes bibliographical references and index.
    ISBN:9781450-718677 (alk. paper)
    1.   Academic libraries—United States. 2. Libraries and Colleges-United States.
I. Title.
    Z675.U5 A443x 2012
    027.70973-dc23   1450718671

To all academic and research
librarians whose work and services
shape the new generations of scholars
and researchers world-wide.

TABLE OF CONTENTS

INTRODUCTION

This book is partially based on the contents of the course on Academic Library Management which I have been teaching at the University of Wisconsin-Milwaukee. The contents are designed to be used in connection with additional readings to be selected from the extensive lists of references at the end of each chapter as well as from other databases available to students in university and public libraries and library systems. Examples of best practices found in some academic libraries are mentioned in order to blend theory with practice.

Placing the academic library in the context of the higher education, its evolution, and the changes that impacted American college campuses is the subject of the first chapter. American higher education has gone through many changes and phases from its early days in 1638, when nine colleges were established and patterned after the English model, in particular Oxford and Cambridge. Most of the colonial colleges were either private or church-related and higher education was for the sons of the affluent upper class. The primary objective of these colleges was teaching, not research. Their graduates became members of the clergy, or the civil service, or joined the family's business. The subjects taught were limited to religion, literature, philosophy, Greek and Latin and the classic texts.

The early academic libraries built small collections that emphasized the same subjects being taught. Managing the early college library was simple, with one person—mostly the college president who was also the college librarian, and a teaching faculty. As college education extended beyond the colonies and grew with the young nation, publicly funded institutions began to emerge. The Morrill Act of 1862, the Hatch Act of 1887, and the legislations that followed provided income from public lands for the establishment of land-grant institutions; the number of institutions grew faster and further. Two world wars contributed to the influx of young GIs to colleges; college education was no longer limited to members of the upper class. College education however was not as accessible to women and non-white minorities.

With the turn of the century, higher education opened the gates to the poor, as well as the middle class. The composition of the college student body changed, as did the diversity of the student body. More minorities, females and older students were registered on college campuses, with the numbers expected to grow as the American demographics change. Higher education emphasized research in addition to teaching and extending its resources and know-how to the rural and urban societies they serve. Academic library collections began to reflect these changes, with their collections growing faster with the additional funding that came in the years of the Great Society and the great expansion of higher education in the late 60s and early 70s. More libraries were built and more graduates of library schools were hired to handle that historic expansion.

In addition to acquiring books, journals, and non-book materials from a growing publishing industry, academic libraries had to look for and acquire foreign materials that faculty and students demanded. Librarians developed collection development policies to accommodate new technologies as well as to ensure balanced collections and be able to resist efforts of censorship or bias and defend academic and intellectual freedom.

While the financial health of the academic libraries has grown stronger, they have not been able to build what some believed to be comprehensive collections. Academic library budgets, even in the best of times, did not keep up with the inflationary prices of books and journals and the emerging technology that produced databases and e-books and various media. Cooperation and consortia emerged as libraries tried to supplement their collections with resources available at other libraries and institutions that could be made available through inter-library loan and facsimile transmission. Consortia also helped with negotiating book and journal subscription prices with publishers and distributors. The complexity of academic library services and resources and the poor preparation of incoming freshman as to how to use these resources effectively have resulted in the introduction of formal and informal bibliographic instruction, with academic librarians added a teaching responsibility to their growing list of professional tasks.

The recent decline of the financial support for academic libraries has left many libraries understaffed, as retired librarians are not being replaced and some libraries are under budget and hiring freezes. The budget crunch has forced many academic librarians to join the ranks of their fellow academic deans and directors in seeking extramural funding and applying for gifts and grants to supplement their current budgets. Such outside funds have been used to buy materials, endow library collections or positions, build additions, and renovate old buildings into facilities such as information commons. These information commons which emulate the popular coffee shops in large book store chains have contributed to a less policing atmosphere in academic libraries. They have also contributed to the expansion of technology in terms of more computers and the addition of wireless access, throughout the library buildings and beyond and more comfortable and ergonomically designed seating furniture.

A new phenomenon that has impacted academic libraries is the widespread use of the Internet, not just for accessing information online, but also the extent to which Web centric distance education is being used on American campuses. Academic librarians have inserted themselves into the development of distance education programs as early as 1995. The papers by Mr. William Kopycki and Dr. Betsy J. Schoeler are good examples of the development and growth of a Web centric academic program that was a pioneer on the campuses of the University of Wisconsin System and throughout the United States. The impact of social networking will certainly bring libraries to the forefront as they attempt to be present on such social networks as Face Book, You Tube, Twitter, and the like.

Today's academic librarians have recognized the vital importance of marketing and outreach in support of their parent institution's stated vision and mission. Activities and events such as exhibits, displays, public lectures, and promotional materials are commonly and regularly used in order to attract traffic to the campus library. Displays often include aspects of collections that the library is able to highlight through public events. Many academic libraries have recently opened coffee kiosks that serve a variety of coffee and drinks and selected pastries, as well as access to cable television, wireless access, newspapers and light reading materials nearby. This has resulted in making the library part of the social networking on campus where old fashioned policing is no longer in effect, at least in these areas and similar library commons. Also with coffee and other amenities, libraries have added more comfortable tables and chairs in a more informal and pleasing section of the library.

Evaluation of library services, programs and products is not new. There has been the old fashioned way of asking clients or library users about how they found the library service and were there satisfied. Former Mayor of New York City Ed Koch, made it a practice as he walked the streets of his city to stop and ask citizens "How am I doing" in an effort to learn how they viewed the performance of his administration and the delivery of services. Asking and listening are always useful exercises and the results can help in taking actions to improve services, products and programs. A reference librarian should ask if the user has found the information sources handed to him/her helpful. The library staff member who is checking books at the circulation desk should ask the patron if he/she found what he/she was looking for. These and other queries are similar to what Mayor Koch used to ask his New York constituencies. Assessment, accountability, and outcome measures are familiar to the teaching faculty and academic administrators, and they are now part of the academic librarians' vocabulary and practices. New tools have been used to examine academic library services and collections as part of regional and national accreditation and to determine the level of user satisfactions/expectations and to compare the results with peer institutions. Evaluation instruments such as SERVQUAL and LIBQUAL+ were introduced and the latter is now used by many academic libraries to determine the levels of user satisfaction.

These and many other issues and practices are some of the timely subjects treated in this book's thirteen chapters. It is my sincere hope that the information and discussions contained in this book will help prepare the future generations of academic librarians in the United States and abroad. They are the information intermediaries and teachers who are integral part of the instructional and research team of their campuses.

There are many individuals to thank for producing this book. First and foremost, I wish to express my sincere thanks to my wife Mary Jo Aman, who provides the moral and valuable literary support through her keen editorial skills and loving criticism, not only for this book, but throughout our married life of close to four decades. My thanks also to my fellow academic librarians and especially those cited or mentioned in this book. Special thanks to Mr. William Kopycki and Dr. Betsy J. Schoeler for their contributions on the evolution and development of the highly successful distance education program in the School of Information Studies at UWM, from its early inception to the present. Special thanks to my doctoral student and Research Assistant Mr. Ismail Osman for his valuable assistance with the production of the manuscript and the preparation of its index. Any deficiencies found in the book are my own.

1

ACADEMIC LIBRARIES IN HIGHER EDUCATION

Charles Haskins pointed out "universities, like cathedrals and parliaments are a product of the Middle Ages," In the United States, the history of higher education can be traced back to 1638 when nine colleges were established and patterned after the English model in particular Oxford and Cambridge. Their small library collections emphasized certain subjects such as religion, classics, texts in Latin and Greek. Like their parent institutions, the primary objective was teaching, not research. In the small colleges, it was not unusual for the college president to be the librarian. Nineteen colleges were established between 1782 and 1802. During the first half of the 19th century the educational mission of the colonial colleges was transplanted westward. New colleges were established in territories as they gained independence and citizens lobbied their legislatures to support state colleges. The libraries of the literary societies were literary in nature and filled a void left by the weak collections of college libraries.

By late 1850, there were 217 colleges in the United States. However, hard times in the 1830s and 1840s contributed to the demise of fifty colleges that went bankrupt. Before the Civil War, most of the growth in higher education was in private colleges, as expansion in state colleges was hindered by national and state politics and economics.

The Morrill Act of 1862 (named after a congressman from Vermont named Justin Smith Morrill) was originally passed to establish institutions in each state that would educate people in agriculture, home economics, mechanical arts, and other professions that were practical at the time. The Hatch Act of 1887 followed, with additional federal grants and funds for each state establishing agricultural experiment stations in association with the land-grant college. The Land Grant System was revolutionary at the time. It opened college classrooms and made college degrees accessible to the working classes. Its agenda of scholarship did not exclude any topic. It provided access to knowledge to those who would never qualify, nor want to be in its classrooms. Other legislation that followed provided income from public lands for the establishment of land-grant institutions and the number of these institutions grew faster and further. The second Morrill Act expanded the system of grants to include previously excluded black institutions. These and other acts were successful in integrating research and extension

As the subjects taught in colleges expanded, the idea of introducing elective courses was advanced at Harvard College by then President Charles William Elliot; this idea gained momentum elsewhere. By the turn of the century, electives were in place at most major institutions. The old recitation methods of instruction were replaced by lectures and the German-imported seminars. When Johns Hopkins University opened in 1876 as a graduate school for advanced study, the German style of graduate education was adopted. Also imported from Germany was the idea of lehrfreiheit which stands for academic freedom, or the right of the professor to freedom of inquiry and teaching.

When World War II broke out, students as well as faculty left their campuses to serve the war efforts, and libraries began to function as information centers and as depositories of scholarly materials. The demand for technical literature to support the war effort overcame the traditional college libraries' emphasis on humanities and social sciences in their collections. After the war, American colleges and universities benefitted from the large numbers of young soldiers who began to pursue their education with funding from the newly introduced GI Bill. In addition to the GI Bill recipients, and following the end of WWII in 1945, a greater percentage of high school graduates were pursuing a college education. It is interesting to note that the University of Wisconsin's Memorial Library built in 1953 was so named to honor those who served in the armed forces.

In its report of 1947, the President's Commission of Higher Education stated that one half of the youth in the U.S. had the ability to pursue a college education. The report also pointed out that the major burden of equalizing educational opportunity would fall on publicly supported institutions, and that such expanded opportunities would have to be provided in the communities in which people lived. With the conclusion of WWII, the former GIs returned to America's college campuses in large numbers, and enrollment soared from 1,676,851 in 1945-46 to 2,616,262 the following academic year—1947-48. The American college education system brought college education to where people lived and worked, unlike Europe where colleges were built in the capitals like Paris, Berlin or other large urban centers. The urban university is a newcomer to the American scene, unlike the European pattern, where the university tradition has been strikingly urban (Klotsche, 1972). Residential campuses were the norm until commuting to campus became the norm, and students combined education with full or part-time work, and even family responsibilities on top of that.

From the end of WWII to the end of the 1990s, higher education went through what can be described as three distinct phases:

- Phase I (end of WWII to the 1960s): can be described as a period of unrestricted growth and "massification" of higher education;
- Phase II (1960s–1970s): the period of critical self-examination as the public disfavored the prevailing political turmoil on campuses; and
- Phase III (1970s-1990s): the period of critical examination of all aspects of higher education by outsiders. Public agencies, both federal and state, devoted increasing attention to the issues of higher education;

One can add a Phase IV to describe the spread of information and communication technology on American campuses; the changing population of students from the traditional young high school graduates to the influx of the adult "non-traditional" learners who are pursuing part-time education, holding full or part-time jobs and even raising families.

The 'massification' of higher education had a significant impact in the early part of the past century, when higher education was no longer restricted to the rich and the upper class. Of great significance was the open door admission policy of some city and state universities in the mid and late sixties in New York and California, followed by others, and the noticeable spread of community colleges around the country. This new concept of college education emerged in the late 50s and early 60s, with the introduction of the concept of junior colleges, whose education mission included remedial education and training students in technical subjects in only two years, with the possibility of continuing their education beyond the two years at four-year institutions. The past few decades have seen tremendous growth in college enrollment numbers. Indeed, college enrollment in the United States has risen from only 25% of the population in 1967 to almost 40% in 2006 (U.S. Census Bureau, 2009). With more students on campus comes more diversity. As more and more students are seeking out post-secondary education, colleges have needed to evolve to accommodate this demand for a wider, more diverse student population and more diversified faculty and academic staff on campus. Today, higher education offers a variety of choices, from the very elite Harvard's of this world to the people's colleges. Enrollment and employment soared, and in 2008, the National Center for Education Statistics reported about 74.1 million people were enrolled in American schools and colleges.

During the era of the Cold War, the rivalry between east and west, particularly the U.S. versus the then Soviet Union, created a demand for more science and engineering research and manpower, and colleges found themselves in the center of the race to develop new war, peace and space technologies. Commitment to research became an integral part of higher education. As a consequence, currency of information became the key principle in the acquisition of library materials. Support for liberal arts and the traditional subjects taught earlier in classrooms and acquired in library collections began to decline.

The present diversity and complexity of higher education in the U.S. is reflected in the recent Carnegie Classification of Institutions of Higher Learning, (CC) published by the Carnegie Foundation for the Advancement of Teaching. Today's higher education institutions are classified in one of the following types: secular state; secular private (independent); religious, or religion affiliates. Within these types, they are further classified into: a) Doctoral granting institutions; b) Master's colleges and universities; c) Baccalaureate colleges; d) Associate colleges; e) Special focus institutions; and f) Tribal colleges. There are 26 unclassified institutions. The CF classification of institutions of higher education comes primarily from the Integrated

Postsecondary Education Data System (IPEDS) and the College Board. Further classification can be found under each classification as follows:

Doctoral granting universities: Those institutions that grant at least 20 doctorates.

- Research Universities (RU/VH) Very high research activity
- Research Universities (RU/H) High research activity
- Doctoral/Research Universities (DRU)

Master's Colleges and Universities: Those institutions which "awarded at least 50 master's degrees in 2003-04, but fewer than 20 doctorates."

- Master's Colleges and Universities (Master's/L) (larger programs)
- Master's Colleges and Universities (Master's/M) (medium programs)
- Master's Colleges and Universities (Master's/S) (smaller programs)

Baccalaureate Colleges: Those institutions at which "bachelor's degrees accounted for at least 10 percent of all undergraduate degrees and they awarded fewer than 50 master's degrees (2003-04 degree conferrals). They are further classified into:

- Baccalaureate Colleges---Arts & Sciences (Bac/ A&S)
- Baccalaureate Colleges—Diverse Fields (Bac/Diverse)
- Baccalaureate/Associate's Colleges (Bac/Assoc)

Associates Colleges: Associates colleges are defined as institutions whose "highest degree conferred was the associate's degree, or if Bachelor's degrees accounted for less than 10 % of all undergraduate degrees (2003-04 degree conferrals)." They are classified further according to their size (small, medium, or large); and their location (urban, rural); single or multi-campus; public or for profit, etc.

Special Focus Institutions are those classified "based on the concentration of degrees in a single field or set of related fields, at both the undergraduate and graduate levels. Institutions were determined to have a special focus, with concentrations of at least 80 % of undergraduate and graduate degrees. In some cases this percentage criterion was relaxed if an institution identified a special focus on the College Board's Annual Survey of Colleges, or if an institution's only accreditation was from a body related to the special focus categories." Examples of these special focus institutions include:

- Theological seminaries, Bible colleges, and other faith-related institutions (Spec/Faith)
- Medical schools and medical centers (Spec/Medical)
- Other health profession schools (Spec/Health)
- Schools of engineering (Spec/Engg)
- Other technology-related schools (Spec/Tech)
- Schools of business and management (Spec/Bus)
- Schools of art, music, and design (Spec/Arts)
- Schools of law (Spec/Law)
- Other special-focus institutions (Spec/Oth)

Tribal Colleges and universities is another category for the 32 colleges and universities that are members of the American Indian Higher Education Consortium.

The last category in the CE classification is the "unclassified" which refers to 26 such institutions. Today's incoming college students' profiles are different from the traditional profiles of yesteryear, that being white and under the age of 18. Today's college students are diverse in race, gender, sexual orientation, physical fitness, and so on. They are of different economic, ethnic, cultural, national and religious backgrounds, much older, stay in school longer, have full or part time jobs.

It is expected that these and other trends such as globalization, immigration, and rising social economic inequality, as well as the need to educate for an information-driven society will shape the future focus in higher education. Continued emphasis on academic partnerships with business, research, rising costs of higher education and the continued expansion of distance learning will continue to accelerate and dominate nationally and internationally. In his book *Universities and the Future of America,* Derek Bok (1990), former president of Harvard University identified the contributions universities can make to greater competencies, to search for a better society, and to moral education. He suggested ways and means wherever universities can organize themselves to engage the world and not to "succumb to its blandishments, its distractions, its corrupting entanglements …diminishing the more profound obligations that every institution of learning owes to civilization to renew its culture, interpret its past, and expand our understanding of the human condition" (pp. 103-04).

The term "engaged university' resulted from the deliberations of the Kellogg Commission, which in 1999 published a report titled *Returning to Our Roots: The Engaged Institution*, which is credited for starting the discussion on university engagement. Engagement means exposing students and their faculty to the society that houses their university. This goes beyond the traditional outreach activities of universities and is a far cry from what Harvard's Bok was expressing in 1990. Stephen R. Graubard (1997) traces the origin of the service interest of the American academy with the Morrill Act of 1862 which established the Land Grant colleges of agriculture. He captured the essence of the engaged university when he wrote:

> Without wishing to deny the importance of the influence of the German and British universities, the uniqueness, the uniqueness of the American system needs to be emphasized, and not only because of the Morrill Act and the innovations introduced by the land-grant principle, with its emphasis on research and agriculture and many other fields as well. The concept of "service" took on a wholly new meaning in state universities that pledged to assist their citizens in ways that had never previously been considered. (Gaubard, 1997, p. v)

Urbanization and globalization are factors that will continue to affect higher education in the twentieth century. Dr. Martin Klotsche, former chancellor of the University of Wisconsin-Milwaukee and a leading voice in the urbanization of higher education wrote a book on the subject and the changes that befell universities starting in the 1960s.

The mission of an urban university is to create new knowledge and educational models to address one of the nation's most significant and enduring questions: *how* do we produce reliably excellent schooling for children growing up in urban America? The global reaches of American universities are equally significant, with many campuses competing for international students for good causes such as diversifying their student populations, but also out of greed, especially in attracting students from oil-rich countries. Many American universities have established branch campuses in the Middle East. Examples are: Carnegie-Mellon University, Johns Hopkins Medical School, Commonwealth of Virginia, and others in Qatar and in the United Arab Emirates. This is a new phenomena capitalizing on the old and well-established American universities in Cairo and Beirut. These are not to be confused with newly established American universities in Kuwait, Sharjah and similarly named others that have nominal but not strong or formal affiliation with major American universities in the U.S. In either situation, and with the emerging new private colleges and universities in many countries overseas, there is a strong belief in, and recognition of the value of quality assurance, assessment and even international accreditation of institutions and programs of higher education. This is one of the reasons why the above-mentioned examples of American or American-affiliated campuses overseas require their academic library staff to have the ALA accredited master's degree in library and information studies. Many of the public and private universities overseas are, now more than ever pursuing accreditation of their academic programs and specific disciplines or professional programs from American accrediting agencies such as AACSB and IACBE (for business education); ABET (for engineering programs); NCATE (for education programs); LCME (for medical schools); ADA (for dental schools); and the list goes on. Regional accrediting agencies such as Middle States Association of Colleges and Schools; North Central Association of Colleges and Secondary Schools; and others are responsible for accrediting schools and colleges within their respective regions as well as schools for American children overseas and children of other English-speaking countries. Some of the regional accreditation agencies have also taken interest in extending their accreditation to cover colleges and universities overseas. Examples are the Instituto Tecnologico y de Estudios Superiores de Monterrey (ITESM) in Mexico, and the American University in Dubai; both are accredited by the Southern Association of Colleges and Schools (SACS). These developments could have a positive effect on the quality of higher education in these developing countries as they strive to reform their systems of higher education and to keep abreast of the pedagogical and technological developments of the 21st century.

REFERENCES

Bok, D. 1990. *Universities and the Future of America*. Durham, NC: Duke University Press.

Bowker, A. H. 1972. *Higher Education in the Seventies: the Challenge of Growth*. New York: Newcomen Society in North America.

Cangemi, J. P. 1982. *Higher Education in the United States and Latin America*. New York: Philosophical Library.

Chambers, M. M. 1950. *Universities of the World outside U.S.A.* Washington, DC: American Council on Education.

Cunningham, J. 1980. *Sources of Finance for Higher Education in America*. Washington, D.C.: University Press of America.

"Education in the United States." http://en.wikipedia.org/wiki/Education_in_the_United_States. (accessed Dec 6, 2009).

Eschbach, E. S. 1993. *The Higher Education of Women in England and America: 1865-1920*. New York: Garland.

"From battlefield to GI Bill," *New York Times*, Jan. 9, 2010 available at: http://www.nytimes.com/2010/01/09/nyregion/09gis.html?th&emc=th (accessed Jan 9, 2010)

Gitlow, A. L. 1995. *Reflections on Higher Education: a Dean's View*. Lanham, MD: University Press of America.

Gruber, C. S. 1975. *Mars and Minerva: World War I and the Uses of the Higher Learning in America*. Baton Rouge: Louisiana State University Press.

Haskins, C. H. 1923. *The Rise of Universities*. New York: Henry Holt.

Henderson, A. D. 1974. *Higher Education in America: Problems, Priorities and Prospects*. San Francisco: Jossey-Bass.

Hofstadter, R. 1952. *The Development and Scope of Higher Education in the United States*. New York: Columbia University Press, for the Commission on Financing Higher Education.

Hutchins, R. M. 1978. The Higher Learning in America. New York: AMS Press.

Jackson, E. M. 1986. *Black Education in Contemporary America: a Crisis in Ambiguity*. Bristol, IN: Wyndham Hall Press.

Jacoby, R. 1994. *Dogmatic Wisdom: How the Culture Wars Divert Education and Distract America*. New York: Doubleday.

Jeynes,W. 2007. *American Educational History: School, Society, and the Common Good*. Thousand Oaks, CA: SAGE Publications.

Klotsche, J. M. 1972. *The University of Wisconsin-Milwaukee: an Urban University*. Milwaukee: University of Wisconsin-Milwaukee.

Leslie, S. W. 1993. *The Cold War and American Science: the Military-Industrial-Academic Complex at MIT and Stanford*. New York: Columbia University Press.

Locke, R. R. 1989. *Management and Higher Education since 1940: the Influence of America and Japan on West Germany, Great Britain, and France*. Cambridge; New York: Cambridge University Press.

Lowell, A. L. 1970. *At War with Academic Traditions in America*. Westport, CT: Greenwood Press.

Lucas, C. J., 1996. *Crisis in the Academy: Rethinking Higher Education in America*. New York: St. Martin's Press.

Miller, B. W. (1984). *Higher Education and the Community College*. 2nd ed. Lanham, [MD]: University Press of America.

Neusner, J. & Neusner, N. M.M. 1995. *The Price of Excellence: Universities in Conflict during the Cold War Era*. New York: Continuum.

Osburn, C. B. 1979. *Academic Research and Library Resources: Changing Patterns in America*. Westport, CT: Greenwood Press.

Richards, T. F. 1999. *The Cold War within American Higher Education: Rutgers University as a Case Study*. Raleigh, NC: Pentland Press.

Roebuck, J. B. and Komanduri S. M. 1993. *Historically Black Colleges and Universities: Their Place in American Higher Education*. Westport, CT: Praeger.

Schmidt, C. 1998. *History of Universities*. Oxford: Oxford University Press.

Schuman, D. 1982. *Policy Analysis, Education, and Everyday Life: an Empirical Reevaluation of Higher Education in America*. Lexington, MA: D.C. Heath.

Taylor, J. M. 1972. *Before Vassar Opened: a Contribution to the History of the Higher Education of Women in America*. Freeport, NY: Books for Libraries Press.

The Carnegie Classification of Institutions of Higher Education. 2001. Menlo Park, CA: Carnegie Foundation for the Advancement of Teaching.

The Wide Variations in the Black-White Higher Education Gap in America's Largest Cities. *The Journal of Blacks in Higher Education*, No. 40 (Summer, 2003).

Turnaround: Leading Stressed Colleges and Universities to Excellence. 2009. By: James Martin, James E. Samels & Associates. Baltimore: Johns Hopkins University Press.

Veblen, T. 1957. *The Higher Learning in America; a Memorandum on the Conduct of Universities by Business Men*. NY: Sagamore Press.

Wallenfeldt, E. C. 1986. *Roots of Special Interests in American Higher Education: a Social Psychological Historical Perspective*. Lanham, MD: University Press of America.

Zimmer, A. B. 1938. *Changing Concepts of Higher Education in America since 1700*. Washington, D.C.: The Catholic University of America.

2

GOVERNANCE OF HIGHER EDUCATION

Structures of colleges and universities in the U.S., as well as other countries vary from the single campus, like Carleton College, in Northfield, Minnesota, to a multi-campus—such as Long Island University, with campuses in Brooklyn, Manhattan, Long Island, and South Hampton—to a state-wide system, such as the University of Wisconsin System, with 13 four-year university campuses, 13 freshman-sophomore UW college campuses and a state-wide Extension.

Regardless of their type or size, American institutions of higher education and their counterparts overseas are governed by governing boards that have the same concept, but with different names, such as a board of trustees, or a board of regents, or a board of supervisors, who are responsible for the overall management of the institution, the appointment of the president or chancellor of the institution, and other major decisions. The essential function of the board is policy making and responsibility for sound management. The board formulates and determines the general, educational and financial policies for the administration and development of its college or university in accordance with its stated purposes, existing laws and bylaws. Normally, the board will exercise the following:

- Determine and review aims and purposes of the educational program of the college/university;
- Authorize the establishment and discontinuance of programs and departments;
- Elect a president and chief executive officer, who shall be the chief administrative officer of the college, and remove the president from office, with or without cause; and appoint such other persons as the president recommends as officers of the college, and remove them , with or without cause;
- Evaluate periodically the effective implementation of duties of all college officers, taking appropriate action;

- Approve appointment, promotion and dismissal of faculty members upon recommendation of the president;
- Set terms and conditions of employment, salary policies and schedules for faculty members, administrative officers and staff, and all other employees of the college;
- Authorize the awarding of all earned degrees upon the recommendation of the faculty, and the awarding of all honorary degrees upon the recommendation of the president;
- Determine or approve policies that relate to the instruction, extracurricular activities, campus and residential life of students;
- Oversee the fiscal affairs of the college, including approval of budgets, supervision of investments and fixing of tuition and fees;
- Authorize the acquisition and disposition of all property and physical facilities, including the construction of new buildings. Where circumstances warrant, this power may be delegated by the full board to a board committee; and
- Approve plans for and obtain necessary funds from all possible sources for academic and physical development and maintenance purposes.

Many of the responsibilities for running the daily affairs of the college/university are normally delegated to the president and his/her deputies. Faculty maintain control over the curriculum, teaching loads and responsibilities, faculty promotion and tenure. Regardless of the classification of the institution, independent/private, or public, the internal management of the institution normally consists of a president or the equivalent CEO title such as chancellor; their deputies (vice president or vice chancellor or provost; assistant presidents and associate and assistant vice chancellors or presidents; academic deans; non instructional deans and heads of units; academic department chairs and program directors who supervise their faculty and academic staff and librarians.

Internal governance of the institution consists of faculty; instructional faculty; academic staff, clerical, professionals, technicians, custodians and an unlimited supply of student employees. Most institutions pride themselves on adopting the concept of shared governance and its style of management which is different from what is practiced in a corporate structure.

In American universities, faculty play a major role in the selection of their college presidents, and all other major administrative appointments on their campuses. They also evaluate holders of these positions every five years, on average and can vote a "no-confidence" in their college president or dean at their senate meetings, if and when the situation warrants such a drastic measure.

Such a vote will definitely receive the attention of the governing body of the institution or university system, and local/national media.

The American education system of higher education remains a cradle of democracy when it comes to shared governance, as faculty legislative bodies have a say in work load, curriculum, personnel actions, budget matters, and other academic and administrative matters. This privilege was not given to faculty on a silver platter. These rights and responsibilities were the result of collective bargaining, strikes and legal fights in courts and outside courts to protect faculty's academic freedom, freedom of expression, and intellectual freedom. The American Association of University Professors (AAUP) and the American Federation of Teachers (an affiliate of the AFL/CIO) have done so much to protect these rights, as well as to improve salaries and benefits and work conditions for faculty and academic librarians on most campuses in the U.S. It is because of this culture that American academic libraries are governed in a similarly democratic fashion, which is almost a mirror-image of how academic departments on campuses are organized and governed, except that there are not just librarians or faculty/librarians, but also administrative, paraprofessional, technical and student staff that are, or should be included in the governance of the academic library.

In government-run colleges and universities overseas, the governing body is vested in the Ministry of Education or the Ministry of Higher Education and Scientific Research, which is headed by a minister appointed by the country's king or president. In some cases, the president of the government-operated (state or public) university may have a title of vice- chancellor while the president or head of the state is the chancellor or president of every university in the country (example Kenya). Unlike the American system of shared governance, the faculty may not have a voice in the choice of a university president or vice chancellor, or whatever the title might be, or even their dean.

REFERENCES

Amaral, A., G. Jones and B. Karseth. 2002. *Governing higher education: national perspectives on institutional governance.* Dordrecht ; Boston : Kluwer Academic Publishers.

Jeffires, E. and N. Smith-Tyge. 2000. *Higher education in the 50 states: a survey of higher education funding, governance, and other related topics in the states.* Lansing, Mich.: Senate Fiscal Agency.

Kezar, A. 2006. "Rethinking Public Higher Education Governing Boards Performance: Results of a National Study of Governing Boards in the United States". *The Journal of Higher Education (Columbus, Ohio) 77*, no. 6: 968-1008.

King, R. 2007. "Governance and accountability in the higher education regulatory state." *Higher Education 53,* no. 4: 411-30.

Lindblad, S., and R. Lindblad 2009. Transnational Governance of Higher Education: On Globalization and International University Ranking Lists. *Yearbook (National Society for the Study of Education), pt2,* 180-202.

McLendon, M., R. Deaton, and J. Hearn 2007. "The Enactment of Reforms in State Governance of Higher Education: Testing the Political Instability Hypothesis." *The Journal of Higher Education (Columbus, Ohio) 78*, no. 6: 645-75.

Mills, M. (2007). "Stories of Politics and Policy: Florida's Higher Education Governance Reorganization." *The Journal of Higher Education (Columbus, Ohio) 78*, no. 2: 162-87.

Shattock, M. 2008. "The Change from Private to Public Governance of British Higher Education: Its Consequences for Higher Education Policy Making 1980-2006." *Higher Education Quarterly 62*, no. 3: 181-203.

3

Vision, Mission and Planning

Like business and industry, colleges and universities must have their own vision and mission. A vision of any organization or institution is like a dream. It is a clearly articulated statement of what the organization or institution's intent, or wish to become, i.e. a future-oriented statement (Penniman, p.51). A good vision statement should express the institution's aspirations, core values, and philosophies. Such a statement should be very general and not achievable—at least in the near term. The lifetime of a vision is at least five years and can be much longer. It should be stated in the present tense and be short of seven words or less.

The vision statement of a college or university should be in lockstep with the mission of the parent institution. Furthermore, the vision statement should be shared with the participants (staff, customers and management). Those affected by it should help write it, or at least be able to provide input, and definitely read it. An institution's vision may not be the one everybody else sees, but at least it will provide a framework for future decision-making, and will enable a college or university and its library to evolve within the dynamic academic and professional environment. As can be observed from the examples below, a vision statement can be described as a very idealistic statement that describes what the organization will be or hope to be like in the future and can be used as a motivational tool.

"The world's leading resource for scholarship, research and innovation" (The British Library)

"Unity with diversity, open communication and trust, collaboration, innovation, initiative" (Harvard College Library)

THE MISSION STATEMENT

In its simplest definition, a mission statement should be aspirational and broad rather than concrete and particular. Danner (1997) defines a mission statement as being broad, aspirational, and idealistic, yet it should not be merely a statement of good intentions. "It should set forth the unique role the library plays within its institution" (p.8). Danner offered a sample set of questions the planning team may want to ask itself, including the nature and characteristics of the library, the basic needs and problems the library exists to address, the ways in which the library recognizes or anticipates and responds to those needs or problems, the manner in which the library responds to and satisfies stakeholders, and the library's philosophies and core values (p.28). Jacob (1990, p.61) highlights the elements of a well-crafted mission statement. According to Jacob, the mission statement should: "identify the community or communities the library serves, describe the way in which it serves these communities," establish a vision of what the library will become, "provide a sound base for decentralized decision making, and stand without modification for a considerable period." On the other hand, Jacob stated that a mission statement "should not be a detailed laundry list of library services, but instead be a multi-paragraph, multi-page statement, be continually modified, and reflect only today's goals."

The mission statement differs from the vision statement in that it is shorter, and presents a clear description of the organization's main purpose. It should contain those basic values that the institution holds dear and describes how the organization accomplishes its vision. Jacob argues that the mission statement should identify the communities the library serves, describe the way in which it serves the communities, establish a vision of what the library will become and be able to withstand changes to the library environment.

For colleges and universities, the mission statement is an affirmation of the academic institution's goal to support the teaching and research goals of the university. Among some, there is confusion between vision and mission statements. Unlike a vision statement, the mission statement may be realized in the midterm and unlike a vision, a mission is achievable. According to Penniman (1999) "a vision statement is a statement of: 1) what the institution does; 2) for whom it does it; 3) how it does it; and 4) why. The mission statement should contain measurable objectives and targets. It also "defines in broad terms the enduring fundamental and distinctive purpose of the organization and its roles in the community—what it is trying to accomplish" (Corrall, 1994, p.21).

The mission statement can be longer than the vision statement, but still should be relatively short—one hundred words or less. The mission statement should be unambiguous and understandable, reflect consensus, accepted by the stakeholders, measurable, achievable, concrete, concise, (but complete) memorable, and relevant to the mission of the organization. It should be simple and user friendly. It must be noted that a mission statement is an attainable goal, for the present, rather than the vision's looking to the future. Essentially, it is an announcement to all concerned, including faculty, students, staff and public that "reflect(s) the unchanging values of the organization" (Jacob, 1990). Gary Hartzell states that a mission statement should be "crisp, clear engaging—it reaches out and grabs people in the gut;" "people get it right away; it requires little or no explanation." He added "a vision statement should be broad, fundamental, inspirational and enduring, and it grab's the soul" (Hartzell, 2002).

Most universities mission statements are written in a lofty manner to express what the organization will be in the near or foreseeable future. In general terms, the mission of college and university libraries is to preserve the record of knowledge and to provide access to that record and its contents. A well written library mission statement is an affirmation of the academic library's goal to support the teaching and research goals of its parent institution. Beyond the instruction and research, outreach (also referred to as extension or continuing education) is, in most cases included in the mission statement. In general, the term "outreach" refers to the proactive relationship that exists between the campus and the community ("town and gown") at large.

The 1996 Learner's Library document tied a library's mission to that of a college's and affirmed "The library's mission is to prepare students to be lifelong learners who can and do solve information problems." (Gremmels & Pence, 1996, p.17).

EXAMPLES OF UNIVERSITY MISSION STATEMENTS

The University of Wisconsin-Madison Mission Statement (2009) reads:

> The primary purpose of the University of Wisconsin-Madison is to provide a learning environment in which faculty, staff and students can discover, examine critically, preserve and transmit the knowledge, wisdom and values that will help ensure the survival of this and future generations and improve the quality of life for all. The university seeks to help students to develop an understanding and appreciation for the complex cultural and physical worlds in which they live and to realize their highest potential of intellectual, physical, and human development.

EXAMPLES OF ACADEMIC LIBRARIES MISSION STATEMENTS

The mission statement of the University of Wisconsin-Madison Memorial Library states: Memorial Library provides world class collections, staff, facilities, and services to ensure the success of students, faculty, researchers, and staff in the humanities and social sciences. As the major research library in the state, Memorial also serves the local community and beyond." (University of Wisconsin-Madison: c. 2009).

"The University of Calgary Library "...is to provide and create information resources that support the University's role as a place of education and scholarly inquiry."

The mission of the American University Library is: "to serve as a gateway to information and to promote intellectual discovery for the American University community. Towards these ends the Library provides quality service, collections and facilities that support the University goals for learning, teaching and research."

The mission statement for Drake University's Cowles Library broadly states that the mission of the Cowles Library is to advance "the educational goals of Drake University by providing services, collections, technology, and learning opportunities that make it possible for faculty and students to successfully access and use information" (Jurasek, 2008).

The mission statement of the University of North Carolina – Chapel Hill states that the university is a research institution. The faculty is involved in research, scholarship, and creative work. The mission of the university is to serve all the people of the state, and the nation, as a "center for scholarship and creative endeavor." The university exists in order to teach at all levels in an environment composed of research, free inquiry, and personal responsibility. The University works to expand the body of knowledge and to improve the condition of human life through service and publication in order to enrich our culture."

"The mission of Northwestern University Library is to provide collections and information services of the highest quality to sustain and enhance the University's teaching, research, professional and performance programs. The library provides a setting conducive to independent learning and a resource for users, both within the library and throughout the university and broader scholarly communities. The library's mission statement reflects the fact that the administration wants it to be thought of as an integral part of the learning experience. The Library "is committed to meeting the needs of users by taking a leadership role in linking the University to information in a rapidly changing environment. The Library develops innovative strategies to select, organize, provide access to, and preserve information resources and to educate users about their utilization. It forges effective partnerships outside the Library to connect users with the resources they need."

"The mission of the USC "University of South Carolina" Information Services Division (ISD) is to provide the information, central technologies, and services necessary for the university to achieve its educational, research, clinical, artistic, professional, and public service goals." This statement emphasizes the currency of the technology that is to be provided, and also emphasizes highly qualified staff. Because the libraries are just one part of ISD, alongside the promise to provide "next-generation libraries" and research computing are promises to provide an infrastructure supporting administrative systems, and the USC webpage architecture and homepage. Also, just as the University emphasizes its position, not just as a regional or national institution, but as an international one (and a leading-edge international institution at that); the final statement indicates that ISD exists to support that position: "By leading the development of the university's information and technology infrastructure, ISD helps position USC as a global center of intellectual activity for the 21st century." The USC ISD mission statement can be found at:

http://www.usc.edu/isd/strategicplan/private/pdf/append3_missions.PDF

The Virginia Commonwealth University (VCU) articulates in its VCU Creed, under the subheading "Philosophy for an Academic Community," its commitment to the academic success of its students, research community and health care community by providing excellent "collections, services, spaces and staff." The values section of the statement includes the belief that great universities are built upon great libraries, and again reaffirms the library's commitment to the student body. It ends with a stated commitment to academic integrity and freedom. http://www.library.vcu.edu/about/mission.html.

Marquette University, a private Jesuit University located in Milwaukee, Wisconsin has as its mission "the search for truth, the discovery and sharing of knowledge, the fostering of personal and professional excellence, the promotion of a life of faith, and the development of leadership expressed in service to others. All this we pursue for the greater glory of God and the common benefit of the human community." In harmony with its parent institution (MU), the Raynor Memorial Libraries incorporates into its mission the University-wide mission in the following manner: "The mission of Raynor Memorial Libraries is to foster growth in learning, scholarship and discovery in an environment of service and stewardship and in support of the university's mission. We value self-reflection, diversity and engagement within and beyond the Marquette University community."

Cornell Law Library's mission statement embodies the above mentioned principles—it is succinct, identifies the library's role within the larger university and how it serves its communities, and it will withstand the test of time. It states

"The mission of the Cornell Law Library is to advance legal research, scholarship, and education by providing outstanding and innovative information services and resources in the most efficient manner to the Law School, the University, and the transnational research community" (Cornell University Law Library).

GOALS AND OBJECTIVES

Goals are defined as long-term objectives that guide the institution's daily decision-making. They are the accomplishments by which management can judge whether success has been achieved. Goals are necessary to effectively focus time and energy spent on the task at hand. They are a powerful way to motivate the organization to great achievements.

Goals define "the broad strategies an institution will pursue in support of its mission" (Jacob, 1990, p.64). While goal statements are intended to capture broad aims, objectives are short-term, specific and measurable statements (Jacob, 1990, p.65). Objectives are designed to carry out the library's goals (Danner, 1997, p.11). They should be achievable, realistic targets (Danner, 1997, p. 11; Jacob, 1990, p. 65). They imply a resource commitment on the part of the library (Riggs, 184, p. 35). For example, the University of Iowa Libraries promises to carry out its environment goal by accomplishing the following related objective: "Plan and build a remote storage facility to provide high-quality, environmentally sound space for all types of library materials" (The University of Iowa Libraries).

The focus of goals is on outcomes rather than the methods used to obtain them (Danner, 1997, p.10). Goal statements should be crafted to reflect "doing something," describing in a straightforward manner a library's broad aims with respect to its programs and services (Jacob, 1990, p.64; Danner, 1997, p.10). Riggs identified three types of goals for libraries: service goals, resource management goals, and administrative or directional goals (Riggs, 1984, p.32-33). Jacob suggests that goals should be limited to less than eight in number (Jacob, 1990, p. 64). An example of a resource management goal statement that reflects these criteria comes from the University of Iowa Libraries' strategic plan: "Environment: Provide an attractive, comfortable, and flexible environment for study, research, work, and creative/intellectual exchange, as well as for access to and preservation of the collections" (2004).

There are certain criteria by which goals of academic institutions and their libraries can be judged. On the whole goals should be:
1. Specific
2. Measurable, so you know that you have achieved them
3. Clear, not vague or abstract

4. Achievable, unlike vision or mission statements
5. Realistic, practical and feasible
6. Timely, set dates for start and finish
7. Predetermined
8. Flexible
9. Demanding
10. Agreed to by those who must achieve them

A comparison of the goals statements of the academic libraries mentioned in this book points to three types of goals for academic libraries:

1. Service Goals: include service levels, users served, and types of services;
2. Administrative Goals: deal with organization, coordination, and cooperation; and
3. Resources Management Goals: cover three areas; collections (weeding targets, acquisition policies, materials availability, and delivery time); staff (productivity, morale, training, and conditions), and facilities (accessible, automation, adequacy, and use).

An example of goals statement is that of Drake University's Cowles Library which announce outcomes that more specifically further its mission; for example, the second goal in the strategic plan states that Cowles Library strives to "[p]rovide an exceptional collection of print and digital information resources that support the learning objectives of the Drake Curriculum" (Jurasek, 2008).

Objectives, on the other hand, can be defined as statements of intent. They answer questions such as: What we do; why are we here? Objectives are often confused with goals, but they are not the same. Objectives are the environmental scan put into short, specific, measurable statements. They are suitable for, and supportive of the mission of the institution and need to be acceptable to those involved. Objectives must also be achievable, flexible, motivating, and understandable. Objectives should state what the institution wants to do, how the institution would know when it succeeded in achieving its objectives and who is accountable. They should identify timetables and dates of completion. Objectives must be: focused; consistent; specific; measurable; related to time; and attainable.

Objectives can be classified into three types: 1. Routine objectives; 2. Innovative objectives; and 3. Improvement objectives.

Princeton University Libraries supports the PU Mission by providing the following objectives:

1. User instruction – teaching patrons to find and use library resources.
2. Bibliographic control of the collections – bringing more of our resources under bibliographic control in order to make them more available to users, and creating more links to external resources.

3. Online content – providing more digital representation of our collections and linking these to our web presence.
4. Speedy turn-around – providing quick delivery of library materials and reducing the turn-around time associated with other library services.

STRATEGIC PLANNING

Academic librarians view strategic planning as a tool for managers to see where the library has been, the problems that have been faced and where the library is going and how the problems will be addressed. However, Riggs (1984) offers three definitions evidencing business or corporate influences. For example, one of the definitions speaks in terms of the "continuous process of making present entrepreneurial (risk-taking) decisions systematically ..." (p.1). However, Riggs ultimately settles on a more simplistic definition, "the strategic plan gives the goals and objectives of the library and the means by which the library intends to reach them." (Riggs, 1989). Danner (1997, p.2) advanced the following more sophisticated but still library-appropriate definition, "[S]trategic planning is the systematic analysis of an organization's basic mission as well as its long and short term goals and objectives in light of external threats and limitations. Riggs' analysis provides the framework for strategies and action plans designed to capitalize on opportunities and strengths and to deal appropriately with threats and limitations" (p.3). Danner emphasized that the process takes into account the library's current and future environment, is premised on change, considers the library as a whole and as a part of the university system, considers alternatives among organizational goals and objectives and the strategies for achieving them and is formal and documented (p. 3). A strategic plan should incorporate a time limit, which is usually initially set at three to five years (pp.3-4).

There are many types of strategies, including organizational, personnel, growth, opportunistic (to take advantage of new ideas), innovation (the drive to be new and different), financial, and retrenchment (downsizing). (Riggs, 1984, pp. 49-50).

Strategic planning (SP) is "the process of deciding objectives, on the resources used to attain these objectives and on the policies that are to govern the acquisition, use and disposition of these resources. SP deals with the future of current decisions, identifies future opportunities and threats, exploits the former and avoids the latter; changes can be introduced as the need arises. SP is an attitude and a process that links three major types of plans: strategic, medium range plans, and operating plans.

ADVANTAGES OF STRATEGIC PLANNING

Strategic planning is an attitude of thinking strategically; new ideas that may seem disparate often come together in support of the mission and major goals of the organization. Strategic planning allows an organization to ask the question "what do we want to be down the road?" When done well, planning enables an institution to develop a vision for the future and a strategy for implementing and managing that vision. This enables managers and employees to anticipate, rather than react to events in the future. The plan enables both managers and subordinates to agree to common goals, share in the advancement of their institution and take credit and pride for its success and accomplishments or learn from their mistakes and revise the plan to achieve better results.

Strategic planning serves a variety of purposes in organization, including to:

1. Clearly define the purpose of the organization and to establish realistic goals and objectives consistent with that mission in a defined time frame within the organization's capacity for implementation;
2. Communicate those goals and objectives to the organization's constituents;
3. Develop a sense of ownership of the plan;
4. Ensure that the most effective use is made of the organization's resources by focusing the resources on the key priorities;
5. Provide a base from which progress can be measured and establish a mechanism for informed change when needed;
6. Bring together everyone's best and most reasoned efforts that have important value in building a consensus about where an organization is going;
7. Provide clearer focus of the organization, producing more efficiency and effectiveness;
8. Bridge staff and board of directors (in the case of corporations);
9. Provide the glue that keeps the board together (in the case of corporations);
10. Produce great satisfaction among planners around a common vision;
11. Increase productivity from increased efficiency and effectiveness; and
12. Solve major problems.

There are many advantages to strategic planning in colleges and universities in general, among them: to enable the university to make better use of its human and financial resources, enhance communication between members of the campus community and with the "global village", and prepare students that graduate to live and work in the world of technology.

The benefits of strategic planning to an academic library are well-documented. There is no question that a well-thought out strategic plan could lead to accountability. Academic institutions are increasingly holding their libraries accountable for instituting a planning process that incorporates the parent institution's missions and goals and that "close[s] the loop" through comprehensive evaluation and assessment practices. By adhering to the strategic planning process, a library can "identify the monetary, technology, and facilities resources, as well as the personnel and skills" necessary to the development and maintenance of library programs, resources and services. The library can then report on these findings to the parent institution (Ryan, 2003, p. 208).

A strategic plan allows a library to be proactive rather than reactive. For example, the environmental scanning process will alert the library to the external forces that may have an effect on the library "far enough in advance to be able to make intelligent decisions about their impact on an organization" (Danner, 1997, p.46). It prevents missed opportunities and minimizes exposure to threats. A strategic plan will allow the library to prioritize its initiatives based on verifiable internal and external data. Some libraries like the James Cabell Library at Virginia Commonwealth University use the Balanced Scorecard approach to strategic planning ,which uses performance measurements that are balanced into areas such as: user perspective, internal processes perspective, innovation/learning perspective and financial perspective. The scorecards are strategic goals with their own specific objectives or tasks listed. This approach is reflected in VCU's Strategic Plan to be reached in 2020. The plan can be viewed at http://www.vcu.edu/cie/pdfs/vcu 2020_final.pdf

From an operational point of view, strategic planning is considered a continuous process that involves several key steps: environmental scanning, identification of the library's stakeholders and analysis of the library's Strengths Weaknesses, Opportunities and Threats (SWOT), formulation of the strategic plan, implementation of the plan, and evaluation of the plan. For example, after conducting a SWOT analysis, the library may find that one of the threats to its existence is a projected campus student enrollment decline due to the economic downturn, or losing them to the competition. The library can then use that knowledge to implement a more aggressive marketing campaign touting its unique services, facilities or programs in the first year of the plan and save another less pressing initiative for the second or third years of the plan. A strategic plan will allow the library to make data-driven decisions. For example, following an annual review of the plan, the library will have data regarding the cost of carrying out the strategies. The library can then conduct a cost-benefit analysis to determine whether the strategy for carrying out an objective needs to be modified. A strategic plan ensures effective use of library resources. For example, a SWOT analysis should reveal a library's weaknesses, such as insufficient weekend reference desk hours, and the library can then reallocate funds toward part-time weekend reference help. Finally, a strategic plan will ensure buy-in from stakeholders. For instance, change is more acceptable to employees when they have had a voice in creating it than if it is externally imposed (Riggs, 1984, p.102).

The strategic planning process will require contributions from all levels of staff. Because these internal stakeholders will have been able to provide input into the planning process, they will be more likely to buy into the benefits of the plan and engage in its successful implementation. While it is important that successful strategic planning should involve as many staff members in the organization, there is disagreement in the ranks of managers and in the literature about management as to whether strategic planning should be "top-down" with the director of the library initiating, overseeing and supporting the process (Riggs, p.14). Others have questioned the wisdom of a strictly "top down" strategic planning approach and call for more involvement of librarians and support staff. In either case, total involvement of staff in the strategic planning is highly recommended. Dougherty (2002, p.40) states, "[a]ll levels of staff from the director to the newest circulation clerk ought to be represented in the planning process." Danner pointed out that the most commonly offered piece of advice in Richard Clement's 1994 survey of Association of Research Libraries member libraries that had engaged in strategic planning was to "involve library staff; give everyone a voice" (Danner, p.14). Participation in the process increases the likelihood of staff buy-in of the final strategic plan, thereby increasing the chances of a successful implementation (p.13). However, the key to success, as Danner observed, is to ensure that the zeal for participation does not result in a planning team that is too large to function effectively (p.14).

Peter Drucker (2008) and others mention some of the steps recommended for strategic planning and they include:

1. Define the situation and problem.
2. Identify knowledge gap and constraints.
3. Develop alternatives.
4. Analyze alternatives.
5. Select the best alternatives and identify why.
6. Implement the decision.
7. Evaluate the decision.

The elements mentioned above constitute a major component of the planning process. The result of the planning process should be the planning document for the organization. The planning document is a symbol of accomplishments and a guide for action. The core of the strategic plan consists of the following:

1. The vision and mission statements;
2. A summary of the environmental forces and market trends;

3. The key objectives and priorities of the plan, with annual, measurable library goals and objectives; where you are now and you will be or like to be in the future;
4. Human resources and financial projections along with technology and where these resources will come from;
5. A time plan for the implementation of the plan; and
6. Methods for gathering feedback, evaluation, and adjustment to plan.

IMPLEMENTING THE PLAN

A good plan is of no value if not implemented, regularly reviewed and evaluated. The purpose is to decide what needs to be changed, create a new plan incorporating the changes, and develop a tactical plan. Tactics implement strategies. Strategic plans are for the future, tactical plans are for the present. The strategic plans provide the framework for the tactical plans. The latter include procedures and budgets, and plans for day-to-day activities.

Just because a library did all the right things mentioned above, does not mean that its plan will succeed. A number of plans have failed due to one or more of the following reasons:

1. Poor or unrealistic assumptions made;
2. Political considerations;
3. The goals may have been over ambitious; or
4. Resources were not made available, downward change in the economy, reduction in staff, change in management or ownership of the parent organization.

When applying these criteria, students in my academic library classes discover that a significant number of academic libraries do not have strategic plans, or the plans some of these libraries have are too old and outdated. As these students observe and the literature proves some of the excuses or "reasons" cited by some of the academic librarians for not having a plan include: It is expensive and time consuming; it will limit flexibility and creativity; things have always been done that way at this library or institution; it will create more paperwork, and other similar excuses. (Evans and Wards, *Management Basics*, 2007)

Lessons learned from the corporate world show that failing to plan leads to sure failure. If you don't know where you are, as the saying goes, it doesn't matter how long it takes to get there. Planning is about managing change. It keeps you on course. Planning helps you to do the right thing. Planning also gives the staff an idea of where the organization is going, thus helping assure their commitment to the library's future. Planning creates confidence in your unit by the parent institution, where it is going and how it will get there. It can also improve future funding. Furthermore, when done right the process improves staff morale and staff motivation, helps make them less reactive, and instills in them team spirit and a sense of community and corporate identity due to a shared purpose. High staff morale contributes to customer satisfaction.

STAKEHOLDER IDENTIFICATION AND SWOT ANALYSIS

The results of the environmental scan should inform the second step of the process, the identification of stakeholders and analysis of a library's SWOT. The identification of stakeholders ensures that user perspectives are in the forefront of the planning process. While naming stakeholders should be a straightforward exercise, Danner suggested that if guidance is needed, the library's planning team should use the following questions to frame its discussion: (1) "Who does the library affect through its services and programs? (2) Who affects the library and resources available to it? In what ways does each influence the library and its activities? (3)What factors does each use to judge the library's performance? and, (4) Which stakeholders are most influential and important to the library?" (Danner, 1997, p.24).

The purpose of the SWOT exercise is to put the library in a position to develop plans and strategies that take advantage of its strengths and opportunities and minimize or overcome weaknesses and threats (Dougherty, 2002, pp. 38-39). The library should identify and evaluate its own strengths and weaknesses in relation to its environment, not only as they are viewed by the planning team members, but as they might be seen by the stakeholders (Danner, 1997, p. 25). Threats are usually external and are defined as "those factors that can lead to stagnation, decline, or even death of an institution or one of its programs unless corrective action is taken" (Danner, 1997, p.25). Opportunities, on the other hand, are areas in which a particular organization is likely to have competitive advantages (Danner, 1997, p.25)

FORMULATION OF A STRATEGIC PLAN

A good strategic plan does not have to be too detailed. One should document the plan with current and historical statistics; use appendices to include more details; make sure reference is made to the mission and objectives of the parent institution; supplement the text with graphs and pictures instead of tables. Finally, give your plan a title, perhaps taken from the vision or mission statement.

Steps in the planning process include: agreement on the goals, and mission of the institution, selection of specific objectives from a variety of possible objectives, gathering and analysis of data in order to determine appropriate objectives, selection of the most appropriate means of achieving the objectives, and development in detail of the way in which the objectives are to be achieved. Each plan in the strategic plan must fit within an objective and each objective within a goal. The budget allotted for each strategy should be noted.

The next step in the strategic planning process is the development of the plan itself. "The elements of the final plan move from the broad to the specific, from the ideal to practical, and become increasingly more quantitative the deeper one goes into the plan" (Danner, 1997, p.7). These elements, from the broadest and most idealistic to the narrowest and most practical, include a mission statement, vision and values statements, goals, objectives, and strategies. Thus, the strategic plan elements form a hierarchy of sorts. The mission statement is the umbrella under which all other elements are placed; the goals should fit within the mission statement; the objectives should fit within one of the goals; the strategies should fit within one of the objectives (p.8).

The next elements of the strategic plan are the examination of the existing vision and values statements, or the formulation of new ones, if none existed before. As both Danner and Jacob indicated, a vision statement can be developed for a library using the same methods used to develop the mission statement (Jacob, 1990, p.61; Danner, 1997, p.9). The difference between the mission and vision statement is that the mission statement focuses on the current mission of the library whereas the vision statement recognizes "the range of possible futures for the library and states a desirable future" (Danner, 1997, p. 9). Values offer a structure for decisions, policies, planning, and accountability (p.10). The vision statement of the academic library articulates where the library would like to be in the future and the values statements reflect the library's shared culture of service. The vision statement provides, in part, "[a]s a center for engagement in the discovery of knowledge and critical reflection at the parent institution, the libraries will further campus' efforts to: Optimize access to information in and beyond the collections…." The strategic plan announces several values, but the first example is "[W]e value service by ensuring our decisions and activities are useful to our community of users."

BENEFITS OF STRATEGIC PLANNING

The benefits of strategic planning to an academic library are well-documented. There is no question that a well-thought out strategic plan could lead to accountability. Academic institutions are increasingly holding their libraries accountable for instituting a planning process that incorporates the parent institution's missions and goals and that "close[s] the loop" through comprehensive evaluation and assessment practices. By adhering to the strategic planning process, a library can "identify the monetary, technology, and facilities resources, as well as the personnel and skills" necessary to the development and maintenance of library programs, resources and services. The library can then report on these findings to the parent institution (Ryan, 2003, p.208).

A strategic plan allows a library to be proactive rather than reactive. For example, the environmental scanning process will alert the library to the external forces that may have an effect on the library "far enough in advances to be able to make intelligent decisions about their impact on an organization" (Danner, 1997, p. 46). It prevents missed opportunities and minimizes exposure to threats.

ENVIRONMENTAL SCAN

The first step, which actually should be ongoing throughout the process, is to perform environmental scanning and analysis (Feinman,1999, pp.18-19; Danner, 1997, p.19). Environmental scanning is "a process for examining the external environment through potentially available information on the developments, early warning signals, trends, issues, and forces which might affect some aspect of an organization's operation, goals, or strategies" (Danner, 1997, p.19). Scanning allows "planners to take into account what is happening in the environments beyond the walls of an organization, e.g., within the community, on campus, and among groups of faculty, young adults, unserved, and so forth" (Dougherty, 2002, p.38).

Environmental scanning should help the planning group address the following concerns: (1) the major trends in the environment; (2) the implications of those trends for the library; (3) the most significant opportunities for the library in the planning period; and, (4) the foreseen threats (Danner, 1997, p.19). In carrying out the environmental scan, members of the planning team should rely on background readings of library literature discussing the effects of change on libraries and information service, documentation from the library's own policies and mission statements, and relevant documents from the university, comparative data from similarly situated institutions, and, information regarding the library's primary users and other constituents (Feinman, 1999, p.20; Danner, 1997, p.20; Jacob, 1990, pp.47,50). Because environmental scanning and monitoring should be an ongoing part of the planning process, the library should put in place a system where selected members of the staff engage in scanning activities as a part of their regular work duties (Danner, 1997, pp.45-46).

A strategic plan will allow the library to prioritize its initiatives based on verifiable internal and external data. For example, after conducting a SWOT analysis, the library may find that one of the threats to its existence is a projected campus student enrollment decline due to the economic downturn. The library can then use that knowledge to implement a more aggressive marketing campaign touting its unique services, facilities or programs in the first year of the plan and save another less pressing initiative for the second or third years of the plan. A strategic plan will allow the library to make data-driven decisions.

For example, following an annual review of the plan, the library will have data regarding the cost of carrying out the strategies. The library can then conduct a cost-benefit analysis to determine whether the strategy for carrying out an objective needs to be modified. A strategic plan ensures effective use of library resources. For example, a SWOT analysis should reveal a library's weaknesses, such as insufficient weekend reference desk hours, and the library can then reallocate funds toward part-time weekend reference help. Finally, a strategic plan will ensure buy-in from stakeholders. For instance, change is more acceptable to employees when they have had a voice in creating it than if it is externally imposed (Riggs, 1984, p.102).

The final elements of a strategic plan are the strategies that show how the objectives will be accomplished. The action plan approach to strategy formation requires team members to identify with specificity who will do what to carry out the strategy, when, and at what cost (Danner, 1997, p.13). Effective strategy statements will describe each of the major components of the library's strategy, indicate how the strategy will lead to the accomplishment of the corresponding library objective and goal, and describe the strategy in functional terms and as precisely as possible (Riggs, 1984, p.45). The University of Iowa Strategic Plan does not include strategies—instead, it includes indicators. However, a strategy for the objective noted above might be: An off-site storage facility for lesser-used library materials will be built in the west campus by 2012.

IMPLEMENTATION AND EVALUATION

Implementation of a strategic plan can prove difficult. First, the library may already be cash-strapped, will need to make financial resources available for the new initiatives. Danner (997, pp. 44-45) suggests relieving some of the budgetary discomfort by implementing only a small number of the strategies each year. Second, the implementation of the strategies devised during the planning process will require staff members to alter the way they do their work and change can cause considerable apprehension for those workers most affected (Riggs, 1984, p. 102). Riggs offered several tips for making the changes more palatable for staff, including carefully documenting responsibilities, establishing a positive attitude about the new plan, improving staff understanding of the planning, and recognizing the efforts of staff who work to successfully carry out the strategies (Riggs, pp. 102-106).

The final step, which is ongoing, is the evaluation of the plan. The library should conduct an inquiry into whether the strategies produced substantive, cognizable results in achieving the goals and objectives (Danner, 1997, p. 45). The plan should be evaluated at least once a year and the next year's annual plan should build upon what was learned during the implementation of the plan over the previous year (Danner, p. 45). The methods used to evaluate the plan will vary depending on the library (Riggs, 1984, p. 111; Danner, p. 45). Riggs (p. 116) offers a form for evaluating the planning system and, what he calls, strategic checkpoints to help control the progress toward the accomplishment of library strategies.

The decision-making process includes: gathering information and preliminary problem review, review goals and objectives on which decisions rest, develop a model of the situation under consideration based on the elements and relationships involved, list alternatives, and evaluate alternatives, then select the most feasible alternatives.

The next step is to analyze the results of the previous steps and develop alternative futures for the institution. This is also known as the scenario planning. According to Giesecke (1998), "using scenario driven planning, managers develop scenarios, or stories, to design possible futures. Managers can then design strategies that will help move the organization forward"

According to James King (King, 1998, pp.8-15), some of the steps for developing scenarios include:

- Identify the central point to be made (how can we serve our users better?);
- Identify the key forces in the environment (be they are cost, compensation, staff);
- List and analyze those important driving forces. What is their probability? Identify trends, or rate of change. Are they controllable;
- Rank the forces by importance or by uncertainty;
- Choose the main themes or assumptions to develop the scenarios;
- Create or develop the scenarios;
- Look at the scenario implications; and
- Identify indicators that will help in monitoring changes as they develop.

EXAMPLES OF STRATEGIC PLANNING IN ACADEMIC LIBRARIES

The University of Calgary Library has developed an excellent strategic plan which can be viewed on the Web http://lcr.ucalgary.ca/files/lcr/BusPlan.pdf. The plan contains the main elements described above, like vision, mission, and it covers the SWOT analysis, and looks at the demographic, market, fiscal, work and technological trends. The three main goals are listed, and each has one or two objectives, four strategic initiatives, expected outcomes, key performance measures and target costs for each of the next five years. All of this data makes the goals comprehensive and measurable, realistic and timely. The goals cover the main goal types, e.g. service (to provide high quality research and scholarship), administrative (provide accountability for results), and resources management (dedicated and professional faculty and staff). Each goal has a main strategic priority. For example for the goal (providing a high quality learning environment), the main strategic priority is the construction of the Taylor Family Digital Library. The objectives are focused, consistent, formulated for short term, and serves as a yardstick for performance.

The following example of a library SWOT illustrates the relations between goals, objectives and action plan and the assignment of tasks to staff members. The example also shows strengths, weaknesses, opportunities and threats.

Goal 1: To plan creative and innovative programs of library service which will be student and faculty centered

Objective 1: To develop a marketing plan that will promote the library within the university community by May 2011.

Action 1: Members of the staff will be assigned to a subcommittee to develop the plan current volunteers include: Jane, John and Mary

Objective 2: To develop an information literacy program by May 2012.

Action 1: Based on the information from the ACRL conference and their experience. Rogelio, Adam and Fatima to develop the plan.

Goal 2: To provide both a physical and virtual environment which enhances the teaching and learning for students and faculty.

Objective 1: To continually seek internal and external resources which will enable the Library to provide ownership of, access to, the information resources needed by students and faculty.

Action 1: Identify and apply for appropriate grants to increase staff and collections;

Action 2: Meet with the University grant writer;

Action 3: Meet with faculty to discuss inclusion of library staff and resources in grants being written in their areas.

Objective 2: To continue the long-range building planning process begun with the VC for Administration & Finance.

Action 1: David can provide a timeline.

Objective 3: To improve the look and functionality of the existing facility by June 2012.
  Action 1: Complete the painting as soon as possible;
  Action 2: Establish a subcommittee to review the existing layout and make suggestions for a more efficient layout. Implement changes;
  Action 3: Meet with the Visual Arts department and other area artists about artwork for the library;
  Action 4: Arrange for and install new furniture, carpeting, and appropriate display hardware.

OPPORTUNITIES

A. Staff: dedicated, collegiality, flexibility, customer-oriented, willing, small/not bureaucratic, knowledgeable, embracing change, opportunities for staff development, teaching/helping mentality, able to participate, fun.
B. Library: accessible by users, loyal/committed students, participate in external consortia, comfortable atmosphere, and good relationships with faculty, students and community, educational /research focus, good follow-up to issues/concerns, consortia with sister campuses, making do.
C. Technology: accessible, keeping pace.

WEAKNESSES

A. Building: building design, uncomfortable furniture, sick, internal access, inadequate signage both internally and externally.
B. Budget: lack of resources, under funded, takes backseat to departments in funding decisions.
C. Staff: understaffed, inadequate training, small staff-multiple duties, underappreciated, lack of time, too many hats, status unclear: academic? department? teachers? who? small in comparison to other campuses.
D. Library: isolated, lack of understanding of what we do, not high priority with administration, location, dated equipment, lack of recognition for what we do, lack of cooperation/working relationships with other libraries in the area, reactive rather than proactive, lack of electronic literacy, inability to reach everyone, identity on campus, need consistent message about the library.

OPPORTUNITIES

A. Library: improve image by taking care of library's image, lines of control/consortia, use new technology and be a leader, have a greater presence in the community, enhance programs, building renovation, friends group, faculty being advocates for library, full use of technology, more proactive.

B. Staff: act as a unit in making decisions, virtual library service/education, expand information literacy, allow for more initiatives, in-house staff development.

C. Funding: fund-raising/development, changing criteria for campus funding.

THREATS

A. Campus: campus administration, societal attitudes, have/have not technology, responses to problems.

B. Collections: thought books are going to go away, we don't need books, and it is all on the Internet... it's free.

C. Library: censorship, copyright issues, low morale, sick building, ergonomic issues, problem patrons.

D. Technology changes: mergers, breakups, obsolescence, new staff, inability to interface, technology support.

E. Staff: low starting wages for students, low funding in general, inflation, pricing models.

The website http://www.managementhelp.org/plan_dec/str_plan/str_plan.htm offers a list of benefits as to why strategic planning is so important.

ORGANIZATIONAL STRUCTURE

Organizational structures of academic libraries vary from the very flat, simple and streamlined to the very complex and top heavy management, with layers of managers and supervisors. Most academic librarians report directly to the chief executive officer of the college or university who may delegate the authority to the chief academic officer, like vice president, provost or vice chancellor. The latter may delegate the daily supervisory authority to an associate vice chancellor or associate vice president for academic affairs. The title of the chief librarian varies from vice president for information services or chief information officer (with responsibilities for libraries in addition to computer, information and telecommunication services), or dean of libraries with academic title of full or associate professor, to director, or chief librarian or just plain college librarian with or without faculty rank.

The college librarian may be assisted by an associate librarian who also runs the library in the absence of the director. A number of assistant librarians or heads of departments are responsible for the various major units in the library (technical services, access/public services, archives/special collections, systems and technology, administrative affairs (human resources, fiscal planning and budget, marketing, development, etc.). There can be a third layer of managers under the chief officer depending on the size and complexity of the organization.

There is usually a standing university library committee whose members are elected by the faculty and academic staff in campus-wide elections. These committees can be advisory or executive in nature and this determines the extent of their level of authority and responsibility. A good working relationship between the librarian executive and the chair of the library committee will contribute to a positive and constructive relationship between the library and the campus faculty much to the benefit of all on campus especially students who are the ultimate beneficiaries of quality education supported by quality library collections and services.

A typical example of the organization of a medium to small college library may look like this:

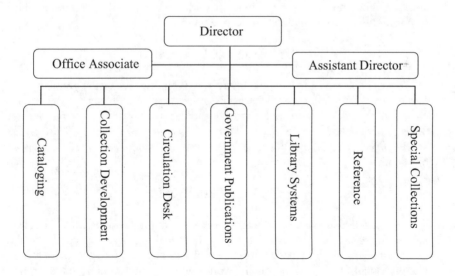

MANAGEMENT STYLES

According to the *ACRL Standards*, the library should be administered in a manner that permits and encourages the most effective use of available library resources. The *Standards* further require the library director/dean to report to the president or to the appropriate chief academic or instructional officer of the institution. Internal policies and procedures of the library should be in place. The responsibilities of the library director/dean's should be defined in writing. The *Standards* also require a standing library advisory committee. The library should also abide by the ALA "Library Bill of Rights," and, I might add, the AAUP's *Principles of Academic Freedom.*

Management styles in academe may vary according to the governing system used, the culture and prevailing traditions at the institution. The management style can be directive, controlling, or participatory (including representation from students, faculty, academic staff, unions, governing committees, administrators, etc.). Some use tools of scientific management such as operations research. The conceptual or behavioral style of management can vary from one campus unit on to the next, depending on the education, orientation and experience of the respective department or unit heads and the extent of the subordinates' will and desire to exercise their rights and express their opinions and standing up for their rights in addition to fully accepting their responsibilities in running their respective units.

STYLES OF SUPERVISION

Styles of supervision can be: a) Directive (you do what I want you to do); b) Participative (let's talk about what needs to be done, how, when and by whom, etc.); and c) Laissez-Faire (everybody does his/her own thing). Lucille Wilson notes in her book, *People Skills for Library Managers: A Common Sense Guide for Beginners* (p.117), that the usage of these styles is not always independent of one another.

TEAM APPROACH

Organizations have created teams simply by taking the department structure and renaming the departments as teams without making any changes in how the group functions or is managed. There are different kinds and levels of teams: interdivisional teams, horizontal work groups, and other collaborative arrangements are replacing many of the traditional functional and hierarchical structures in organizations.

Jon Katzenbach and Douglas Smith, in their book *The Wisdom of Teams*, provide a succinct definition of a team. They describe a true working team as a small number of people with complementary skills who are committed to a common purpose, performance goals, and approach for which they hold themselves mutually accountable.

To be a team, the group needs to be small enough (20-25 people) in order for people to interact regularly and effectively. Team members get to know each other, build working relationships, and meet regularly. Team members must also share accountability and agree to take responsibility for their own work and the work of the team. Teamwork is an attitude, a frame of mind and a commitment, not just a program. In a team, group goals are more important than individual goals. Team members believe in the value of group process and work to ensure that processes complement productivity. Decision-making systems, communication systems, and work processes are equally important in meeting the team's goals.

THE MANAGER'S ROLE IN TEAMS

In order for a team to be successful, it must have a team leader or manager who understands and is committed to the team concept including:
1. Select team members;
2. Look for complimentary skills;
3. Develop people skills;
4. Facilitate information flow;
5. Work effectively with other team leaders;
6. Pay attention to first meetings;
7. Set clear rules for behavior;
8. Spend time together;
9. Provide positive feedback and constructive advice;
10. Keep goals relevant;
11. Create opportunities for others; and
12. Do real work.

STAFF COMMITTEES OR GROUP THINK

Involving employees in decision-making is a must in a democratic society. It is good for business as well as for employee's morale. Some of the far-reaching decision-making in some organizations are made by groups and this is known as "group think". It is rare that an organization does not have or make use of committees, task forces, review panels, study teams, or similar groups as vehicles for making decisions. On the average, managers spend more than 40 % of their time in meetings, defining problems, arriving at solutions, determining the means for implementing the solutions. Committee structure is a method of combining the mechanistic and organic organizations.

Staff committees may be permanent or temporary in nature. A temporary committee is similar to a task force. Permanent committees facilitate the unity of diverse input as does the task force, but they offer the stability and consistency of the matrix. Members of committees can meet at regular or irregular intervals to analyze problems, make recommendations or final decisions, coordinate activities, or oversee projects. They are the mechanisms for bringing together the input of various departments. Universities rely heavily on committees, under the system of shared governance, for everything from student admissions to searching for faculty and administrators, to promotion and tenure of faculty and academic staff, to operating facilities, receiving complaints and appeals, deciding on budgets, selecting a president or deans, etc.

A task force, on the other hand, is a temporary structure created to establish a specific well-defined and complex task that requires the involvement of personnel from a number of organizational subunits. Members serve on the task force until its goal is achieved. Then the task force is disbanded. The task force is a common tool of consumer product firms especially when they are contemplating the introduction of a new product. In libraries, a task force may prepare for accreditation visit, introduction of a new service or product, new building and remodeling project, look into the introduction of a new computerized system, or the launching of a major new service to the community. Once the system is implemented or the new program is approved and integrated into the library programs and operations, the task force is disbanded.

ADVANTAGES OF GROUP DECISIONS

There are advantages and strengths to group decisions, but there are also disadvantages and constraints. Group decisions provide more complete information—"two heads better than one." A group will bring to the table diverse opinions, experience and perspectives, which can impact the decision process better than one individual acting alone.

Groups also generate more alternatives than can an individual. This is more evident when the group represents different specialties. Furthermore, group decision-making increases acceptance of a solution. Individual decisions may fail because the people who will be affected by them reject them. The group decision-making process is consistent with democratic ideals. Therefore, decisions made by groups may be perceived as more legitimate than decisions made by one person.

DISADVANTAGES OF GROUP DECISIONS

Group decision-making is not a panacea. As is the case with individual decisions, group decisions may not be effective all the time. The axiom "a camel is a race horse put together by a committee," has some validity to it, because group decisions have their drawbacks. They are time-consuming, it takes time to assemble a group. The interaction among the group may not be efficient and the group can take longer to reach a decision in contrast to one individual making a decision. Members of a group are never perfectly equal. Some are more knowledgeable about the problem, have more experience, influence with other members, have better verbal skills, assertiveness, etc. This could result in having those members take over the meeting, overwhelm, or intimidate others and dominate the meeting and have influence on the outcome of the meeting and the decisions reached. In other words, they have their own agenda which may not be in the best interest of the organization or they wish to undermine the leadership. In other words, they can be destructive, using the democratic process as a shield.

There is also the problem of conformity due to social pressures to conform in a group "group think." Group decisions rely on give and take, and this takes time. This is a form of conformity in which group members withhold deviant, minority, or unpopular views, in order to give the appearance of agreement. Group decisions may appear to enjoy unanimity, but this is an illusion. If a member of the group does not speak, it does not mean that s/he is in full agreement with the group.

Groupthink undermines critical thinking in the group. There is also ambiguity as far as responsibility is concerned. Group members share responsibility, but who is actually responsible for the outcome? In an individual decision, we know who is responsible. In group decision, the responsibility is watered down. If decision effectiveness is defined in terms of speed, individuals are superior.

There are ways to make group decision more effective:
- Brainstorming;
- The nominal technique;
- Adelphi techniques; and
- Electronic meetings.

Brainstorming is one way to overcome pressures of conformity that can adversely affect the development of creative alternatives. The process encourages all alternatives while withholding any criticism of those alternatives. It is a good process of generating ideas, without criticism from others.

Nominal technique restricts discussion during the decision-making process. Group members are present, but they operate independently. Independent thinking is encouraged as is the case in traditional interacting group.

Delphi technique is similar to the nominal group technique except that it does not require the physical presence of the group members. In the Delphi technique, group members do not meet face to face and therefore, group members are shielded from the influence of others. Members can be all over the national or global maps. The Delphi technique has its drawbacks as it does not have the rich feedback that face-to-face interaction and debate could provide

Electronic meetings: This is the most recent approach to group decision-making. It blends the nominal group techniques with the sophisticated computer technology. Issues are presented to participants who then type in their opinion onto their computer screens. The messages are transmitted to other members of the group who can debate the merits of each suggestion and even vote on the final outcome. The major advantages of electronic meetings are anonymity, honesty, and speed. It is estimated that e-meetings can be as much as 55 % faster than traditional face-to-face meetings.

References

Aamot, G. 2007. "Getting the Most out of Strategic Planning. *College & Research Libraries News* 68, no. 7: 418-426.

Alexander Campbell King Law Library. 2007. Strategic Plan. University of Georgia Law School Web site: http://www.law.uga.edu/library/libraryinfo/policies/stratplan.pdf (accessed April 10, 2009)

Association of College and Research Libraries. Environmental Scan 2007. American Libraries Association:
http://www.ala.org/ala/mgrps/divs/acrl/publications/whitepapers/Environmental_Scan_2007%20FINAL.pdf (accessed April 10, 2009)

Bahavar, S. 2008. Strategic Planning for Reference in a Team Environment: the Preferred Futuring Model. *Reference & User Services Quarterly* 47, no. 4: 356-363.

Bryson, J. M. 1995. *Strategic Planning for Public and Nonprofit Organizations: a Guide to Strengthening and Sustaining Organizational Achievement*, rev. ed., San Francisco: Jossey-Bass Publishers.

Cornell University Law Library. Mission and history. http://library.lawschool.cornell.edu/WhoWeAre/MissionAndHistory/ (accessed April 10, 2009)

Corrall, S. 1994. *Strategic Planning for Libraries and Information Services*. London: Aslib.

Danner, R. A. 1997. *Strategic Planning: a Law Library Management Tool for the '90s and Beyond.* 2nd ed. Dobbs Ferry, NY: Glanville Publishers, Inc.

Dougherty, R. M. 2002. Planning for a New Library Future. *Library Journal* 127, no. 9: 38-41.

Drake University Law School. Environmental Scan 2007. http://www.drake.edu/selfstudy/resources/2/EnvScanLaw.pdf (accessed April 10, 2009)

Drucker, P. F. 2006. *The Essential Drucker*. New York: Harper.

Duke University Libraries. Connecting People + Ideas: a Strategic Plan for the Duke University Libraries 2006-2010. Duke University libraries: http://library.duke.edu/about/planning/Perkins-Library-strategic-plan-2006-2010.pdf. (accessed April 10, 2009)

Einasto, O. 2009. Using Service Quality Monitoring to Support Library Management Decisions: a Case Study from Estonia. *International Information & Library Review* 41, no. 1, 12-20.

Evans, E. and Ward, P. L. 2007. *Management Basics for Information Professionals*. NewYork: Neal-Schuman Publishers.

Feinman, V. J. 1999. Five Steps toward Planning Today for Tomorrow's Needs. *Computers in Libraries* 19, no. 1: 18-21.

Fiels, K. M. (2009). Strategic Planning. *American Libraries* 40, no. 11: 10-11.

Franklin, B. 2009. Aligning Library Strategy and Structure with the Campus Academic Plan: a Case Study. *Journal of Library Administration* 49, no. 5: 495-505.

Giesecke, J., ed. 1998. *Scenario Planning in Libraries*. Chicago, IL: American Library Association.

Green, R. 2007. *Library Management: a Case Study*. New York: Neal-Schuman Publishers.

Gremmels, J. and J. Pence. 1996. *The Learner's Library: a Library for the Future*. Waverly, IA: Wartburg College.

Hallmark, E. K. 2007. Developing a Long-range and Outreach Plan for Your Academic Library. *College & Research Libraries News* 68, no. 2: 92-95.

Hartzell, G. 2002. Controlling Your Own Destiny: Why Vision and Mission Statements are Indispensable. *School Library Journal* 48, no. 11: 37.

Hayes, R. M. 1993. *Strategic Management for Academic Libraries: a Handbook*. Westbrook, CT: Greenwood Press.

Hulseberg, A. 2009. Strategic Planning for Electronic Resources Management: a Case Study at Gustavus Adolphus College. *Journal of Electronic Resources Librarianship* 21, no. 2: 163-171.

Jacob, M. E. L. 1990. *Strategic Planning: a How-to-do-it-Manual for Librarians*. New York: Neal-Schuman Publishers.

Joseph, M. 2009. Public Library Strategies for the Over 50s: Everything Old is New Again — Or Is It? *APLIS* 22, no. 3: 115-119.

Jurasek, K. 2008, October 9. Cowles Library Strategic Plan 2009-2010. Drake University Cowles Library: http://library.drake.edu/pages/cowles-library-strategic-plan-2009-2010 (accessed Dec 15, 2009)

King, J. 1998. "Scenario Planning: Powerful Tools for Thinking about Alternatives", In: Scenario Planning for Librarie. Joan Giesecke, ed. Chicago: ALA. pp. 8-15.

Kronenfeld, M. R. 2008. Using Strategic Goals to Guide the Development of Library Resources, Services, and Web Sites. *Journal of Electronic Resources in Medical Libraries* 5, no. 4: 325-337.

Lampert, C. 2009. Success Factors and Strategic Planning: Rebuilding an Academic Library Digitization Program. *Information Technology & Libraries* 28, no. 3: 116-136.

Linn, M. 2008. Planning Strategically and Strategic Planning. *Bottom Line: Managing Library Finances* 21, no. 1: 20-23.

Marquette University. Our Mission. Marquette University: http://www.marquette.edu/about/mission.shtml (accessed Dec 10, 2009)

Matthews, J. R. 2005. *Strategic Planning and Management for Library Managers*. Westport, CT: Libraries Unlimited.

Mittrowann, A. 2009. Strategic, Digital, Human: the Library of the Future: a View on International Developments by a German Library Supplier. *Public Library Quarterly* 28, no. 3: 193-203.

Paley, N. 2008. *Mastering the Rules of Competitive Strategy: a Resource Guide for Managers*. New York: Auerbach Publications.

Penniman, W. David, 1999. Strategic Planning to Avoid Bottlenecks in the Age of the Internet. *Computers in Libraries* 19, no. 1: 50-53.

Riggs, D. E. 1984. *Strategic Planning for Library Managers*. Phoenix, AZ: Oryx Press.

Raynor Memorial Libraries. Envisioning the Future: The Next Seven Years 2007-2013. Marquette University Raynor Memorial Libraries:

http://www.marquette.edu/library/staff/plans/stratplan2007-2013.pdf (accessed Dec 10, 2009)

Ryan, S. M. 2003. Library Website Administration: a Strategic Planning Model for the Smaller Academic Library. *Journal of Academic Librarianship* 29, no. 4: 207-218.

Schachter, D. 2007. Developing Your Library's Strategy Requires More than a Once-a-Year Planning Session. *Information Outlook* 11, no. 8: 42-43.

Schonfeld, R. C. 2007. Getting from Here to There, Safely: Library Strategic Planning for the Transition Away from Print Journals. *Serials Librarian* 52, no. 1/2: 183-189.

Sehanovic, J. and Zugaj, M. 1997. Information Technologies and Organizational structure. *Library Management* 18, no. 2: 80–87.

Sheldon, B. E. 1991. *Leaders in Libraries: Styles and Strategies for Success*. Chicago: American Library Association.

Stamp, G. 1989. Management Styles. *Management Decision* 27, no. 4: 23-30

Texas Tech University Libraries. Mission, Vision and Values. Texas Tech University Libraries: http://library.ttu.edu/about/admin/mission.php (accessed Dec 10, 2009)

Thelen, L. N. 2003. *Essentials of Elementary Library Management*. Worthington, OH: Linworth Publishing.

The University of Iowa Libraries. Strategic Plan 2004 – 2009. http://www.lib.uiowa.edu/about/stratplan04-09.pdf (accessed Dec 10, 2009)

United States Census Bureau. Population Finder. http://www.census.gov (accessed April 10, 2009)

University of Iowa Libraries. 2004. University of Iowa Libraries Strategic Plan 2004-2009. University of Iowa Libraries. http://www.lib.uiowa.edu/about/strategic.html (accessed April 10, 2009)

University of Missouri-Kansas City School of Law. UMKC School of Law Strategic Plan. University of Missouri-Kansas School of Law: http://www1.law.umkc.edu/strategic_plan-footer.htm#web (accessed Dec 10, 2009)

University of Wisconsin Stevens Point Libraries. Environmental Scan—January 2009. University of Wisconsin Stevens Point Libraries. http://library.uwsp.edu/admin/StratPlan/Environmental_Scan_final_draft_march_17.pdf (accessed Dec 10, 2009)

Wilson, L. 1996. *People Skills for Library Managers: a Common Sense Guide for Beginners*. Englewood, CO: Libraries Unlimited.

4

FISCAL MANAGEMENT

A budget is defined as an itemized summary of probable expenditures and incomes for a given time period. Usually it involves a systematic plan for meeting expenses, a planning document used by an organization, generally prepared and presented in standard accounting formats emphasizing dollar revenues, expenditures, and costs, or an assessment of revenues that can be realistically anticipated. Another definition of a budget connects planning to control, by referring to budgeting as the process by which necessary resources are determined, allocated, and funded. In other words, budgets are tools for control, no matter the type of organization. For most libraries, the budgetary process is annual, and the budget is relatively the same from year to year.

Budgeting can help management development, communication and coordination across programs. Budgets for service organizations, like libraries, usually focus on labor, as they are labor intensive organizations. Next to labor come materials (books, journals, electronic sources, etc.). These materials are viewed as fixed assets.

As was mentioned in the history section of this book earlier, the late 1960s was a period of expansion for American colleges and universities, and their libraries benefited greatly. Since that time, the funds available to libraries, including college libraries, have fallen behind. For the past few years academic library budgets have had to deal with a flat budget which resulted in fewer titles being purchased. At the University of Wisconsin System level, for example, libraries have not received an increase in state funding for the past ten years. The present financial situation facing academic libraries can best be described as uncertain. There are many challenges facing academic libraries today and for the near future. Among them:

- Inflationary prices for books, serials, a/v and other types of library materials;

- Budget cuts and demands on budgets for technology, databases, special programs and services;
- Space issues as a result of the growing student population, adding more new technologies in addition to the traditional books and journals, more staff and more computers;
- Professors' growing expectations for publishing to meet the requirements for promotion and tenure;
- Demands from multidisciplinary studies, new programs, etc. demographic changes; and
- Expectations for more community outreach and service.

As a planning document, a budget can be used to express objectives set forth in financial terms. As a political document, the budget can show the importance of given services relative to other services provided by the library. A well designed budget must be flexible, forecasting and predicting future expenses, it should identify sources of funding (origin), and it should measure the financial performance of organization. The main issues of a budget plan are to create a stable environment, enable a library to add better services using the same budget or for additional increase in next year's budget, reflect current and future costs of print and electronic collections including costs of space (the need for additional space), and staff (the need for more staff).

When planning a library budget, financial planning models could provide means for assessing the effects of alternative financial policies and external environments upon the financial structure. Historical financial data, especially for sources and uses of funds provide good input. A budget model permits the testing of alternative policies and alternative assumptions about internal and external factors.

The budget for each year can be considered to be the short-range or operational plan with price tags attached to the various items. Previous library budgets are excellent indicators for determining where the library has been. Looking back five years can, in most cases, be most instructive and reveal patterns and trends. Long-range budget planning is one of the library administrator's most important duties.

Most academic libraries allocate a portion of their library materials budget to programs and instructional departments on campus based on a formula combining a base allocation and the elements of the number of faculty, academic, majors, minors, graduate students, and the cost of U.S. and foreign imprints in the field as cited in the *Bowker Annual of Library and Book Trade Information.*

On average, college and university libraries budgets are allocated according to the following formula: salaries, followed by book budget and other operating expenses: 50-65% for salaries, 35-25% for collections with serials consuming about 45-57%, and 10-15% for other expenses. Journal subscriptions and electronic databases now consume the lion's share of today's academic library budgets. Whatever remains after that can be allocated for discretionary funds to order purchases in support of each of the university's programs. As a result, some of the following coping strategies are being implemented by most academic libraries:

- Continue to reallocate money toward journals/databases;
- Buy fewer books;
- Continue to cancel journals;
- More reliance on resource sharing; and
- Reliance on outside sources to supplement the library's budget.

Today's academic librarians are responsible for running libraries that vary in the size of their budgets from more than $20 million to a few hundred thousand dollars. Presidents who support their college and university libraries have been able to boost and supplement their libraries' budgets by raising private funds (development/foundations), grants (federal, state and private), supplemental (sweeping end-of-year salary savings and budget surplus, if any, at the end of the fiscal year to benefit the library's acquisitions program).

Most of library budgets increases, if any, are incremental and take into account cost increases for books, journals and databases. Very few libraries use the zero-based budget practice. Most of the year-to-year budget is usually described as an operating budget. These are the funds to carry out the library's program for the year. Operating expenditures include supplies, utilities, insurance, service and repairs, along with less expensive items of equipment or furniture. The four variations of an operating budget, as mentioned before, are: 1) Line item (object-of-the-expenditure (books, salaries, materials, utilities). This kind of budget builds on previous year's budget; 2) Program Budget, which identifies long-range goals for the library, then breaks these goals into objectives; 3) Performance Based Budget, a refinement of program budgeting system. In this kind of budget variation, each item must be justified and feedback provided; and 4) In addition to the operating budget, there is the capital budget which is for long term projects such as buildings, major remodeling, furnishings, purchase of major equipment such as computers, and usually in excess of certain amount of money to be defined by the parent institution or its governing body (state, central or provincial government and the like), and could be funded from a number of sources.

A budget is simply a planning document which sets out in summary form the categories and amounts of expenditure which appear necessary to maintain the library's program. Therefore, a budget with clear and realistic estimates for what is needed during the year is easier to maintain and administer. This does not mean that external factors such as price increases for goods and services should not be taken into account when planning a budget. Library administrators prepare their budgets on the basis of current and past practices, taking into account new developments that may occur during a budget year and make the needed adjustments. In addition to internal factors, there are external factors such as taking into account professional standards and findings from the library literature on budget matters. Budget expenditures can be grouped into one of the following 1) Operating budget, which outlines the cost of operating an agency such as personnel costs, costs of maintaining the physical plant, of purchasing supplies and similar operating costs; and 2) Emergency budget, which is a one-time activity designed to meet an unexpected critical need.

The major budget distinction is that between expenditures for current operations and for capital improvements. There is also the special-purpose budget to meet specific needs and departmental budgets (reference, special collections, etc.) which are left to departments to administer. The general types of operating plans most often discussed are the traditional line-item budget, and the performance, program and zero-based budget systems. Budgets can be defined according to the classification of expenditures as either program-oriented, or means-oriented.

The line item, or object of expenditure budget is the most common form of library budgets. It is based on line-item accounting and lists those items necessary to conduct an activity, such as personnel, equipment, supplies, and books. This type of budget is developed based on increments to the base figures from the previous year. Line item budget does not require much planning since it is based on past library activities.

Performance budgeting, also referred to as program budgeting emphasizes the services that have been developed and assesses the dollar allocations that serve the needs of the clientele. Program budgeting requires the presentation of alternative ways of providing necessary services at different and priority levels. Performance budgeting is defined as activity budgeting, that is efficiency-oriented and places emphasis on the work to be done and its unit cost.

There are a number of steps involved in planning and controlling budgets. They can be summarized as follows:

- Preparation of a budget request for the fiscal year, and possibly part of a long-term budget planning cycle and based on future needs;
- Presentation of the budget;
- Casting of an actual budget following a negotiation process;
- Monitoring of expenditures during the fiscal year which, in most academic institutions start on July 1st.
- During the fiscal year, the director/dean of the college library and his/her budget team may have to respond to:

- Budget cuts and position freeze, which seem to be happening more frequently in recent years, in addition to the most recent phenomena of furloughs on college campuses;
- Sudden changes in programs and institutional needs;
- Shifting of funds to meet unexpected university needs; and
- Cancelling or reducing programs in mid-year

FORMS OF BUDGETS

In its simplest form, a budget may consist of three or four lines which summarize categories of expenditures. Whether the budget is long or short, detailed or abbreviated, as an object, a budget is merely a representation of what will be done with the allocated sums of money. It becomes a process by the carrying on of the transactions implicit in the accounts (salaries, fringe benefits, acquisition of book, travel, supplies and expenses, etc).

The three aspects of the budget are: planning, management, and control. Planning is concerned with budget preparation, and reflects the continuous process by which the objectives of an organization are assessed, changed, and restated. Management is the process by which the necessary resources are obtained and used in order to achieve these objectives. Control is the process by which adherence to policy is ensured. Planning proceeds at the beginning of the fiscal year, while the audit side of control will begin at the end.

SOURCES OF FUNDING

Sources of funding can be either internal or external. Examples of the internal sources of funding are: tuition, income from local utilities such as photocopies, vending machines, and fees (such as rental fees, fees for online searches, fees for interlibrary loan, and the like). External types of funding include research grants and contracts, endowments, friends of the library. State, provincial and/or federal funds, and church-supported, when applicable, can be classified as internal and/or external, depending on the nature of the sources and designation. On average, academic institutions allocate about 4% of their total educational and general (E & G) expenditure budget to their libraries. The fortunate ones may receive more, but the majority may receive less. The former *ACRL Standards for College and Research Libraries* have called for 6%, which many institutions fail to meet. Today the academic library is receiving proportionally less and less of the resources of the university at a time when more and more demands are being made on it. The lucky ones receive about 4% of their campuses' E & G budget, others even less.

Due to the fact that academic library budgets have become so large and complex, directors and deans of academic libraries must now rely on professional budget experts, business managers and accountants. Responsibilities of these budget officers can be summarized as: 1) placing, processing, purchasing orders and paying bills; 2) checking monthly ledgers and reports; 3) guarding against budget overruns; 4) determining insurance inventories and coverage; 5) inventorying equipment; 6) paying staff salaries and benefits; 7) transferring funds from one budget category to another; and 8) collecting and reporting fines. Academic librarians must factor in inflation for book budgets and periodical subscriptions. They should also plan on priorities for budget cuts in times of retrenchment, which seem to be more in vogue due to recent global economic recession.

PRIMARY TYPES OF FUNDS

1. Operating Funds: The major fund for most institutions is the Operating Fund, frequently called the current fund. At the end of the fiscal year, the librarian prepares the Balance Sheet which includes assets and liabilities and fund balances; Statement of Revenue, Expense and Changes in Fund Balances, and the Statement of Changes in Cash, Sources of Cash, and Use of Cash.

2. Endowment Funds: A second major fund is the endowment fund or trust fund. This fund, or group of funds, has restrictions placed on them by donors or sources of these funds. Endowment funds are usually established to create ongoing sources of revenue by preventing use of the principal for current activity. The principal is usually protected and its gains in value and earned income are usually distributed by the institution according to a prior agreement between the managers of the institution, or perhaps the original donor. Proceeds may be transferred to another fund and then used for purposes within the restrictions of the new funds guidelines

3. Plant/Building Funds: These funds are used for major construction related to the library. The Plant Fund is most commonly used to establish reserves for repair, maintenance or replacement of facilities and equipment.

4. Fiduciary Funds: This group of funds is similar to, but broader than endowment funds and includes pension trust funds, agency funds and loan funds. Typical fund activities include motor pools, printing, duplication, and data processing.

5. The Balance Sheet: The balance sheet provides a snap shot of the financial health of the institution or organization on a specific date and

answers the question: How did we stand at that point in time? As a financial inventory, the balance sheet presents financial information in an orderly manner. It offers a comparison of the status of assets and liabilities at the end of an accounting period.

KINDS OF BUDGETS

- Revenue Budget: is a budget that projects future sales;
- Expense Budget: a budget that lists the primary activities undertaken by a unit and allocates a dollar amount to each;
- Profit Budget: a budget used by separate units of an organization that combines revenue and expense budgets to determine a unit's profits;
- Cash Budget: a budget that forecasts how much cash an organization will have on hand, and how much it will need to meet expenses;
- Capital Expenditure Budget: a budget that forecasts or includes major expenditures such as construction, remodeling, a bookmobile, and furniture and equipment costing more than a predetermined sum (such as $1,000);
- Fixed Budget; a budget that assumes fixed costs without regard to potential changes in the institutional internal activity or the external environment; and
- Variable Budget: A budget that takes into account those costs that vary with volumes of purchasing.

BUDGET FORMATS

There are four budget formats to choose from:
1.   Line-item;
2.   Program;
3.   Performance; and
4.   Zero-based.

1. *The Line-Item Budget* format is the traditional method of budgeting and it focuses on expenditures. Most libraries operate on a line item budget formula that shows in the aggregate what is going to be spent in a particular year. It assumes that all categories of expenditures made one year must be continued in the next, and that all activities included last year are not only essential, but are performed in the most cost-effective manner. It further assumes that last year's level is incremented for increases in costs, and that the spending level is further incremented for new projects and programs. For each year's budgetary forecast, costs are adjusted simply to reflect

inflation. There are advantages to line-item budgeting. It is simpler to construct than other formats and is easy to construct and compute. The individual lines are clearly defined; they emphasize control and tradition; they are comprehensible; little added explanation is necessary. Line items are the focus of analysis and control, and they are usually clearly defined, comprehensible and require little explanation. The disadvantage of the line item budget is that it does not stress the library's services to the public. Rather, emphasis is on services or commodities to be purchased by the library. Cost centers are not identified, and there is not sufficient historical data with which to discern major trends. The incremental (traditional) budget is the most popular budget approach. It has two identifying characteristics. First, funds are allocated to departments, or organizational units. The managers then allocate budgets to units as they deem appropriate. Second, the incremental budget develops out of the previous budget. Each period's budget begins by using the last period as a reference point. Only incremental changes in the budget request are reviewed.

2.   The *Program Budget Format* groups expenditures of all kinds by program. This kind of budgeting places less emphasis on objects as such. In the Program Budget, each service unit budgets its expenditures in response to its service goals and objectives, incorporating these goals and objectives as an integral part of the financial planning process. The program's goals and objectives would precede the calculated expenditures: personnel, materials, and operating costs. The program budget formulates spending plans and then makes appropriations on the basis of expected results. Expenditures are plotted to reflect quantified objectives. The program budget is derived for each area of service within a department, and then brought together for the department as a whole. The department budget is projected for the personnel, materials, supplies, communications, and other categories of expenditure necessary to meet objectives. Program budgeting is a complex process. It is difficult to assign fiscal responsibility for programs that span several departments. If goals and objectives are vague, then the strength of the resulting data is vague.

3.   *The Planning, Programming, Budgeting System (PPBS)* combines both the preceding methods, adding cost benefit analysis and management by objective

4.   *The Performance Budget Format* is a functional budget built around the library's service units. It uses the goals and objectives and figures of the program approach and adds to them workload performance measures—or service output, and unit costs. It is based primarily on the establishment of relationships between the investment of resources and the production of services. Performance budgets define the work performed to provide that

service. They emphasize output measures. Calculation of unit cost is added. Services are provided so that they can be described in terms of work input and service output. Program elements are broken down into their functions, activities into their individual components. Performance budgets are useful in evaluating alternative means of carrying out the same activities.

5. *The Zero-Based Budget (ZBB)* Format is popularly defined as an operating plan through budgeting that requires managers to justify their entire budget in detail from scratch, hence zero-base or cut back management, and to show why they should spend any money at all. This approach requires that all activities be identified in decision packages that are evaluated systematically and ranked in order of importance, combining the goals and objectives of the program format with the service output measures of the performance format and adding to them its own unique features—a priority ranking of services. This listing builds an element of control over cutbacks by indicating to funding decision makers where cuts will be made if resources are not sufficient to support services as projected. The lowest priority is cut first. This helps ensure that no arbitrary reductions will be made. ZBB requires managers to justify their entire budget from scratch. Every year, managers have to look at each service unit and determine whether or not it should be funded by asking questions such as: Should the service be abolished or continued? If the budget increases next year, will the costs outweigh the benefits? ZBB, like incremental budgeting has its set of drawbacks. It increases paperwork, and requires time to prepare. Its eventual outcome rarely differs much from what would occur through an incremental budget. ZBB is rarely used and when implemented, it asks that each year be constructed from the bottom up. ZBB provides for more flexibility.

6. Formula Budget (FB): is based on the use of standards and quantitative measurements in the allocation of funds.

PREPARING FOR CAPITAL BUDGET EXPENDITURE

A major step in justifying capital outlay and STRATEGY is to follow a planning process and gather data inputs. Data inputs include: Current and projected resources and space needed to house those resources; review of the changes in service and resources which may occur as a result of technological advances, demographic changes, or other long-term trends. Initial planning should be done by the library staff, preferably with the help of an experienced consultant. The planning report will be presented to governing boards responsible for a budget approval and allocation. Preparing for capital expenditures requires several steps among them:

SUPPLEMENTING THE LIBRARY'S BUDGET

In order to boost their university libraries' budgets, most universities have decided to return a percentage of grant indirect costs (about 5%) to support library and information technology infrastructure. On a yearly basis, a university like UWM anticipates that this will translate into about $300,000 for the first year, increasing as the University's research portfolio expands.

Most academic librarians no longer rely solely on their library allotments from their campuses' E & G budgets. Part of their responsibilities as chief officers of their libraries is to do what other academic deans and program directors on campus—to obtain additional funds through gifts and grants. A good source of gifts and donations are the libraries' friends' groups or associations, and parents' groups which consists of students' parents willing to make donations to the college library. We will discuss grants, grant writing and fundraising in chapter 12.

The *ACRL Standards* require that library budgets to be "prepared, justified and administered by the library director/dean in accordance with agreed upon objectives; that the budget should meet the reasonable expectations of library users when balanced against other institutional need." It further recommends that the library "should utilize its financial resources efficiently and effectively," and that the library director/dean should "have authority to apportion funds and initiate expenditures within the library budget and in accordance with institutional policy. Needles to say that the budget should support appropriate levels of staffing and adequate staff compensation."

REFERENCES

Byrd, Gary D.. 1989. "Financial Implications of Strategic Planning." North Carolina Libraries 47: 6-10.

Bowker Annual of Library and Book Trade Information, 53 ed. 2008. NY: R.R. Bowker.

Corry, E. 1982. Grants for the Smaller Library: Sources of Funding and Proposal Writing Techniques for the Small and Medium-sized Library. Boulder, CO: Libraries Unlimited.

Finding the Sites and Resources for Fundraising & Grants. Retrieved Dec 16, 2009, from: http://librarysupportstaff.com/find$.html

Graff, I. 1977. Library Financial Management System: Budget Forecast Program: Instruction Manual. Niles, IL: Graff.

Hallam, A. 2005. Managing Budgets and Finances: a How-to-do-it Manual for Librarians. NY: Neal-Schuman Publishers.

Holt, Glen. 2002. "Long–range financial planning for libraries." The Bottom Line 15, no. 3: 125-8.

Lomax, J.O, et al. 2000. A Guide to Additional Sources of Funding and Revenue for Libraries and Archives. 2nd ed. London: British Library.

Martin, M. S. 1978. Budgetary Control in Academic Libraries. Greenwich, CT: Jai Press.

Prentice, A. 1983. Financial Planning for Libraries. Metuchen, NJ: Scarecrow Press.

Roberts, Stephen A.. 2001. "Trends and developments in financial management of collections in academic and research libraries." The Bottom Line 14, no. 3: 152-63.

Roberts, Stephen A.. 2003. "Financial Management of Libraries: Past Trends and Future Prospects." Library Trends 51, no. 3: 462-93.

Rolen, Rhonda. 2009. "Tips for Writing Grants." Louisiana Libraries 71, no. 3: 16-18.

Seer, Gitelle. 2000. "Special library financial management: the essentials of library budgeting." The Bottom Line 13, no. 4: 186-92.

Singh, S. P. 1978. Capital Expenditure Decisions: an Analytic Approach. Allahabad: Wisdom Publications.

Stueart, R. D. and Moran, B. B. 2007. Library and Information Center Management. 7th ed. Westport, CT: Libraries Unlimited.

Usry, M. F. 1966. Capital-Expenditure Planning and Control. Austin, TX: Bureau of Business Research, University of Texas.

5

Human Resources

Academic libraries are staffed with professional librarians who hold an accredited graduate degree in library and information studies. They are assisted in their daily work by other professionals with graduate and/or undergraduate education in other fields, and paraprofessionals and clerical staff of various education and skills performing other supportive duties. In addition, academic libraries are fortunate to have a built-in workforce that is willing and able to work in these libraries. They are the campus undergraduate and graduate students who provide an intelligent, enthusiastic and cheap work force.

In most academic libraries, the head librarian or his associate/assistant librarian is also responsible for human resources issues. But in larger university libraries there may be a small human resources department with a full time person in charge of personnel matters. Where a department exists, it acts in conjunction with the office or department of human resources on campus. The responsibility of the library's HR department is to recruit all types of library staff, evaluate library staff, manage personnel files and other matters such as vacation, sick leaves, retirement, and other human resources related issues

The full time staff in an academic library has a myriad of titles and responsibilities. Among such titles are: librarians, bibliographers, curators and conservators, archivists and historians, fundraisers, systems and programming specialists, financial managers, architects and facilities planners, library assistants, clerical staff, maintenance and technicians, security officers, among others.

The ALA *ACRL's Guidelines* advise academic institutions to have a sufficient staff in size and quality to meet the pragmatic and service needs of its primary users. It requires academic librarians to have ALA accredited graduate degrees and perform professional activities. Special emphasis is placed on staff training and development through continuing education. Personnel policies and procedures should be guided by the ACRL *Standards for Faculty Status for College and University Librarians* (http://ala.org/acrl/guides/facsta01.html).

One of the important functions of a supervisor/manager's job is to make good hires and to help those hires become successful on the job. A good manager wants to be successful on the job and also leave a lasting positive influence on the organization. The supervisor's ability to recruit and select employees is a skill likely to be examined at interviews for any management position. Selection and interviewing are core management skills. This can be developed over time, with experience. There is a cost to pay for bad hiring. Ineffective or high maintenance individuals will drain energy, not only from the rest of the team, but also from the organization as a whole. If one is building a house, use good foundation. If one is building a department, use good employees. A U.S. Department of Labor study shows that 50 % of new hires last only six months in the position for which they were hired. There are hidden and direct costs for bad hiring. The cost of bad hires can be calculated by a formula known as CPH (cost per hire)—total cost for the recruitment of all hires in a given period (usually a month or quarter) divided by the number of hires. Good hiring benefits the director and the organization and gives a sense of satisfaction. There are factors that can contribute to good and to bad hires.

There are essential questions that should be considered by the library management as soon as a position is open: 1) Is the job necessary as it is defined at the present time?; 2) When a job opens up you should identify if the job has changed and if so how? 3) Has the job increased or decreased in responsibility to warrant a different title and salary scale?; 4) How frequent is the turnover in the position? And 5) If turnover is frequent, you need to address why. It could be due to the fact that the job description does not match the real world requirements of the job. Perhaps the job is too much for one person to handle, and needs to be split into two or more separate functions.

It helps to get answers to these questions in order to reduce the confusion and costly turnover of hiring someone to do an impossible job, or getting a candidate whose skills don't match the practical requirements of the position. Another secret to the success of a good hire is to re-examine the current job description for the vacant position, as this will help determine the appropriateness of the position for the current and future needs of the organization.

Among the steps to follow in developing a sound job description are the following: Have your staff develop their own job descriptions as these job descriptions will identify the strengths and weaknesses and this will give you insight into possible training programs to enhance staff competencies and also alert you to key criteria for successful new hires. List the five or ten major functional responsibilities of each position. Make a list and prioritize the functions, then go back to each function and identify skill sets or special knowledge required to execute that function successfully.

There are steps that should be taken in defining realistic job description and needs. Your central HR department can help in each of these steps:

1. Write down the job title;
2. List the major functional responsibilities and the skills required for the position;
3. Determine educational requirements;
4. Identify the depth and quality of experience required;
5. Determine the requirement for stability. What are the reasons for the applicant's job-hopping;
6. Consider the position's interaction with other people, levels, departments, and customers. What kind of communication skills and customer skills are required in the position; and
7. Future role for person and position. Training can lead to promotion.

STEPS TO TAKE TO ENSURE SUCCESSFUL HIRES

Don't use the same old job description and hiring practices; the odds are that the same old problems will continue to crop up down the road. Give the department a "once over" and ask some questions that will help define the real needs of the job: Is the department living up to the institution's expectations? If not, where is it falling short?; Has the institution made any recent directional changes that should affect the manpower and skill set makeup of the team?; What positions are needed to successfully meet a department's goals?; Could money be saved, and productivity increased by providing existing staff some other resources, such as another administrative assistant?; What specific skills are needed to execute each job or position?; What level of experience is required?; Who in the HR department can help to mentor the manager in this evaluative process?.

Other traits include: collegiality, flexibility, customer-oriented, willing, small/not bureaucratic, knowledgeable, embracing change, opportunities for staff development, teaching/helping mentality, able to participate, have a sense of humor.

RECRUITMENT

For beginning positions, the process can be begun by looking within the organization. In a library where a student employee has completed his/her graduate degree in library and information science, it may be a good idea to

encourage this person to apply for the position when an announcement is made
public. This is not at the exclusion of outsiders who may apply for the position,
and should not be discriminated against or given the impression that the position
is already "cooked" or spoken for and an internal candidate has already been
identified, perhaps in violation of the institution's commitment to equal
opportunity and affirmative action. If everything else is equal and the internal
candidate surfaces to the top of the list, then there are advantages to hiring
someone who has a vested interest in the organization, is loyal, and familiar with
its structure and the community it serves.

Regardless of the availability of an internal candidate, others should be
encouraged to apply; library staff should be invited to make recommendations, if
they know someone. Or contact fellow professionals in the field, as
'networking' is another way to cast your search net wide. Seek the assistance of
the HR department for posting help-wanted ads, contacting temporary-help
agencies. Other outlets include headhunters for mid and upper management
positions, job fairs, online recruitment, and resumé banks.

In addition to sound professional education, what colleges and universities
expect from new or old library staff can be summarized as follows: flexibility,
willingness to do what is necessary, comfortable with technology, knowledge of
users' needs, orientation to service, proactive and outgoing, good marketing
skills since libraries are in the business of marketing and promoting their
libraries' services and products and subject expertise in one or more academic
disciplines.

The interview process is a very important step in the organization's efforts
to select the right person for the right job at the right price. There are steps to
take in managing and conducting the interview process. Initial interviews can be
done via phone or conference calls between the search and screen committee
and the applicants. Coupled with the right selection of the committee members
and the questions to be asked, the result will be a further weeding of unqualified
applicants and narrowing down the list of potential applicants. It is expected that
the search and screen committee will be looking for a person who is:

Able and willing, a team player, is manageable, and has skills such as
technical, interpersonal and conceptual.

Recruiting librarians is a very important managerial decision which
involves, not just deans and directors of libraries, but also members of the staff,
the campus human resources and diversity offices on campus. Most interviews
are individual and group interviews. The organization can decide who will be
included on the search and screen committee, as well as the group conducting
the interview in addition to the individual interviews. Group interviews with
counterparts in the department or unit of hiring will help both candidates and
staffers to decide on the level of comfort with one another and can reveal to

either side information about the organization and the candidate that may have not been ascertained otherwise. Interview questions can be chronological versus behavioral questioning.

The graying of the library profession is evidenced by the number of expected retirements. According to the U. S. Department of Labor's Bureau of Labor Statistics "two out of three librarians are 45 years of age or older" and will retire within the next ten years. Recruitment of a new generation of librarians must also take into consideration the importance of recruitment of minorities to the profession. In an article titled *Responses to Diversity: a Comparison of the Libraries at Stanford and UCLA,* Lee Anne H. Paris observed that "American academic libraries' lack of response to diversity in academic libraries has resulted in insufficiently diverse library staff and few effective information service for minority communities." She further suggests that academic libraries "need to strengthen their resolve to benefit from the emerging character of a multiracial and multicultural society." (Paris, 1997). More on diversity at the end of this chapter.

EMPOWERING EMPLOYEES

Empowered employees are happier, more productive and loyal. To empower employees, the literature recommends:
1. Be sure that employees have the abilities and motivation to perform empowered tasks. They should therefore be screened for their ability to perform in an empowered setting or be appropriately trained to do so.
2. Be specific about what employees can and cannot do.
3. Specify employees' range of discretion. There has to be a limit to the amount of freedom they may exercise. The supervisor should be consulted when the employees reach the outside range.
4. The supervisor should inform others that empowerment has occurred so they know that the employees are not acting on their own or without approval.
5. Establish feedback controls. Empowerment does not mean abdication. The ultimate responsibility lies with the supervisor. Getting feedback on what is happening in the unit is the job of the supervisor.

While motivation and education are very important to a successful workforce, in the library profession, as in hospitality, education and health related professions, having "people skills" is of utmost importance to librarians. It is easier to hire the right attitudes than it is to change long-established wrong ones. Having good recognition skills needs to be one of the criteria for hiring new librarians, or library managers for that matter. This is why companies like

Walt Disney, Southwest Airlines, and other successful businesses recruit people-oriented individuals, regardless of the position. Southwest Airlines, for example adopts a policy to "hire for attitude, train for skill." All employees at Disney, for example, are required to attend Traditions 101 and learn the values of the organization, including the importance of how people are treated and what these values look like in practice. In any organization, and especially in libraries of all types, people skills are very important and must be used as criteria for hiring and promotion. Librarians and managers who are not competent people-developers should receive additional training. It is unfortunate when some libraries, mistakenly focus more on technical and theoretical preparations and operations than they do with soft skills related to working with and/or managing others.

MOTIVATION AND DIFFERENTIATION THEORY

Differentiation is a way to manage people and businesses. Here is what Jack Welch has to say about differentiation in his book, *Winning* (2005):

> Basically, differentiation holds that a company has two parts, software and hardware. Software is simple, it is your people. Hardware depends. If you are a large company, your hardware is the different business in your portfolio. If you are smaller, your hardware is your product lines.

Applying differentiation to hardware and products is easy and straightforward. Every company has strong business or product lines and weak ones and some in between. Differentiation requires managers to know which is which and invest accordingly. To be strong, a product will have to be number one or number two in its market. If not, the managers will have to fix it, sell it, or as a last resort, close it. Differentiation among people, however, is different. It is a process that requires a manager to assess employees and separate them into three categories in terms of performance: top=20%, middle=70% and bottom=10%. Differentiation requires managers to act on that distinction. When people differentiation is real, the top 20 % of employees are showered with bonuses, stock options, praise, love, training and a variety of rewards to their pocketbooks, and souls. (p. 41)

The middle 70% are managed differently. The management needs to keep them motivated and engaged. After all, they are the majority. That is why so much of managing the middle 70% is about training, positive feedback, and thoughtful goal setting.

Differentiation is about managers looking at the middle 70%, identifying people with the potential to move up, and cultivating them. Everyone in the middle 70% need to be motivated and made to feel as if they truly belong. You do not want to lose the vast majority of your middle 70%—you want to improve them. As for the bottom 10 % in differentiation, there is no sugar coating this, they have to go; unfortunately, that is easier said than done. Protecting underperformers always backfires. The worst thing, though, is how protecting people who don't perform hurts the people themselves.

Differentiation has its proponents, like Jack Welch who applied it when he was CEO of GE, and detractors who view it as pitting people against one another and undermining teamwork, or differentiation is enormously de-motivating to the middle 70 %, who end up living in an awful kind of limbo.

LABOR MANAGEMENT RELATIONS

In some libraries, the management of human resources is governed by policies and procedures spelled out in the labor contract. In a unionized environment, labor and management can work closely together to make their organization better, avoid conflicts and possible strikes. When we talk about collective bargaining, we refer to the negotiation, administration, and interpretation of a labor contract. Federal regulation requires a union to secure signed authorization cards from 50% of the employees, after which the union is automatically certified. Once a union is certified, the management has to negotiate with that union. Negotiations begin with union presenting a list of demands. These demands are derived from information gathered from other organizations, like what they are doing with their labor unions such as compensation, overtime, safety, and cost of living data. On these bases, the union and the management can negotiate terms of the contract. Labor unions can make firing a big issue, as unions are credited with providing their members with job security. We are also living in an increasingly litigious society, and supervisors are concerned about being named in a law suit against them or the institution they work for, or both dealing with discrimination and the like. Supervisors have become gun shy lately and are reluctant to weed the bad public or unionized employees especially those who lack the knowledge and soft-people skills.

STAFF TRAINING

There are several implications of a more diverse future workplace, many of which can be seen as beneficial to organizations. As the workplace grows more diverse, an obvious implication is the need for increased training, not only for management but for all employees. The focus of this training would be on the differences and similarities of cultures, attitudes, and expectations of a diverse workforce. There are many benefits to providing staff with training opportunities, among them: elimination of insensitive and intolerant behaviors at work, reducing an organization's liability for discrimination and harassment claims, transforming the organization, creating harmonious relationships between team members, and retaining high quality employees.

Hall and Parker's article titled *"The role of workplace flexibility in managing diversity"* states that by including the views of a diverse workforce it will improve the overall creativity and cooperation of any organization (Hall & Parker, 1993). Hall and Parker also argue that a major implication of an increasingly diverse workforce will be the need for organizations to be more flexible in order to "…encourage higher levels of involvement in the activities and relationships that make up a job—and, as a result can produce better work performance"(p.6). Another argument for increasing flexibility of an organization in order to meet the needs of a diverse workforce is the equal (versus identical) treatment or benefits. Organizational flexibility in this regard can be defined as "…providing different members of different groups with different mechanisms through which they can bring their whole selves to work and perform to their full potential" (p.9). Finally, another benefit of workplace diversity would be for the library staff to reflect the diversity of the community that they serve. Reflecting and even improving upon this diversity would help enable the library to gain public trust and respect as being an organization which values and encourages diversity and therefore encouraging all patrons to take advantage of their services. For management, this means developing skills to attract, grow and retain diverse job candidates and staff. By acknowledging and encouraging a diverse workforce, organizations can increase overall retention and job satisfaction of all employees.

STEPS FOR IMPLEMENTING DIVERSITY IN ACADEMIC LIBRARIES

- Listen to staff members;
- Hire staff who represent the spectrum of American society and utilize their talents and ideas;
- Train existing staff to help them understand different cultural attitudes and beliefs, cultural responsiveness for existing non-ethnic library staff personnel;
- Avoid conflicts and misunderstanding and alleviate resentment toward new cultural groups;
- Conduct periodic outreach/recruitment efforts to identify potential multicultural staff;

- Establish and highlight special events from each representative community group, e.g. African American Awareness or Black History Month, Hispanic family week, etc;
- Provide orientation sessions for ethnic groups; and
- Maintain ongoing line of communication and cooperation with leaders from each representative ethnic community group

There are a number of helpful sources to aid library managers in their efforts to diversify their staff, among them is the diversity web site, www.diversityweb.org, which is a project of the Association of American Colleges and Universities Office of Diversity, Equity and Global Initiatives. The main objective is to foster diversity in today's colleges and universities, and to make diversity an educational priority. The ACRL has an excellent web page describing instruction for diverse populations: http://www.ala.org/ala/mgrps/divs/acrl/about/sections/is/committees/idp.cfm.
The print and electronic resources have been authored within the last few years and describe teaching diverse groups within an academic library context. Ten to twenty resources are listed for each diverse population group. http://www.ala.org/ala/acrlbucket/is/publicationsacrl/diversebib.htm.

STAFF EVALUATION AND PERFORMANCE REVIEW

The quality of academic library service is directly related to the quality of the library staff. A well qualified, experienced and happy library staff provides good quality and efficient service. Therefore, it is important that the library hires, trains, retains, promotes and rewards high quality staff. Most academic librarians, particularly in the U.S., or American universities or their branches overseas require their college librarians to have a master's degree from one of the ALA accredited library schools in North America. In addition, some are requiring a second Master's degree in another discipline, and even the doctorate for middle and upper management positions in academic libraries. Membership in professional library associations like the ALA, ACRL, and other relevant organizations within the ALA, LITA, SLA, EDUCOM, and or their equivalents is equally important for a professional staff that should keep abreast of developments in the profession, interact with other academic librarians and library leaders in the profession. These and many similar organizations offer continuing education programs and workshops. Their journals and newsletters are good read for a library staff who should be informed about research and development in their profession, best practices, who is doing what where, grant opportunities, and the like.

The academic library needs constantly to take stock of its workforce and to assess its performance in existing jobs for three reasons:

- To improve performance via improving the performance of individual contributors (should be an automatic process in the case of good managers, but (about annually) two key questions should be posed:
  - What has been done to improve the performance of a person last year?
  - What can be done to improve his or her performance in the year to come?
- To identify potential, i.e. to recognize existing talent and to use that to fill vacancies higher in the organization, or to transfer individuals into jobs where better use can be made of their abilities or developing skills.
- To provide an equitable method of linking payment to performance where there are no numerical criteria (often this salary performance review takes place about three months later and is kept quite separate from 1. and 2. , but is based on the same assessment).

On-the-spot managers and supervisors, not HR staff, are the ones responsible for the evaluation of their subordinates. The HR personnel role is usually that of:

- Advising top management of the principles and objectives of an evaluation system and designing it for particular organizations and environments.
- Developing systems appropriately in consultation with managers, supervisors and staff representatives. Securing the involvement and cooperation of appraisers and those to be appraised.
- Assistance in the setting of objective standards of evaluation / assessment, for example:
  - Defining targets for achievement;
  - Explaining how to quantify and agree on objectives;
  - Introducing self assessment; and
  - Eliminating complexity and duplication.
- Publicizing the purposes of the exercise and explaining to staff how the system will be used.
- Organizing and establishing the necessary training of managers and supervisors who will carry out the actual evaluations/ appraisals. Not only training in principles and procedures, but also in the human relations skills necessary. (Lack of confidence in their own ability to handle situations of poor performance is the main weakness of assessors.
- Monitoring the scheme; ensuring it does not fall into disuse, following up on training/job exchange etc. , recommendations, reminding managers of their responsibilities.

Full-scale periodic reviews should be a standard feature of evaluation schemes since resistance to evaluation / appraisal is common and the temptation to water down or render schemes ineffectual is ever present (managers resent the time taken, if nothing else).

Basically an evaluation / appraisal scheme is a formalization of what is done in a more casual manner anyway (e.g. if there is a vacancy, discussion about internal moves and internal attempts to put square pegs into "squarer holes" are both the results of casual evaluation). Most managers approve merit payment and that too, calls for evaluation. Staff evaluation is a standard routine task; it aids the development of talent, warns the inefficient or uncaring and can be an effective form of motivation. The purpose of staff evaluation should be spelled out clearly in the evaluation process and the form should be completed by the library staff. A good introduction to the evaluation form outlining the objectives of evaluation and its value to both the library and the person being evaluated will create a feeling of good-will and help remove the sense of apprehension that surrounds performance assessment. For example: the staff performance appraisal "is designed to enhance counseling and communication, professional development, personnel decisions such as consideration for promotion, tenure or salary increases.

In order for the evaluation to be fair and successful, the criteria and the procedures should be clearly explained to the newly hired staff members, if not before, by placing the evaluation guidelines and criteria on the library's web site. This way, expectations are clear and there are no surprises or hidden agendas.

Performance expectations should be clear and made known to employees. The performance evaluation process should give the staff member ample opportunity to respond to the supervisor's evaluation, regardless of agreement or disagreement with the supervisor's evaluation. The evaluation should mention areas of strengths, weaknesses, and areas in need of improvement which can be used as goals for the staff member to strive to achieve before the next evaluation. The evaluation should be kept confidential; the information is used only for personnel actions and decisions. Most HR specialists prefer not to have the annual performance evaluation tied to annual salary increases, although the evaluation plays a part in this process. Other criteria and traits to be used in the evaluation include, but are not limited to: knowledge, communication skills (verbal and written), personal and work ethics, dependability, team-work, and technical and soft skills, to mention a few.

Frequency of evaluations varies. A newly appointed librarian may be evaluated six months after joining the library, while in other cases, an evaluation is conducted at the conclusion of the first year of appointment and annually thereafter. At the conclusion of six years, and after a rigorous campus evaluation process, an academic librarian may be promoted to tenure or the equivalent, such as indefinite appointment. Awards, some financial and recognitions, verbal or written can be bestowed on staff members who demonstrate exceptional qualities. This creates a healthy competition among staff and gives users the opportunity to name staff members of distinction. This is good for staff morale and the positive image of the library.

Listed below are examples of the major areas of performance and criteria that a supervisor could use in completing the annual evaluation of a librarian using a scale of 1-5 (with 5 being outstanding/excellent; 4: Above average; 3: Average/satisfactory; 2: Improvement needed; and 1: Unsatisfactory; 0 or N/A for not applicable.

1. Personal attributes (initiative, stability, adaptability, judgment, sense of responsibility);

2. Professional qualities (professional competence, professional activities, professional ethics, relations with library users, awareness of academic community and current affairs);

3. Job responsibilities and performance (designed to gather information on the employee's attitude, organization of work, quality of work, planning and decision-making, acceptance and use of criticism, supervisory skills, supervisory relations;

4. Specific questions to ask include:
   - Does the employee clearly understand what his/her responsibilities are?
   - Does the employee achieve what is expected within these responsibilities?
   - Does the employee understand how the job relates to other jobs? How his/her job contributes to the whole?

5. Technical competence:
   - Does the employee possess the skills required to do the job effectively and does s/he apply them well?
   - Does the employee use technologies to the level required by the job?

6. Work quality:
   - When mistakes are made, are they subsequently corrected or is assistance sought?
   - Is the employee's work accurate?
   - Has the employee made adequate personal contributions to the success of the department by effective execution of responsibilities?
   - Are there positive or negative opinions of the employee's work from coworkers or customers?
   - Are same mistakes made on an ongoing basis?

7. Judgment:

- Does the employee make sound decisions in areas that affect job performance?
- Does the employee manage multiple or conflicting tasks well? Does s/he prioritize tasks well?
- Does the employee seek assistance when necessary?
- Does the employee understand the business environment in which s/he operates?

8. Dependability:
- Are project deadlines regularly met or missed?
- Does the employee effectively track project or work status?
- Is the employee punctual when coming to and leaving work, and attending meetings?
- Is the employee dependable?
- Is the employee organized in his approach to the working day and the projects at hand?

9. Teamwork and professionalism:
- Does the employee treat workers with respect?
- Does the employee get along with members of another sex, race, or belief system?
- Does the employee adhere to any required business dress code?
- Is the employee's work professional with customers, clients, and the public when representing the institution?
- Does the employee adhere to all college and library policies and procedures?

10. Communication:
- Does the employee communicate with others effectively when necessary?
- Are written communications adequate (Layout, grammar, syntax, tone, etc.)?
- Are verbal capabilities appropriate to the needs of the job?
- Is communication with peers, customers, and management appropriate?

11. Initiative:
- Are there instances that exemplify a commitment, or lack thereof, to the job's responsibilities and the success of the work group?
- Does the employee suggest ideas and solutions?
- Does the employee identify needed tasks and perform them, or wait until they are brought to his/her attention?
- Does the employee suggest new ideas to improve productivity, workflow, teamwork, or the like?

- Is the employee a self-starter, or does s/he wait for instructions?

12. Customer satisfaction:
    - Does the employee understand the needs of his customers, internal or external to the work group and the organization?
    - Does the employee work to satisfy those needs? Is the employee committed to customer satisfaction?

In addition to the rating scale similar to the one mentioned above, there is always a section on the form for narrative appraisal. Both staff and supervisor should sign the completed form even when there are disagreements. In this case the subordinate can express his disagreement in the appropriate space provided on the form.

While not all colleges and universities require their librarians to publish, most academic librarians are frequent contributors to the library literature as writers of journal articles and even books. Some universities require their academic librarians to publish in order to be considered for promotion and tenure or the equivalent of the latter, known as indefinite appointment. Also important is to serve on state, regional and national professional associations, as well as being active on campus committees as part of satisfying the service requirement in academic faculty and staff evaluation and future promotion. This is part and parcel of staff involvement in the campus and broader community, and of keeping in touch with the academic library constituencies.

To help incoming academic librarians adjust to their new responsibilities, the peer mentoring system which matches experienced librarians with the newcomers is being practiced in some libraries. It is patterned after the mentoring system used for faculty and can be helpful in orienting, training and advancing the new cadre of academic librarians at the hands of the more experienced "old hand or old guards".

INDIVIDUAL DEVELOPMENT PLAN

The library, with help and guidance from the HR may use what is known as the IDP (Individual Development Plan) to assist in the assessment of library employees. The IDP will also facilitate the review of position descriptions on an annual basis and allow for updating as needed. Updated position descriptions will be signed by the supervisor and employee and forwarded to Human Resources for approval. Components of the IDP include:

1. Position Description
    It is vital for the position description to be accurate and up-to-date. The position description dictates position expectations and describes major duties and responsibilities of a position. The position description should be prepared in the goal and worker activities format. The goal statements

should describe the major duties and responsibilities of a position. The worker activities describe in specific terms what the employee is expected to do to accomplish these goals.

2. Department/Unit Organization Chart

These organizational charts may require revisions. To ensure accuracy, annual revisions should be coordinated through the IDP process and forwarded to the HR unit on campus.

3. Discussion

The discussion component of the IDP encompasses the following:

- Department/Unit Goals

Departmental/Unit goals will be reviewed during the IDP session. These goals are the basis on which the employee and supervisor align the employee career goals and supervisor position expectations.

- Employee Career Goals

Employees and supervisors will discuss employee career aspirations.

- Supervisor Position Expectations

Supervisors will outline, communicate and document specific position expectations for the employee to achieve.

During this exercise, employees and supervisors will determine which career goals can be achieved in the current employment setting and will create a strategic plan to accomplish these goals. This portion of the IDP allows for employment growth and satisfaction. The IDP process facilitates the review and planning of supervisor's expectations.

4. Review Outcomes (Results) from the previous IDP year

Supervisors will review the employee's career goals and the supervisor's position expectations set in the previous year. Supervisors will outline, communicate and document the IDP results with the employee.

5. Planning for the next IDP year

The planning session will document the specific timelines in which to accomplish the established employee's career goals and the supervisor's position expectations throughout the next IDP year.

6. Comments

The comments section allows for the employee and/or supervisor to indicate information not addressed during the IDP session and/or voice concerns regarding the outcomes (results) documented.

DISCIPLINING EMPLOYEES

Disciplining employees is part and parcel of what managers are required to do if the subordinate is performing poorly, as can be judged from regular staff evaluations, lacks required skills, or committed unprofessional or unethical acts. The results of the staff appraisal mentioned above could lead the supervisor to discipline his/her subordinate(s). Listed below are some steps that should be followed when disciplining an employee:

1. Before accusing anyone, investigate the problem. If the infraction was not personally seen, investigate to determine what happened. Document date, time, place, individuals involved, mitigating circumstances, and the like.
2. Ensure that ample warning was provided to the employee. Before any formal action is taken, be certain that the employee has been provided reasonably early warnings, and that these warnings have been documented.
3. Act in a timely fashion. When it becomes apparent that an infraction has occurred, and it has been supported by the investigation, do something, and do it quickly.
4. Conduct the discipline session in private. Good supervisors praise subordinates in public, but keep punishment private. Public reprimands embarrass and humiliate the employee and may not lead to the desired behavior change.
5. Adopt a calm and serious tone. Administering disciplines should not be facilitated in a loose, informal, and relaxed manner. Avoid anger or other emotional responses, and convey your comments in a clam and serious tone.
6. Be specific about the problem. Define the violation in exact terms instead of ambiguous regulations. Explain why the behavior cannot continue by showing how it affects the employee's job performance, the unit's effectiveness, and the employee's colleagues.
7. Keep it impersonal. Focus on the employee's behavior, not the employee. The discussion should be on objective information, not some subjective or evaluative statement.
8. Get the employee's side of the story. Due process demands that the employee be given the opportunity to explain his or her position regarding what happened. If significant deviations occur, the supervisor may need to do more investigation. Active listening is important here to ensure that the supervisor has the relevant facts.
9. The supervisor should keep control of the discussion. Disciplining an employee by definition is an authority-based act. The supervisor is enforcing the organization's standards and regulations. Ask the employee for his/her side of the story and get the facts.
10. Agree on how mistakes can be prevented next time.
11. Disciplines should include guidance and direction for correcting the problem. Have the employee to draft a step-by-step plan to change the problem behavior. Then set a timetable with the follow-up meetings in which progress can be evaluated.

DIVERSITY

The past few decades have seen tremendous growth in college enrollment numbers. Indeed, college enrollment in the United States has risen from only 25% of the population in 1967 to almost 40% in 2006 (U.S. Census Bureau, 2009). As more and more students are seeking post-secondary education, colleges have needed to evolve to accommodate this demand for a wider, more diverse student population and more diversified faculty and academic staff on campus. There are very strong reasons for the need to diversify staff and the change away from the *status quo*. One of the reasons is the shift in the population of the U.S., as Caucasians will cease to make up the majority of the population eight years sooner than previously estimated, According to the U.S. Census Bureau:

> In the next century…. America will be many faces and many races with no one majority group in the workforce. The question is not whether there will be a change but how we manage that change so that all may benefit. It is not so much a choice as a challenge.

Minorities, now roughly one-third of the U.S. population, are expected to become the majority in 2042, with the nation projected to be 54% minority in 2050. By 2023, minorities will comprise more than half of all children. This growth in minority populations will transform the U.S. into a white-minority country by 2042, according to the latest Census Bureau estimate. By 2050, the minority population — everyone except for non-Hispanic, single-race whites — is projected to be 235.7 million out of a total U.S. population of 439 million. The black population is projected to increase from 41.1 million, or 14% of the population in 2008, to 65.7 million, or 15% in 2050. The Hispanic population, on the other hand, is projected to nearly triple, from 46.7 million to 132.8 million during the 2008-2050 period. Its share of the nation's total population is projected to double, from 15% to 30%. Thus, nearly one in three U.S. residents will be Hispanic. More than 36% of the Hispanic population is under eighteen years of age and, unlike the old generation of Hispanics, the young ones are pursuing higher education as, evidenced by the growing number of Hispanics on American campuses, and especially the growing number of Hispanic-serving institutions (HIS) which have become important college destinations for Hispanics' access to college education and improving their economic opportunities.

As with the Hispanic population, the Asian population is projected to climb from 15.5 million to 40.6 million. Its share of the nation's population is expected to rise from 5.1% to 9.2%. Among the remaining race groups, American Indians and Alaska Natives are projected to rise from 4.9 million to 8.6 million (or from 1.6 to 2% of the total population). The Native Hawaiian and Other Pacific Islander population is expected to more than double, from 1.1 million to 2.6 million. The number of people who identify themselves as being of two or more races (biracial) is projected to more than triple, from 5.2 million to 16.2 million.

While recent statistics reveal that the demographics of the U.S. population have considerably changed with minority representation at approximately 30% in 2000, the number of minority representation in librarianship lags far behind 0.4% (Paris, 2007). Although library literature has provided many recommendations to facilitate cultural diversity, Trujillo and Weber (1991) asserted that American academic libraries' lack of response to this issue has resulted in insufficiently diverse library staff and few effective information services for minority communities. The researchers suggested that American academic libraries should resolve to compete with other sectors in society, and to benefit from the emerging character of a diverse society. This means that recruiters for the library profession will soon have a much more diverse applicant pool, workforce, and customer base. The question is will librarians in general and academic librarians in particular be able to welcome these changes, or will intolerant behavior and poor representation of minorities in the library profession put libraries at risk of talent loss, lawsuits, or both?

There is no longer any doubt about the benefits of having a diverse workforce. A diverse workforce at all levels, from librarian to student staff members creates a level of comfort for minority library users. When minority users see an employee of the library that looks like them, their (possible) feelings of apprehensiveness about the library are lessened. A diverse staff increases the comfort levels minority students, faculty, and community members have regarding the library. If a minority user sees another minority working within the library, they will be more likely to feel that they belong in the library in addition to having the impression that the library is a place of inclusivity. The academic library staff should represent the rich ethnic background located within the campus as well as within its local surroundings. Such inclusion of staff with different cultures and backgrounds can contribute to an increased awareness and respect for the cultural differences among minority groups. Brey-Casiano's editorial in *American Libraries* details why diversity is important in the academic library: "Diversity is at the heart of our nation today and, for that reason, must be at the heart of the library profession as well, library personnel, collections, programs, and services should reflect our communities". (Brey-Casiano 2005).

We live in a diverse society and libraries' staff should reflect the local, regional and national population our libraries serve. Pamela Tudor in her article titled "Adding value with diversity: What business leaders need to know," (http://www.aimd.org/files/PamelaTudor.pdf), mentions several types of diversity: "1. Social category diversity: visible demographic characteristics such as age, sex, ethnicity and race; 2. Informational diversity: educational level, organizational tenure and work experience, expertise of the individual; and 3. Goals and values diversity: team and company goals and underlying work values. "This diversity can lead to conflict, but then, if managed well, can lead to creativity. "Diverse (social category and informational) work teams develop more innovative solutions, but take longer to get there, at least initially.... It takes more time to work through some of this newness and difference. However, they are more effective than homogeneous teams." She suggests that "to capitalize on diversity, managers have to think about an appropriate work environment for their diverse work teams. The leader of this team should avoid a stability-oriented environment with a high emphasis on efficiency.... Studies have also confirmed that diverse groups perform better in organizations that implement diversity-oriented HR practices.

Diversity-oriented HR practices assert that diversity is a valuable asset to the organization, and send a clear signal supporting diversity. These practices deem that the organization values differences and that employees can leverage differences by expanding the knowledge base from which the team works to enhance creativity and effectiveness."

In their book titled *The Library Manager's Desk book: 102 Expert Solutions to 101 Common Dilemmas,* Carson and Carson (1995) examine the specific implications of diversity for libraries. They cite statistics that show while minorities are increasing in the workforce the percentage of minorities employed in the library field is still low— as of the time of the article, only 8%were African-Americans and 2% were Hispanic (p.14), which remains the same to this day. "Those figures represent a serious problem, as the pluralistic needs of patrons cannot be met by a homogenous white staff, a diverse staff is essential.... Although a diverse staff may initially pose some issues for the library manager, in the long run service quality may be improved through broader input into decision making and incorporation of divergent value systems into library policies" (p.14). The authors suggest that one solution is to encourage an increase in the number of minorities in library schools through partnerships between administrators and teachers, tuition waivers and monetary support, recruitment of freshman at four year colleges as well as in community colleges, and helping make the library work environment welcoming.

S. Balderrama, in "Deep Change--Diversity at Its Simplest." (2004), presents a pointed analysis of stages of diversity within a library:

> At the first level of diversity, typically our most successful, is programming and collections. No matter what our background we are capable as librarians of displaying,

programming, and building collections with multiculturalism and intellectual diversity in mind.... At the second level of diversity, we focus on staffing. This is who we work with, work for, work above in the organic or mechanical structures of our library organizations.... [We] recruit for diversity in an honest, authentic manner. We actively and purposely look for people who will be different from us. We look for qualifications and the rest is a surprise package.... Regardless, we focus and we go beyond a good faith effort, implement diverse strategies, rearticulate our job descriptions and recruitment brochures, connect with new or mainstream library groups or with those representing the GLBT, multicultural, and people with disability communities, and stretch timeframes if we need to in order to reach a diverse audience of qualified applicants. We do things differently because we are serious about a diverse workforce.... At the third level of diversity we are colorful at the table, reference desk, and on staff development day. We implement a shared library vision. We are able to finally say that we have visible diversity throughout the ranks. We may be able to include true and natural photos of visible diversity in our recruitment brochure. At the fourth level of diversity is a rainbow coalition. It devotes time to creating new and reviewing traditional operating principles, values, and communication methods.... At the fifth level of diversity are mutual reciprocation, respect, and exchange. Skill for skill... Lesson for lesson.... At this level I am recruited to a library; I get the job; I learn about the new "operating principles" and the overall expectations of a shared vision. I am interested and am willing to learn and to practice them. But if there is "true" diversity, then I expect the employer and organization to be interested in learning from me and to consider incorporating my added value into the organization's values. It is not really about "me." It is really about consistent growth, generation, incorporation and evaluation of a work environment and the service/ product provided. As with my employer, I have mutual respect for the user and my colleagues. I am not attempting to "better" or "empower" someone that I am superior to. I share my skill."(pp.17-18).

These steps give libraries something to aim for in the journey to diversity. In its attempts to solve the problem of weak representation of minorities in the academic library profession, the Association of Colleges and Research Libraries (ACRL) Task Force on Recruitment of Underrepresented Minorities submitted a report to the ACRL Board of Directors in 1991. The report identified several key issues in order to improve the situation on campuses among them is the "Institutional Commitment to Change and Accountability." Some libraries like the University of Wisconsin-Milwaukee recognized the need for change and took measures to respond to the ACRL Task Force Report, as early as 1991 by appointing a committee to study the need for a UW system-wide "Minority Studies Librarian" and developed a proposal embodying this idea. The UWM University Library Committee and other UW Library Directors also supported this proposal. The System Administration considered this a very promising idea, but for several years no funding was available to support such a position. It was then that UWM decided to act on its own and used it own budget to fund a newly created position of multicultural services librarian. The position is similar to others on other campuses in the U.S. The holder of the position is considered a catalyst in educating library staff about race relations and involving them in campus-wide diversity programs. In that way, s/he helps promote the university's and the library's commitment to diversity, enhances understanding among various groups, provides cultural sensibility, while avoiding stereotyped attitudes.

Library managers are encouraged to:

- Incorporate the values of cultural and ethnic diversity values in vision and mission statements. The deans or directors are the visionaries and strategic leaders of their academic libraries. They set the agenda for what plans should be implemented.
- Provide and participate in staff training to increase cultural awareness in all employees. Training can go so far as to encourage multilingualism, a plus for customer service as well as for employee relations. Where use of the English language is mandatory, managers can encourage workers to study English through ESL (English as a Second Language) classes in the community, or sponsoring in-house classes.
- Encourage positive practices in cultural diversity through employee recognition and rewards.
- Reflect various cultural values in benefits and scheduling with an eye toward meeting the wide variety of personal and family needs that a culturally diverse staff requires.
- Promote inclusion by communicating to everyone in the workplace that they are valued contributors to the team effort. Managers run the risk of alienating some employees who may feel that the typical white male is less valued in a new multicultural climate.
- Measure accountability, how successful has the organization been at recruiting and promoting culturally diverse workers? Is there a succession strategy and how effective is it?

DISCRIMINATION AND HARASSMENT

The website for the United States Equal Employment Opportunity Commission. http://www.eeoc.gov/origin/index.html Commission (EEOC) (www.eeoc.gov) offers detailed information about discrimination of all kinds in the work place and how to deal with these issues. According to the EEOC harassment is one of the most common claims raised in national origin charges filed with the EEOC. During the last decade, the number of private sector national origin harassment charges filed with the EEOC increased from 1,383 charges in 1993 to 2,719 charges in 2002. National origin harassment violates Title VII when it is so severe that the person being harassed find the work environment to be hostile. Sexual and ethnic harassment can take many forms, including sexually and ethnically offensive remarks, slurs, workplace graffiti, or other offensive actions because of a person's color, place of origins, ethnicity, culture, sexuality or foreign accent. The hostile environment may be created by supervisors, co-workers, or even non-employees such as customers.

The website, www.hr-guide.com, gives detailed information on many issues such as harassment, employee rights, salaries, hiring practices and many other staff-related issues. According to the website, sexual harassment is a legal term, created for the purpose of ending harassment and discrimination against women in the workplace. The term is constantly being redefined and extended in legislations and court decisions (www.hr-guide.com). Sexual harassment can occur in a variety of circumstances, including:

- The victim as well as the harasser may be a woman or a man, and the victim does not have to be of the opposite sex.
- The victim does not have to be the person harassed but could be anyone affected by the offensive conduct.
- The harasser can be the victim's supervisor, an agent of the employer, a supervisor in another area, a co-worker, or a non-employee.
- The harasser's conduct must be unwelcome.
- Harassment may occur without economic injury or discharge of the victim.

www.diversityweb.org (2007). Diversity Web is a project of the Association of American Colleges and Universities' (AAC&U) Office of Diversity, Equity and Global Initiatives. The site provides valuable information to staff supervisors and managers along with further links to other useful sites.

BEST PRACTICES TO INCREASE MINORITY HIRES IN ACADEMIC LIBRARIES

Academic librarians willing to diversify their staff can also review/revise hiring practices; Identify MLS programs that have African American, Latino or Native American students enrolled; Develop reward/recognition mechanisms for promoting diversity hiring; Create a libraries diversity task force; Conduct a diversity climate survey using the ARL or other model to determine where greatest needs exist and ensure a positive climate for all staff members. Hold a career development event for minority student assistantsSome academic library deans and directors have been creative and more proactive in their serious efforts to recruit minority librarians. Limited-term paid internships are offered in a handful of institutions for recent graduates with the MLIS. The Librarian-In-Residence Program at Notre Dame University is intended "to recruit a recent library school graduate who can contribute effectively to the diversity of the profession and the university while developing career interests in various aspects of academic librarianship." (http://www.library.nd.edu/diversity). Other university libraries offer tuition remission for student workers registered in an accredited LIS program. Hiring campus international students to work in academic libraries may be considered by some as adding to the diversity of their staff, but this the weakest of all efforts to have a truly diverse staff.

At Duke University, it was reported that staff gradually became more accepting of differences and appreciative of the potential value of diversity. On the level of team leadership, different perspectives were sought out because differences no longer were shuttered by the dominant culture (Owens, 1999).

Regardless of the composition of staff, a library should do what it can to motivate its staff and this may encourage others to join the library's work force. Academic libraries have the advantage of providing job security and opportunities for advancement. While job security is high on the list of staff motivation, other benefits such as good salaries and work environment come close second.

LEADERSHIP

The difference between managers and leaders is succinctly made by Bennis (1994) who wrote "Leaders do the right thing, managers do things right." Managers can be either first-line, middle or, top. An effective manager pays attention to many facets of management, leadership and learning within organizations. So, it is difficult to take the topic of "management success" and say that the following ten items are the most important for management success. The most important issue in management success is being a person that others want to follow. Every action you take during your career in an organization helps determine whether people will one day want to follow you. Remember, the real leader has no need to lead. He/she is content to point the way. In the words of the former President and General Dwight D. Eisenhower "leadership is the art of getting someone else to do something you want done because he wants to do it."

Leaders are drawn from the ranks of successful managers. Therefore it is helpful to point out here the important five functions of management that show potential for leadership:

1. PLANNING

Means developing a plan and a strategy to get from here to there. Planning plan nothing will be accomplished. It is the manager's responsibility to develop a plan and to get others to buy into it within and without the organization, manage a team and modify the plan as needed identifying the plan, what is the goal, what the team or group of individuals wants to achieve, in specific terms. Planning also identifies the getting there, that is the structured set of strategies and resources required to achieve the goal. Without a plan, nothing will be accomplished. it is the manager's responsibility to develop a plan and to get others to buy into it within and without the organization, manage a team and modify the plan as needed.

2. ORGANIZING

The next step after planning is to get organized. Organizing means grouping and deploying resources-human and otherwise-in the best possible way to achieve the plan. Creating teams, assigning leadership and responsibility, and delegating tasks are all part of organizing. Organizing usually happens during the beginning of a management assignment or execution of a business plan.

3. STAFFING

Staffing refers to the acquisition and building of a work team. This includes finding people and obtaining the required resources. In many organizations, the functions of human resources have shifted from the HR units to managers

4. LEADING

Leading means not only making decisions and directing the course of action; but also means motivating people to do a good job through effective planning, communication, and rewards for accomplishment. It requires getting people to think in alignment with you and the organization, not simply go through the motions. It requires listening to others and motivating others and providing direction as needed. Leadership also implies managing change and taking the organization to new places.

5. CONTROLLING

Controlling means making sure things are done within the confines of operational rules and planned goals, and taking corrective action where deviation exists. Managers who can plan but cannot keep track of execution or apply corrective action, are less likely to succeed. Controlling includes the assessment of individual performance and coaching and development of that individual and rewarding him/her for a job well done through performance appraisal and reward system.

Traits of a successful manager especially one whom others want to follow:

- Builds effective and responsive interpersonal relationships. Reporting staff members, colleagues and executives respect his or her ability to demonstrate caring, collaboration, respect, trust and attentiveness.
- Communicates effectively in person, print and email. Listening and two-way feedback characterize his or her interaction with others.
- Builds the team and enables other staff to collaborate more effectively with each other. People feel they have become more - more effective, more creative, more productive - in the presence of a team builder.
- Understands the financial aspects of the business and sets goals and measures and documents staff progress and success.
- Knows how to create an environment in which people experience positive morale and recognition and employees are motivated to work hard for the success of the business.
- Leads by example and provides recognition when others do the same.
- Helps people grow and develop their skills and capabilities through education and on-the-job learning.

To paraphrase Lawrence Harrison, author of *The Central Liberal Truth*, some leaders (cultures, in Harrison's words) are progressive borne and others are progressive resistant. Progress resistant cultures in the developing countries is strong. With the same token, one can say progressive-resistant managers can be found in many organizations including some libraries here in the U.S. Such leaders and managers should get out of the way or be replaced in order to allow for a new generation of progressive library leaders to replace them or else we will lose our leadership as the leading libraries of the world, or find our library leaders and managers being replaced with MBAs and other types of graduates from other disciplines.

Developing the skills needed to lead and manage people and institutions is an art, especially when practiced by an inspirational leader (talent), versed in the science of good management. Jack Welch, former CEO of General Electric, notes that, "before you become a leader, success is all about growing yourself. When you become a leader, success is all about growing others," (Welch, 2005).

While the terms 'management' and 'leadership' may be used synonymously at times, they usually have different meanings. Both managers and leaders accomplish tasks and goals successfully in a timely manner, however the way they do this differs drastically. Managers use "values, policies, procedures, schedules, milestones, incentives, discipline, and other mechanisms to push their employees to achieve the goals of the organization" (Nelson & Economy, 2003). Leaders, on the other hand, "challenge their employees to achieve the organization's goals by creating a compelling vision of the future and then unlocking their employees' potential" (Nelson & Economy, 2003).

Leadership is a complicated subject that has roots in societal and cultural changes. In the past, a leader was someone with a solo and unlimited authority and little or no accountability. As we moved away from the concept of unitary or authoritarian leadership towards a pluralistic and more dramatic concept, styles of leadership changed. Thus, a leader in today's society be it in politics, business or academics must be democratic, flexible, adaptive, and proactive. In today's global environment, a leader must possess a global perspective and an appreciation of diversity. S/he must also be a teacher and a preacher (in the broader sense of the words). This means educating subordinates and preaching to them values like work ethics, honesty, integrity, etc.

There has been a debate about whether leadership is art or science and whether one has to be a born a leader. The common belief is that leadership is the art of accomplishing more than the science of management says is possible. Leadership in the workplace is simply the application of a number of learnable behaviors that make people eager to follow your direction. Leadership is mainly a learned set of behaviors.

One can learn much from taking management courses, but this does not necessarily make one a leader, or better yet, a successful leader. I am not sure that leaders are born, even though the animal kingdom shows us there is always a hierarchy in the herd of wolves or elephants. But I think good leaders learn from observation when they are coming up the ladder, learn from his/her mistakes and learn from mentors who are great at leading and setting examples for others, and learn from readings and from recorded history. If you observe carefully around you in your place of work you could judge who is a good leader and who is an average or poor one from college president to library director and beyond. What you find impressive is a sign of good leadership, and what you find depressing is a sign and indication of poor leadership. They can make mistakes, but the better ones can learn from their mistakes.

Leadership requires flexibility and the ability to learn from others and one's own mistakes. A leader is a visionary (a dreamer); a people grower; takes risks and embrace error. A leader has to be creative and innovative, embrace error, conceptualist, and has entrepreneurial vision, even when working in a not-for profit sector like academic libraries.

The issue of diversity in the library leadership is an equally nagging one as the number of non-Caucasian library managers remains very meager. This issue has been written about in the literature and discussed in the various ALA committees and conferences, but there are external powers beyond the library profession as the hiring practices remain in the hands of others who control hiring and funding in these libraries "parent institutions." C. Alire (2001), in her article "Diversity and Leadership: The Color of Leadership," asks rhetorically

> So why should there be such a push to develop minorities as leaders? First, there should be recognition of a basic premise that institutions need to commit to achieving diversity. Minority librarians, who find themselves in leadership positions within a library or other organization, can advocate for organizational change. They can serve as role models, leaders, and spokespersons and provide the necessary linkages to minority communities (however the community is defined), as the minority population grows and as the demographics of the country shift. Who best to articulate diversity and provide the necessary platform to enable library organizations to align their missions with the unique realities of our growing multicultural society than library leaders of color? Minorities can fit well into those changing organizations because of their knowledge, skills, and experiences. Minority leaders bring cultural competencies to their positions" (pp.100-101).

Alire emphasizes the value of diversity again:

> There are other reasons why we need diversity in library leadership. Leaders of color are instrumental in recognizing the value of diversity within their library organizations. These leaders can create an environment where no one is disadvantaged (or preferred) because of race, ethnicity, creed, gender, sexual orientation, et cetera. Who better to lead the efforts in looking for obstacles in achieving diversity in the library organizational policies and procedures? And why is that? It's because minority leaders have the natural awareness and sensitivity to know for what to look. In addition, minority leaders have to heighten sensitivity to diversity within their rank and file and must get organizations to expend their energies in looking for the benefits of diversity.... With this comes the responsibility of minority leaders to provide the necessary staff development that will inform and help employees along. (p.101)

EVALUATION OF THE ACADEMIC LIBRARY LEADER

Evaluation of an ACADEMIC library dean or director is done annually by the provost/vice president for academic affairs or by the president in the case of a small college. It all depends on the organizational structure and what the president has decided on as to which areas to delegate to his/her subordinates, and depending on to whom the library director/dean reports on regular basis. In some universities or colleges the entire campus is requested to evaluate its top administrators (presidents, vice presidents, deans and directors) every five years by the university senate or other appropriate body. In this case a committee is formed usually by the university senate or another appropriate body. A questionnaire is designed and distributed, and some interviews are conducted. Many segments of the campus and representatives of the students, alumni, peers from other institutions, will be involved in the evaluation of the administrators.

The purpose of the evaluation process is to initiate regular, ongoing and constructive review of the dean/director of libraries' performance in meeting the mission, goals and challenges of the library and the campus. The annual and/or five-year review allows a systematic documentation of the achievements and progress of the library and its administrators by obtaining input primarily from the campus faculty, staff, and students. The focus of the annual evaluation is to provide the chief academic administrator an opportunity to review: 1) the library dean/director's leadership, managerial effectiveness, communication skills in relation to achieving the goals and meeting the challenges facing his/her unit; and 2) the mission, goals, performance, and progress of the library, fundraising, etc.

As part of the evaluation process, the dean/director of the library will prepare a self-assessment report dealing with the priorities, plans, and accomplishments of his/her administrative organization. This report should take into consideration the responsibilities and qualities included in the job description used in the latest notice of vacancy for the position of dean of library services. In public universities, a summary of the results of the evaluation is made public. It could also result in the reappointment or even removal of the library dean or director for failing to meet expectations.

The following traits with varying degrees of emphasis are normally considered during the evaluation of an academic library dean/director:

1. Strategic planner who can establish order and routine;
2. Creates structure and standards to achieve;
3. Takes responsibility and is honest with himself and others;
4. Has a history of being fair and ethical;
5. Shows enthusiasm;
   - Be involved in the life of the institution;
   - Take pride in the organization;
6. Looks at the big picture;
7. Advocates and does not get lost in details;
8. Totally responsible for both success and failure;
9. Keeps the end in mind;
10. Is forward looking and futuristic;
    - Puts the past behind him/her;
    - Anticipates challenges and opportunities;
    - Makes careful observations;

11. Breaks down barriers;
    - Creates a success-oriented environment;
    - Gets proper resources and buy-in;
12. Creates an environment of openness and involvement;
    - Stays close to people but do not meddle;
    - Establishes an open-door policy;
13. Assigns jobs effectively;
    - Matches talent and expertise to requirements;
    - Matches people to jobs, not jobs to people;
    - Rotates responsibility;
    - Ensures everyone is keeping pace;
    - Shores up the weak links;
14. Sets expectations clearly;
    - Sets clear goals, measures and consequences;
    - Communicates them effectively;
    - Applies them consistently; always follow through;
    - Revisits and reinforces expectations; adjusts as needed;
15. Delegates effectively;
    - Identifies tasks to delegate;
    - Delegates authority, responsibility and expectations;
    - Empowers subordinates ;
16. Confronts problems directly;
    - Problems solver;
    - Takes responsibility;
    - Let go of the past;
    - Willing to take risks;
    - Creates pride in and reward employees;
17. Excels in the face of Crisis;
    - Reinforces confidence;
    - Gets (and stays) involved;
    - Is strong, but defer to advice from others as needed;
    - Makes necessary changes, is flexible and avoids being rigid; and
18. Builds a Leadership Style
    - Always is consistent (ABC);
    - Recognizes differences in corporate climate;
    - Learns continuously, has evolving leadership style.

IMPORTANCE OF COMMUNICATION IN PERSONAL EVALUATION

"The single biggest problem in communication is the illusion that it has taken place." (George Bernard Shaw)

Library work is a people-oriented profession. The ability of the librarian to communicate with follow workers and with the general public is of utmost importance.

As mentioned under staff evaluation, academic librarians and managers are rated on their ability to communicate with the public and with each other. Library work relies on human interaction as it is a people-oriented profession. The ability of the librarian to communicate with fellow workers and the general public is of utmost importance. The *American Heritage Dictionary* defines communication as the exchange of thoughts, messages, or information, as by speech, signals, writing, or behavior. Managers spend roughly 70% of their time at work engaged in some form of communication. A major part of failing at work is the inability to communicate effectively with clients and/or with fellow staff members.

There are two types of communication: formal and informal. Bob Nelson, President of Nelson Motivation, Inc. offers a descriptive definition of informal communication, "Business communication today is, above anything else, informal and non-hierarchical, fast and furious" (2003, p.155). Nelson goes on to point out that informal communication, where listening and hearing are vital elements, is far more important in today's business world than formal communication. Likewise, Evans considers informal communication to be when most of the discussing takes place orally and very little is written down (Evans, 2003, p.132).

Formal communication is written, and informal communication is spoken. Neither form is right for all situations. A manager needs to learn which form to use under what circumstances. There are similarities and differences between these two forms of communication. There is little room for misunderstanding and a record should be kept for future reference and documentation. A disadvantage of written communication is that it takes time to compose, and it takes time to reach the recipient. Written communication can still be misunderstood. Sloppy written communication can convey the message that the writer is a sloppy worker; no one wants to do business with someone who appears to be sloppy or cannot express himself well. Memos, letters, meetings, minutes, reports, evaluations, mission statements, policies, websites, and e-mails are examples of formal communication within, and from an organization.

Informal communication can be one-on-one meetings, training sessions, staff activities, or grapevines. The value of the communication process, whether formal or informal, lies in its effectiveness. Effective communication occurs when the person receiving the message interprets it with the identical meaning that the sender had in mind. Evans points out that the most important key to effective communication is the ability to listen well. (Evans, 2007). Effective communication is very difficult to achieve in most work situations. It not only requires that the speaker speaks clearly, but also requires that the listener receive, the same message and instructions that the speaker sent. Although this task seems easy enough, it is oftentimes problematic.

The organization's grapevine is the epitome of informal communication. It serves two purposes: to transmit corporate goals, ideas and changes before official communication can occur, often expediting important information and dispelling anxiety and stress over the unknown; and is a socialization mechanism that allows employees to bond. This bonding could create a nurturing work environment that directly impacts productivity, and again, employee communication. However, an uncontrolled grapevine can be both harmful to individuals and the organization as a whole. Grapevines are most active when situations of uncertainty arise. The organization grapevine has gained new strength thanks to electronic communication, making it a more vital tool for relaying information.

As Nelson points out, the culture of a workplace is defined by the day to day interactions of employees (Nelson, p. 191). The type of communication used by the manager greatly affects the culture of a workplace. With an extreme amount of formal communication, a workplace becomes staunch, uncreative, and ultimately less productive. If a manager focuses too much on formal communication, the manager is functioning as a ruler over his/her workers. Workers stand to become little more than cogs in a vast machine (Nelson, p.155).

Informal communication tends to increase creativity and productivity as workers are far more likely to approach management with suggestions. The informal communication creates an environment where workers can discuss and suggest options, learn from each other, and reach a superb conclusion. The same conclusion may be difficult to reach if management did not stress teamwork. Informal communication opens up an environment where workers feel safe and secure approaching their managers with concerns and suggestions. Nonverbal communication plays a larger role in face-to-face communication. The way a person stands, the gestures that are used, and the facial expressions can either credit or discredit what is being said. According to Tobber (2004), nonverbal cues are more important than verbal cues, and can make up to 55% of the total message. The verbal portion accounts for only 70%, and paralanguage-pauses, intonation and sighs account for the remaining 38%.

Communication problems can arise when verbal and nonverbal cues do not match. Our verbal content sends one message, while non-verbal and paralanguage says another. The person to whom we are talking will believe our nonverbal cues over the verbal content most of the time.

Communication skills are very important for professionals and workers in the people business. Librarians should always remember that they are in the people business and not the book business. They have to communicate with the public and with each other. If they fail to communicate, or convey a sense of hostility, boredom or lack of concern, then they would have failed as librarians.

COMPONENTS OF COMMUNICATION

Weingand (1994) lists eight components of communication:
- The sender initiates the message and selects the mode of transmission;
- Encoding translates the thought in some type of symbols being transmitted;
- The message is the series of symbols being transmitted;
- Media or channels are the paths through which the message moves between sender and receiver;
- The receiver receives the message from the sender;
- Decoding by the receiver translates symbols into meaningful understanding; and
- The response is that part of the receiver's response that is communicated back to the sender (and often must be deliberately designed into the overall process).

COMMUNICATION PROCESS

Communication process involves sending a message, transmission of a message, receiving a message, and feedback. Good communication is about effectively transmitting your message. How a person communicates can set the tone for his/her unit. Good communication skills come with practice. When communicating, pay attention to the following and avoid what is known as barriers to communication or noise:
- Be clear: clarity creates a healthy environment. If you are vague, you will set a tone of secrecy and uneasiness;
- Don't interrupt. Interruptions can distract the speaker and cause her/him to lose track of the message;

- Don't distract people with unnecessary details or personal anecdotes. Irrelevant messages can hardly be remembered;
- Avoid being stereotyping as people with bias and prejudices are fond of this practice. Stereotyping can influence how others hear a message;
- Watch your body language, as confusing or conflicting body language can send false communication messages;
- Be calm and composed, as a calm and composed person (non-emotional types) can send or receive clear messages. Emotions can impair sending or receiving a message;
- Be sure that your message is clear and easily identified. If a message is obscure and ambiguous, it will create confusion. Focus and clarity help ensure good response or feedback for the message;
- Know your audience and tailor your message to your audience; and
- Learn to be a good listener. Communication is also about listening. A good adjective to describe a supervisor or administrator is s/he a good listener. Bad managers love to hear themselves talk or brag about themselves. There is also what is known as "the two seconds attention manager" to describe a manager who cannot stand still long enough to listen to someone else talking, without losing interest. Good listeners acknowledge the sender of the message by nodding, injecting an occasional comment such as "yes", or "interesting", or "I see", or "hear you"; and
- A good listener stays focused on the speaker and the message.

IMPORTANCE OF READING AND WRITING

Communication is not just about listening and talking, it is also about reading and writing. Whether it is an employee or supervisor, they should keep up with all reading material and make reading part of the job. Developing an efficient system for the reading of materials can make the job much easier. Acting on correspondence in a timely fashion is a good trait for a professional and a manager. She or he should stay on top of the daily mail, be it snail or e-mail, but avoid getting hooked on or addicted to e-mail or surfing the web on "company's time". A professional or supervisor will need good written communication skills. The supervisor will be responsible for preparing reports, writing evaluations of employees, developing policy statements, and communicating with your supervisors. The supervisor should make sure that all messages or memos are clearly written, checking them for grammar, and word flow.

The ACRL *Standards* describes communication as essential to ensure the smooth operation of the library. The *Standards* recommends that communication should flow from all levels of the library: from the director/dean to the staff, and from the staff to the director/dean, and that the library should have a regular mechanism to communicate with the campus.

REFERENCES

ACRL Task Force on Academic Library Outcomes Assessment, 27 June 1998 http://www.ala.org/acrl/outcome.html (accessed Jan 10, 2010)

Alire, C. 2001. "Diversity and Leadership: The Color of Leadership." *Journal of Library Administration* 32, no. 3/4: 95-109

Atkinson, M. 2007. *What Do You Mean?: Communication Isn't Easy*. New York: Children's Press.

Balderrama, S. 2004. Deep Change--Diversity at Its Simplest. *OLA Quarterly* 10, no. 4: 15-19

Belohlav, J. A. 1985. *The Art of Disciplining your Employees: a Manager's Guide*. Englewood Cliffs, N.J.: Prentice-Hall.

Bennis, W. G. 1994. *On Becoming a Leader*. Reading, MA: Perseus Books.

Bland, K. P. 2009. "American Association of School Librarians Leadership and the Arkansas Connection." *Arkansas Libraries* 66, no. 2: 25-28.

Boyd, M. 2005. "Juanita's Paintings: a Manager's Personal Ethics and Performance Reviews." *Library Administration & Management* 19, no. 1: 31-35.

Bureau of Labor Statistics. 2007, December 18. Librarians, In: *Occupational Outlook Handbook*. 2008-2009 ed. http://www.bls.gov.oco/ocos068.htm (accessed Dec 19, 2009)

Buttlar, L. 1994. "Facilitating Cultural Diversity in College and University Libraries." *The Journal of Academic Librarianship* 20, no. 1: 10-14. Retrieved from http://web.ebscohost.com/ehost/

Carson, P. K., and J. Phillips Carson. 1995. *The Library Manager's Desk Book: 102 Expert Solutions to 101 Common Dilemmas*. Chicago: ALA,

Cogell, R. V. and Gruwell, C. A. eds. 2001. *Diversity in Libraries: Academic Residency Programs*. Westport, CT: Greenwood Press.

Collins, J. 2001. *Good to Great: Why Some Companies Make the Leap and Others Don't*. New York: Harper Business.

Communication   Process.   Retrieved   Dec   22,   2009,   from: http://www.cls.utk.edu/pdf/ls/Week1_Lesson7.pdf.

Dawson, A. 2000. Celebrating African-American Librarians and Librarianship. *Library Trends* 49, no. 1: 49-87.

Definition of communication. Retrieved Dec 22, 2009, from: American Heritage® Dictionary   of   the   English   Language http://education.yahoo.com/reference/dictionary/entry/communication

DeLong, K. 2009. The Engagement of New Library Professionals in Leadership. *The Journal of Academic Librarianship* 35, no. 5: 445-456.

Dewey, B. I., and L. Parham eds. 2006. *Achieving Diversity: a How-to-do-it Manual for Librarians*. New York: Neal-Schuman Publishers.

Diversity Web: an Interactive Resource Hub for Higher Education. http://www.diversityweb.org (accessed Dec 21, 2009)

Equal Employment Opportunity Commission.*http://www.eeoc.gov/origin/index.html*

Evans, G. E. and Ward, P. L. 2007. *Management Basics for Information Professionals*, 2nd ed. New York: Neal Schuman.

Federal Equal Employment Opportunity Commission (EEOC) *http://www.eeoc.gov/abouteeo/overview_laws.html* (accessed Dec 21, 2009)

Ford, W. Z. 1998. *Communicating with Customers: Service Approaches, Ethics, and Impact*. Cresskill, NJ: Hampton Press.

Forrest, C. 2005. "Segmenting the Library Market, Reaching Out to the User Community by Reaching Across the Organization." *Georgia Library Quarterly*, 42(1): 4-7.

Foulger, D. 2004, Feb 25. *Models of the Communication Process*. Retrieved Dec 22, 2009, from: http://davis.foulger.info/research/unifiedModelOfCommunication.htm

Georgia's Policy: Employee Grievance Procedure, 1999, http://www.gms.state.ga.us/pdf/misc/grvpolicy.pdf (accessed Dec 21, 2009)

Hall, D. T., and V. A. Parker. 1993. "The Role of Workplace Flexibility in Managing Diversity." *Organizational Dynamics* 22, (Sum): 4-18.

Hernon, P. & Schwartz, C. 2008. "Leadership: Developing a Research Agenda for Academic Libraries." *Library & Information Science Research* 30, no. 4: 243-249.

Hernon, Peter. 2009. *Academic Librarians as Emotionally Intelligent Leaders*. Santa Barbara, CA: ABC-Clio.

Human Resources Internet Guide. *Questions for Sexual Harassment Investigations.*HR-Guide.com. 2000. http://www.hrguide.com/data/G07202.htm (accessed Dec 21, 2009)

Johnson, D. 2009. "Leadership or Management?" *Library Media Connection,* no.2:106.

Katzenbach, J., and D. Smith. 2003. *The Wisdom of Teams: Creating the High-Performance Organization*. New York: Harper.

Kight, D. V., and C. A. W. Snyder 2002. "Library Staff Development and Training for Assessment of Services." *Library Administration & Management* 16, no. 1: 24-27.

Laden, B. V. 1999. *Serving Colleges and Universities-The History of HSIs and Latino Educational Attainment.* http://education.stateuniversity.com/pages/2045/Hispanic-Serving-Colleges-Universities.html (accessed Dec 19, 2009)

Laughlin, S. 2008. *The Quality library: A Guide to Staff-Driven Improvement, Better Efficiency, and Happier Customers*. Chicago: American Library Association.

Leadership. Wikipedia, http://en.wikipedia.org/wiki/Leadership (accessed Dec 12, 2009)

Librarian-In-Residence Program. http://www.library.nd.edu/diversity (accessed Dec 21, 2009)

Love, J. B. 2001. "The Assessment of Diversity Initiatives in Academic Libraries." *Journal of Library Administration*, 33 (1/2), 73-103.

Ludditt, L. and Atkinson, S. 2008. "Training Staff to Support the Skills for Life Agenda. *Library & Information Update*, 7 (7/8): 35-37.

Merrill, A. N., and E. B. Lindsay. 2009. "Growing Your Own: Building an Internal Leadership Training Program." *Library Leadership & Management* 23, no. 2: 85-87.

Metzer, M. C. 2006. "Enhancing Library Staff Training and Patron Service Through a Cross-departmental Exchange." *Technical Services Quarterly* 24, no. 2: 1-7.

Nelson, B., and P. Economy. 2003. *"Managing for Dummies."* New York: Wiley Publishers.

Nims, J. K. 1999. "Marketing Library Instruction Services: Changes and Trends." *References Services Review* 27, no. 3: 249-253.

Owens, I. 1999. "The Impact of Change from Hierarchy to Teams in Two Academic Libraries: Intended Results versus Actual Results Using Total Quality Management." *College & Research Libraries* 60, no. 6: 571-584.

Paris, L. A. 1997. "Responses to Diversity: a Comparison of the Libraries at Stanford and UCLA." *The Journal of Academic Librarianship* 23: 91-99.

Perry, Emma Bradford, 2000. Winning   money: a team approach to grant writing. Computers in Libraries 20, no. 5 (May): 32-6

Pinkowski, J. 2007, Dec 21. *New Focus Needed to Recruit Minorities for Academic Library Jobs.* Retrieved Dec 19, 2009, from Library Journal: http://www.libraryjournal.com/article/CA6480784.html.

Race/Color Discrimination: http://www.eeoc.gov/types/race.html.

Riggs, D. E. 1997. "What's in Store for Academic Libraries? Leadership and Management Issues." *The Journal of Academic Librarianship* 23, no. 1: 3-8.

Schachter, D. 2004. "How to Set Performance Goals: Employee Reviews are More than Annual Critiques." *Information Outlook* 8, no. 9: 26-29.

SexualHarassment   http://www.eeoc.gov/types/sexual_harassment.html.   (accessed Dec 19, 2009)

Shoaf, E. C. 2009. "Library Leadership in Action: Librarians Express their Views on Administration." *Library Leadership & Management* 23, no. 2: 75-79.

Stanley, M. J. 2008. *Managing Library Employees: A How-to-do-it Manual.* New York: Neal-Schuman Publishers.

The Art and Science of Leadership.
    http://www.nwlink.com/~Donclark/leader/leader.html (accessed Dec 21, 2009)

The Civil Rights Act of 1991, http://www.eeoc.gov/policy/cra91.html.

Thomas, Roosevelt R. Jr. 1991. *Beyond Race and Gender: Unleashing the Power of Your Total Workforce by Managing Diversity.* New York: American Management Association.

Title VII of the Civil Rights Act of 1964 (Title VII) http://www.eeoc.gov/policy/vii.html.

Todaro, J. B., and M. L. Smith 2002. *Training Library Staff and Volunteers to Provide Extraordinary Customer Service.* New York: Neal-Schuman Publishers.

Trujillo, R., and Weber. D. 1991. "Academic library responses to cultural diversity: a position paper for the 1990s." *Journal of Academic Librarianship* 17, no. 3: 157-161.

University of Kentucky. KU Racial & Ethnic Harassment:
        http://www.hreo.ku.edu/policies_procedures/eo_aa_policies/racial_and_ethnic_ha
        rassment.shtml. (accessed Dec 21, 2009)
Van Arsdale, D. G. 2008. "Staff Training as Easy as Making a Peanut Butter Sandwich:
        Using a Wiki for Individualized Hands-on Staff Training." *Arkansas Libraries* 65,
        no. 2: 32-36.
Welch, J., and S. Welch. 2005. *Winning*. New York: Harper Business Publishers.
Whetherly, J. M. 1994. *Management of Training and Staff Development*. London: Library
        Association.
Wilson, L. 1996. *People Skills for Library Managers: A Common Sense Guide for
        Beginners*. Englewood, CO: Libraries Unlimited.
Yang, Z. Y., and B. White. 2007.The Evaluation of a Diversity Program at an Academic
        Library. http://www.webpages.uidaho.edu/~mbolin/yang.pdf (accessed Dec 21,
        2009)

6

TECHNICAL SERVICES AND TECHNOLOGY

Technical Services

The technical services department is the second major department in an academic library after the reference/access services department. Technology and outsourcing have caused the technical services departments to shrink from the big operations they once were for the acquisition, cataloging, and processing materials to be placed on the library's shelves. The cataloging department has made it easy to have OPAC terminals everywhere in academic library buildings. It has also made it easy to access a library's catalog from home, office or dorm. This is in contrast to the old days of the card catalog which had to be duplicated in various areas of the library. Most university libraries are now using the Library of Congress Classification Systems and LC List of Subject Headings, in contrast to public or most school libraries where most of them are using the Dewey Decimal Classification and Sears List of Subject Headings. The majority of academic libraries are also users and members of the OCLC and are members of regional or state library networks. Few do original cataloging and as a result they hire fewer catalogers than they did decades ago.

Responsibilities of the cataloging department in an academic library include the following:

1. Catalog maintenance: number of added copies, withdrawn or volumes, corrections of serious inconsistencies in classification, out-of-date subject headings, inadequate system of cross-references;
2. Special treatment of non-materials, microforms, academic theses, special collections, etc.;
3. Inventory; and
4. Reports and statistics.

ACQUISITIONS

A university library's primary aim is to support the instructional curricula and research agendas of the parent institution. Unlike research universities, teaching colleges and universities do not make supporting faculty research a high priority. On the other hand, in research-focused universities, faculty research interests are supported and the library has to balance between resources spent on instruction and those spent on acquiring materials and resources to support the research mission of the parent institution. Most university libraries have robust collection development policies. The main objective of a collection development policy for a university library is to support the campus' programs and the university community. This is why it is important for a university library's budget to be governed by a university wide policy articulated in the collection development policy which has input from all segments of the campus community.

According to the ACRL *Standards* and *Guidelines*, "the library should provide varied, authoritative, and up-to-date resources that support its mission and the needs of undergraduate users…Undergraduate collections provide ready access to information resources that meet the needs of their primary clientele with focus on the institution's curriculum. The value of undergraduate collections is measured by their usability as well as quality and size. Electronic resources form a significant part of the information network needed and preferred by undergraduates." The *Guidelines* affirm that there is no absolute standard for the size of a collection supporting undergraduate needs. The essential criterion, however, "is that the resources available to undergraduate researchers adequately support their needs." "The library's collection policy should adequately describe this goal. Collection and access should be written, up-to-date, and readily available."

In the case of undergraduate collections, the ACRL *Guidelines for Undergraduate Libraries* recommend that undergraduate collection development policy should consider the following:

1. Because many undergraduate collections require large numbers of students to use the same library materials, direct curriculum support may be provided through research collections of physical or electronic items. Electronic items may be integrated into course management systems;
2. Undergraduate collections provide effective access to information resources through reference sources in a variety of formats. Reference collections for undergraduates provide standard and interdisciplinary indexes and sources;
3. Undergraduate subject coverage encompasses a broad range of disciplines to offer the information needed for papers, essays, presentations, and projects required in the wide variety of courses taken by undergraduates.

More specialized and advanced needs will be met by specific referral to other library sources on campus;

4. The library experience of undergraduates should encourage them to seek information for personal interest. Collection policies should include access to information on current events, cultural interests, careers, and recreational reading, among others, to encourage exploration of information resources as part of everyday life; and

5. Collection policies for separate undergraduate libraries should include withdrawal and relocation practices because of the special nature of undergraduate collections. Collections should be dynamic and responsive to the needs of a changing curriculum and clientele.

COLLECTION DEVELOPMENT POLICY

A written, publicly accessible collection development policy ensures that the entire university community is aware of how and why the library chooses to purchase certain materials and why the library decides to discard materials. Some librarians may argue that creating a collection development policy is time consuming and difficult because of the great amount of data that must be collected (Coughlin & Gertzog, 1992, p.186). However, the data collected concerning an academic library collection will be useful for librarians. This data will indicate the strengths and weaknesses of the library collections. In addition, the data collected will give the library a greater perspective as to what their university is currently focusing on, and how the library's collections do or do not reflect that focus.

The main objective of a collection development policy for a university library is to support the campus' programs and the university community. This is why it is important for a university library's budget to be governed by a university wide policy articulated in the collection development policy which has input from all segments of the campus community.

A collection development policy is quite important to a successful academic library since this is the one area, besides personnel, that consumes the second biggest chunk of a library's budget. Academic libraries spend, on average, 37% of their budget on acquisitions. This translates into several million dollars in the case of large research university libraries. The annual acquisitions budget for the University of Wisconsin-Madison Library, for example, is about $8 million, slightly more than one third of the Library's total annual budget of $26 million.

A good collection development policy should identify who selects items to be added to the libraries' collections. The selection of materials can be performed by subject-specific bibliographers within the library, or it can be outsourced to a book dealer. Both methods have advantages and shortcomings. In-house bibliographers are attuned to the campus needs and wants; therefore their selections for acquisition will be relevant to the university community. When material acquisitions for an academic library collection are outsourced, the library may end up with titles of no interest or use for its students and faculty. Advantages of outsourcing acquisitions include possible lower costs and the possibility that an item's MARC record will be included with the purchase. Time and money issues are two major disadvantages to in-house bibliographers.

Collection development policies may prevent students and faculty from making unreasonable demands for material purchases. Without a collection development policy "it is more difficult to build a library collection effectively and insure that the information needs of the college will be met" (Coughlin & Gertzog, 1992, p.185). The creation of a collection development policy should involve a "working combination of administrators, faculty and librarians" (p. 181). This combination will insure that no one in the university will feel left out.

Traditionally, faculty has enjoyed a major voice regarding collection policies. It is important to include faculty when designing or re-designing the collection policy because university faculties are scholars who are generally highly knowledgeable in their respective subject areas. Faculty may know things about subjects that librarians do not, for example what the current research trends are. However, librarians must be aware of the fact that some university faculty may only select materials relevant to their own research needs, which may not serve the needs of the rest of the university community. The role of faculty should be advisory for the aforementioned reason.

Librarians are obvious addition to the design of a collection development policy because they will be the individuals implementing the policy. They bring knowledge about the current status of the library collection, and student requests to the design of the policy. University administrators will ensure the collection development policy is in line with their university mission statement. Administrators can also help make the policy forward looking, as they may be privy to unreleased information regarding the direction the university intends to follow. In addition, students may make up a small percentage of a committee designing a collection development policy. Students offer input regarding the readability of materials and are the ultimate consumers of library collections (p.184).

WHO SELECTS

In some libraries in the U.S. and in most libraries outside the U.S., selection of materials is usually done by teaching faculty within their particular subject areas. It is a better practice, however, to have qualified librarians and bibliographers make the selection in consultation with library liaisons to the subject areas and regular consultation with them and other faculty members to discuss selection and other issues surrounding collection development and how the library can support classroom instruction and respond positively to faculty research needs and requirements.

Most libraries identify the person or body responsible for collection development. This authority is usually vested in the director or dean of libraries who, in turn, delegates overall coordination and selection to the collection development coordinator or manager assisted by a selection committee. In few cases the faculty reserves this role for themselves, and in others, it could be a cooperative relationship involving librarians and faculty library liaisons who are selected by their faculty peers and provide welcome input into the library's materials selection policies and practices. In either case, it is highly desirable and practiced in most university libraries to have most of the academic librarians on campus to participate in the collection development and selection. Department faculty or liaisons to departments are expected to recommend materials to support instructional programs and where applicable research interests of faculty.

Those responsible for the selection of library materials in academic libraries should make every effort to be familiar, not only with their college library collections, but also with other collections in the community and the neighboring institutions including public libraries. This would help to introduce their clients to the collections as well as to avoid unnecessary duplication of titles and collections.

At Northwestern University, for example, librarians act as liaisons to various campus departments. These departments share with the liaisons course syllabi and personal collection development desires. Most of the departments appreciate the opportunity to participate in the development process and are vocal as to their wants and needs. The liaison program has been very successful at NW. The liaisons then share this information (either specific resource title or general topic) with the acquisitions and cataloging librarians. This relationship is very much like the one described in Scudder (Scudder and Scudder, 1991, p.8).

COLLECTION DEVELOPMENT POLICY ON THE INTERNET

Most academic libraries publish and keep their collection development/selection policies online as part of their libraries' web sites. Updating these collection development policies is another matter as it is a time consuming, but highly desirable practice. Having the policy available for everyone to read helps the library defend itself against internal or external challenges and pressures demanding removal of certain titles.

CRITERIA FOR SELECTION

Most common criteria for the selection of library materials include: Reputation of author(s) and publisher; significance of the subject matter; accuracy and timeliness of the material; usefulness of the title with respect to other materials or services already available in the library; scarcity of materials on the subject; appearance of the title in important bibliographies; lists, and other reviewing sources; current and/or permanent value of material; availability of the material elsewhere; cost, including upkeep costs and format.

Due to budget constraints from which almost all college libraries suffer, there are limitations on spending on the purchasing of new books or subscribing to new journals. In the case of serials, most libraries will subscribe to a new serial only when an existing subscription, or subscriptions are cancelled to offset the new cost. In addition, new periodical titles may be considered only if they are indexed in standard sources, and then preference is usually given to electronic periodicals instead of the print versions. Electronic and machine-readable sources are preferred over print materials, and both are preferred over microforms. Specific guidelines have to be maintained for the selection of machine-readable materials.

Academic librarians hope that scientists and scholars will become more understanding and appreciative of the difficulties academic librarians encounter as they face the skyrocketing cost of science journals and being subjected to criticism for cancelling journals due to limited budgets that did not keep up with these inflated costs. Scientists are developing alternatives to the print-era system whereby scientists and scholars publish their work in electronic journals that charge for access and restrict use. An example of such a venture is the Public Library of Science which provides peer-reviewed scholarship electronically without charge. Funds to support management, editing, and peer review will be built into the authors' research project budgets. Such open access would enormously benefit scholarship.

Academic libraries welcome gifts of books from faculty, alumni, friends and others in the community providing that they meet the library's requirements and its selection policy. If such gifts are also supported by monetary donations to process and maintain the gifted collection, the better the gift is received especially in the prevailing economic difficulties faced by academic institutions, all over the world.

Part of the collection development in academic libraries is the removal of obsolete materials. This is known as weeding or deselection so that unused materials may be withdrawn from the collection in order to maintain a quality and current library collection. This is particularly important in fast changing areas such as science and technology.

A well developed collection development policy can help the academic library guard against censorship. Selectors can rely on The Library Bill of Rights, especially Article I which states that "Materials should not be excluded because of the origin, background or views of those contributing to their creation," and Article II which states that "Materials should not be proscribed or removed because of partisan or doctrinal disapproval." Unfortunately, censorship can occasionally show its ugly face on American campuses.

EVALUATION OF COLLECTIONS

A number of methods are used to evaluate collections, including statistical techniques based on usage and issue count. There are two possible approaches to evaluate a collection: collection-centered and user-centered. The former lays stress on the collection itself and usually involves checking a particular collection against some kind of standard list, which is intended to reveal how 'comprehensive' the collection is. The *conspectus* methodology, developed by the Research Libraries Group (RLG) is the dominant example of this descriptive approach. Codes are given to each subject collection to indicate the collection's strength, linguistic and geographical coverage and intellectual level. The RLG and ARL developed the North American Collection Inventory Project (NCIP) to provide an online database of collection strengths. Similar work in the UK has been undertaken under the aegis of CURL (Consortium of University Research Libraries).

More recently, greater emphasis has been given to user-centered collection evaluation. The techniques used vary, but may include user satisfaction surveys or simply examination of usage statistics. Undergraduate collections can be evaluated using the ACRL Guidelines to answer the following broad questions:
1. Does the collection profile adequately support the undergraduate curriculum?
2. Does the size and depth of the collection adequately support the size and need of the undergraduate population?
3. Are materials appropriately available and accessible for reserve users?
4. Are collections housed and arranged efficiently and effectively for use?
5. Are collections available and accessible to all users? Do circulation policies and practices permit effective access for users?
6. Do appropriate withdrawal policies and practices exist that adequately address the need for collection maintenance?

7. Does the library have adequate, up-to-date technology in place?
8. Are access policies posted to ensure that all users are aware of services and restrictions?
9. Are interlibrary loan and other document-delivery services provided for undergraduates to give them access to materials not owned by the institution?
10. Do undergraduates have adequate access to information technology for accessing and using information?

EXAMPLES OF SOME ACADEMIC LIBRARIES' COLLECTION DEVELOPMENT POLICIES ON THE WEB

Virginia Commonwealth University Library at:
http://www.library.vcu.edu/cm/guidelines/reference.html
Uppsala University Library at: http://www.ub.uu.se/en/Search-website/?quicksearchquery=Search+the+website
Bibliotheca Alexandrina, Alexandria, Egypt (a public/research library):
http://www.bibalex.org/libraries/Presentation/Static/15630.aspx
University of Texas Libraries: http://www.lib.utexas.edu/admin/cird/cird.html

INFORMATION TECHNOLOGY

The technology unit may be part of the technical services department, or a standalone unit responsible for the library's computer operations and computer-based library system. The introduction of technology has enabled libraries to change from individual collecting institutions to cooperating, networking partners in coherent systems for providing access, at national, local, state and even international levels. These cooperating libraries will serve the greatest number of users. Partnerships among libraries, librarians and IT professionals will also be essential in the new IT and information retrieval environments.

More than anything else in recent history, technology has had a profound impact on academic libraries, and more is expected in the immediate future. Used wisely, technology can help libraries manage their material and financial resources better, increase productivity and expand the ways and means they extend information services to their clients.

Technology has enabled educational institutions like universities to link with informal educational institutions like libraries and museums to create new and integrated models of learning, in order to provide people with new and creative opportunities for lifelong learning. Academic libraries were among the early pioneers in using and implementing information technology. The use of microfilm, microfiche and microcards were considered great technology in the 1940s and 1950s, and the use of IBM electric typewriter to produce the 3x5 catalog cards was a technological marvel when most libraries were producing hand-written cards. In the 1950s and 1960s, media centers were established in institutions of higher education to manage the proliferation of films, videotapes, television productions, graphics, photography services, and other media needs of classroom instructors. By the 1970s, it was common in universities to have three directors: one for the library, a second for the media center, and a third for the computer center. Today, one finds one director of the library and media center and one for the computer center/services, or one director for all three operations as the CEO or CIO for library, telecommunication and information services on campus.

The idea of a computerized catalog in the late 50s and early 60s was to have it printed as a computer printout, not searchable online, remotely or by multiple users, as the OPAC is today. The primary area of computer application was circulation control. In the 1970s, library turnkey systems were in vogue. By the 1980s, new technology that combined advances in computer and telecommunication technology, fiber optics, cables and networks, facilitated voice, video, and data storage and transmission. Today the focus is on designing library and information systems to support end user access to recorded knowledge from within and without the campus library. The advent of Transmission Control Protocol/Internet Protocol (TCP/IP) has allowed libraries to connect users to distributed digital resources from all over the world. The cost of owning and operating computers have decreased with the advent of turnkey commercial systems, and academic libraries have moved away from homegrown systems in favor of commercial systems that became more efficient, reliable and less expensive. The rise and fall of some of these commercial systems resulted in the migration from old to new systems. Rapid and widespread use of telecommunication technologies have added value to bibliographic utilities commonly used by academic libraries like OCLC, UTLAS, WLN and RLIN.

Modern technology enhances our ability to share resources, improves productivity, reduces unit cost of operation, improves control, reduces errors, improves speed, improves access, increases range and depth of services, and facilitates local and global cooperation, to name just few advantages.

As information technology evolves, academic library services must continually upgrade hardware, software, and other IT resources to keep pace with the needs and expectations of their clientele. In academic libraries, undergraduate students are most familiar with up-to-date technology and are among the earliest adopters of the latest tools and techniques. Thus, rapid changes in IT demand especially aggressive and proactive planning for undergraduates' services. Resources dedicated to IT should not only be allocated towards maintenance of current facilities, but also towards the development and revision of services and technologies that students will need in the future.

Widespread use of personal computers for research and writing, in homes and offices, by students, faculty and staff as well as the increase in Internet use by all have had a positive impact on libraries, and their adaptation of the new technologies to provide access to information. Students reliance on IT for study, research, and dissemination and increased expectations about its widespread availability, both on and off campus caused libraries to give more emphasis to computer literacy skills; libraries rushed to integrate IT into every aspect of their library operations and class room instruction. With the introduction of distance learning, librarians rushed to support web-based education and serving students who are no longer residing on campus or visiting the library in person, but only from a distance.

The term "virtual library" gained popularity around 1990 in a report about the Coalition for Networked Information. Current usage varies, with the virtual library being closely related to or synonymous with the electronic library or "library without walls." A virtual library as we know it today has three common characteristics: location independence, breadth of contents, and ease of use. The virtual library has been variously called the digital library, electronic library, the library without walls, the "cybrary," the digital spatial library, digitized collections, and the library of the future

In his book, *The Changing Academic Library: Operations, Culture, Environments* (ACRL Publications in Librarianship #56, 2005), John Budd refers in the chapter he titled "Electronic Information and Academic Libraries" to the increasing trend of digitization in the 21st century library and describes the move toward electronic resources as the most significant trend that has affected the academic library. Budd discusses electronic journals, the open-access movement and the financial implications of moving more fully toward an electronic collection. He discusses the role of the librarian in the digital age of information, especially from a reference standpoint: "It is true that the librarian's job is a rhetorical one in the electronic environment; the job is not limited to pointing, directing or locating" (p. 224).

With huge aggregators such as EBSCOHOST making an even larger presence in academic libraries, it is imperative that the academic library weighs the pros and cons (e.g. space and cost) of moving toward the digital realm. Granted, the library must be willing to adapt and keep up with industry changes in regards to the access and dissemination of scholarly information, but Budd does not believe in abandoning print all together. To paraphrase Mark Twain, the demise of the print in favor of the digital text has been vastly exaggerated at least for the time being. Technologies will not replace libraries, we hope. Instead, technology will enable them to extend their resources and help their patrons identify and connect to multiple information sources and products online. Libraries will be part of the larger information resources, accessible next to online bookstores, search engines, and for-pay services. Furthermore, the library of the future will be multi-faceted, providing a place for learning activities along with other means of empowering people with information.

REFERENCES

Anderson, R. 2008. "Future-proofing the library: Strategies for Acquisitions, Cataloging, and Collection Development." *The Serials Librarian* 55, no.4: 560-567.

Anjejo, R. 2006. "Collection Development Policies for Small Libraries." *PNLA Quarterly* 70, no. 2: 12-16.

Atkinson, R. 2006. "Six Key Challenges for the Future of Collection Development: Introduction for the Janus Breakout Sessions." *Library Resources & Technical Services* 50, no. 4: 244-251.

Bailey, P. 2007. "Collection development for knowledge management." *Legal Information Management* 7, no. 4: 247-251.

Brumley, R. 2009. *Electronic Collection Management Forms, Policies, Procedures, and Guidelines Manual with CD-ROM.* New York: Neal-Schuman Publishers.

Buck, T., Headley, S., and Schor, A. 2006. "Collection Development in Public Libraries." *The Serials Librarian,* 50, no. 3/4: 253-257.

Clark, J. 2006. "The Evolution of the World Wide Web as a Collection Development Tool." *Behavioral & Social Sciences Librarian* 24, no. 2: 119-22.

Coughlin, C. M. & A. Gertzog. 1992. *Lyle's Administration of the College Library,* 5th ed. Metuchen, N.J.: Scarecrow Press.

Cowgill, A. 2008. "Training Collection Development Librarians." *Colorado Libraries,* 34, no. 2: 34-37.

Disher, W. 2007. *Crash Course in Collection Development.* Westport, CT: Libraries Unlimited.

Evans, G. E. and P. L.Ward 2007. *Management Basics for Information Professionals,* 2nd ed. New York: Neal Schuman.

Garces, V. E. 2006. Survey on Collection Development Policies and Selection Practices. Buffalo, NY: W.S. Hein.

Gregory, V. L. 2006. *Selecting and Managing Electronic Resources: a How-to-do-it Manual for Librarians,* rev ed. New York: Neal-Schuman Publishers.

Gyeszly, S. 2008. "Advanced Collection Development Project in Partnership with a Vendor." *Collection Building* 27, no.2: 56-62.

Hardesty, L. 1991. *Faculty and the Library: The Undergraduate Experience.* Norwood, NJ: Ablex Pub.

Hoffmann, F. W., and R. J. Wood 2007. *Library Collection Development Policies: School Libraries and Learning Resource Centers.* Lanham, MD: Scarecrow Press.

Huynh, A. 2004. "Background Essay on Collection Development, Evaluation, and Management for Public Libraries." *Current Studies in Librarianship* 28, no. 1/2: 19-37.

Keller, C. 2006. "Collection Development: Electronic or Print Subscription Resources?" *School Library Media Activities Monthly* 22, no. 9: 56-59.

Kennedy, J. 2005. "A Collection Development Policy for Digital Information Resources." *Australian Library Journal* 54, no. 3: 238-244.

Kim, S. 2009. "Learning from Experts: Collection Development in Business." *Collection Building* 28, no. 2: 62-67.

Larson, J. C. and H. L. Totten. 2008. The Public Library Policy Writer: a Guidebook with Model Policies on CD-ROM. New York: Neal-Schuman Publishers.

McPherson, K. 2007. "Using eBay as a Collection Development Tool." *Teacher Librarian* 34, no. 5: 72-73.

Mack, D. C., ed. 2003. *Collection Development Policies: New Directions for Changing Collections*. Binghamton, NY: Haworth Information Press.

McPherson, K. 2007. "Using eBay as a Collection Development Tool." *Teacher Librarian* 34, no. 5: 72-73.

Martin, M. 2004. "Web Sites for Collection Development and Acquisitions." *Mississippi Libraries* 68, no. 1: 17-18.

Moline Public Library. Collection Management Policy. http://www.molinelibrary.com/Collection_Management_Policy.pdf (accessed Dec 26, 2009)

Olaojo, P., and M. Akewukereke 2006. "Collection Development Policies: Ground Rules for Planning University Libraries." *Library Philosophy and Practice* 9, no. 1: 1-5.

Peterson, E. 2004. "Collection Development in California Indian Tribal Libraries." *Collection Building* 23, no. 3: 129-132.

Phillips, L., and Williams, S. 2004. "Collection Development Embraces the Digital Age: a Review of the literature, 1997-2003." *Library Resources & Technical Services* 48, no. 4: 273-299.

Price, A. 2009. "How to Make a Dollar Out of Fifteen Cents: Tips for Electronic Collection Development." *Collection Building* 28, no. 1: 31-34.

Quinn, B. 2007. "Cognitive and Affective Processes in Collection Development." *Library Resources & Technical Services* 51, no. 1: 5-15.

Roger Williams University Libraries. Collection Management Policy. http://library.rwu.edu/About/colldev.pdf (accessed Dec 26, 2009)

Sanchez Vignau, B., and G. Meneses. 2005. "Collection Development Policies in University Libraries: a Space for Reflection." *Collection Building* 24, no. 1: 35-43.

Sandler, M. 2006. "Collection Development in the Age [day] of Google." *Library Resources & Technical Services* 50, no. 4: 239-243.

Schmidt, K. 2004. "Past Perfect, Future Tense: a Survey of Issues in Collection Development." *Library Collections, Acquisitions, and Technical Services* 28, no. 4: 360-372.

Schneider, et al., eds. 1991. *Collection Development in College Libraries*. Chicago: ALA.

Scogin, R. 2004. "Collection Development Resources for Colorado Public Libraries." *Colorado Libraries* 31, no. 1: 28-32.

Scudder, M.C., and J. R. Scudder, Jr. 1991. Faculty Involvement in College Library Collection Development. In J.S. Hill, W.E. Hannaford, Jr., and R.H. Epp, eds., *Collection Development in College Libraries*. Chicago: American Library Association.

St. Cloud State University. Collection Management Policy: Digital Resources. http://lrts.stcloudstate.edu/about/collections/digitalpol.asp (accessed Dec 26, 2009)

Stephens, C., and P. Franklin. 2006. "Collection Development, part II: What do I buy? Developing the Print Collection." *School Library Media Activities Monthly* 22, no. 9: 45-46.

Tucker, J., and M. Torrence. 2004. "Collection Development for New Librarians: Advice from the Trenches." *Library Collections, Acquisitions, and Technical Services* 28, no. 4: 397-409.

Waller, A. 2007. "Technical Services and Open Access: a Few Challenges." *Feliciter* 53, no. 5: 241-243.

Weber State University, Stewart Library. "Collection Management Policy." http://library.weber.edu/libadmin/lppm/collec_manag_policy.cfm (accessed Dec 26 2009)

Weihs, J. 2008. "Education for Librarianship in the Mid-twentieth Century, part 1: Collection Development." *Technicalities* 28, no. 4: 8-11.

Wisneski, R. 2008. "Collection Development Assessment for New Collection Development Librarians." *Collection Management* 33, no. 1/2: 143-159.

Young, C. 2006. "Collection Development and Diversity on CIC Academic Library Web Sites." *The Journal of Academic Librarianship* 32, no. 4: 370-376.

APPENDIX I
COLLECTION MANAGEMENT POLICY
UNIVERSITY OF WISCONSIN-LACROSSE) (UW-L)

General Library Collection Management Policy

GOAL

The goal of the library is to support the mission of UW-L by providing access to a collection of materials which best serves the classroom and research needs of the undergraduate and graduate students. The collection must provide resources to support and enrich classroom instruction for the UW-L curriculum, and when financially possible, should provide some materials to meet the general and recreational needs of the University community. Faculty research efforts will be supported by providing access to information as well as making document delivery services available to fulfill specific information needs. The library recognizes the need for the active participation by the faculty in the development of the library collection.

The library collection includes all formats, i.e., books, periodicals, microforms, audio-visual materials, electronic resources, etc. The University Library upholds and promotes the following statements from the American Library Association:
1. Bill of Rights
2. Freedom to Read Statement
3. Intellectual Freedom Statements

OBJECTIVES

1. To provide resources to support and enrich classroom instruction;
2. To anticipate and fulfill the information and curricular needs of the primary user group (students and faculty) by actively seeking and maintaining communication through the faculty liaison program, purchase requests, and meetings with the faculty;
3. To be cognizant of the resources in subject areas taught at UW-L, and to acquire these materials as funds permit;
4. To be aware of and responsive to the dynamics of curriculum change based on the course descriptions provided by the undergraduate and graduate curriculum committees;

5. To maintain and develop current and easily accessible collection through judicious weeding or de-selection, plus continuously review the scope and depth for adequacy of support. Whenever possible, qualitative and quantitative measures are employed in the evaluation (selection/de-selection) of resources;

6. To budget the resources allocated to Murphy Library in order to best meet the instructional needs of each department;

7. To emphasize the purchase of materials which correspond to the UW-L mission statement;

8. To subscribe to online information services related to the disciplines of each college;

9. To acquire electronic and citation services which will support faculty research and scholarly work; and

10. To develop and support a number of services to provide faculty with access to information and research related to their research and scholarly work.

RESPONSIBILITY FOR SELECTION

1. All materials acquired with library funds are university property available for the use of the entire campus community.

2. The collection development rationale is informed selectivity rather than comprehensiveness.

3. It is the responsibility of the library faculty, with the advice of the departmental liaisons, to maintain a library collection which conforms to the collection development guidelines.

4. Librarians will consult with the faculty and departments in the selection of specific information services.

5. Scope, mission relatedness, annual fees, and startup cost will have a bearing on the selection process.

FACULTY LIAISON

Each academic department will select one faculty member to serve as its Library Liaison. The Liaison will maintain communication between the department he/she serves and the library by relating departmental needs and issues to the library's collection management librarian. As the library's communication resource within each department, the Liaison:

1. Will serve as the channel through which departmental requests for library purchases will be made;

2. Will review and clarify the category of each book purchase request;

3. Will respond to questions from the library on the status of departmental purchase requests;
4. Will receive reports from the library on the status of departmental purchase requests and budget allocations;
5. Will receive and circulate a periodic list of books received by the library as the result of departmental orders; and
6. Will meet with the collection development librarian to discuss existing and evolving departmental needs.

The assistance of the teaching faculty is solicited in the selection process to assure appropriate strength in the subject areas of their teaching. The final responsibility for selection rests with the library.

Recommendations for purchase may be initiated by any member of the UW-L academic community: faculty, academic staff, staff, or students.

New academic programs should be communicated to the library faculty so that acquisition of the needed resources may be accomplished in an orderly and timely way. Additional funds will be needed.

The library is committed to making diverse viewpoints fully and freely available. No material will be excluded because of social, political, cultural, or religious views expressed.

The library faculty carries the responsibility for the correction of imbalances and weaknesses in the collection. It is the library's responsibility to ensure the adequacy and quality of selection and the building of a balanced collection. The library has the ultimate responsibility for collection development and acquisition policies, and for the coordination of resource development of the library as a whole.

COLLECTION DEPTH

It is recognized that the requirements for library materials vary in different subject areas. The UW-L catalog and the mission statement will be consulted to aid in establishing the selections. The faculty liaison will be consulted in determining the depth and breadth of the collection.

DEFINITION OF LEVELS OF SELECTION

1. Minimal. A subject area in which few selections are made beyond very basic works and reference sources. No course work is offered at UW-L.
2. Basic Information Levels. A collection of up-to-date general materials which serves to introduce and define a subject and to indicate the varieties of information available elsewhere. A basic information collection is not sufficient to support any advanced undergraduate course or independent study in the subject areas involved.

3. Instructional Support Level. A collection that is sufficient to support undergraduate and some graduate instruction and research. A collection adequate to maintain knowledge of a subject required for limited or generalized purpose. It includes a wide range of basic monographs, complete collections of the works of more important writers, selections from the works of secondary writers, a selection of representative journals, access to appropriate non- bibliographic date bases, and the reference tools pertaining to the subject.

4. Research Level. A collection that includes the major published source materials required for dissertations and independent research including materials containing research reporting, new findings, scientific experimental results, and other information useful to researchers. Older material is retained for historical research. UW-L will not collect at this level.

5. Comprehensive Level. A collection in which a library endeavors, so far as is reasonably possible, to include all significant works of recorded knowledge (publications, manuscripts, other forms) in all applicable languages, for a necessarily defined and limited field. This selection level is one that seeks to maintain a "special collection". The aim, if not the achievement, is exhaustiveness. UW-L will not collect at this level.

GUIDELINES FOR THE SELECTION OF LIBRARY MATERIALS

The library requires that all purchase requests are categorized before submitting them.

1. Essential - Needed at Library regardless of duplication around UWS.
2. Desirable - To be purchased if funds are available, or must be readily available in another UWS library (delivery via Universal Borrowing).
3. Remotely Accessible - available via interlibrary loan (or Universal Borrowing) and not likely to be purchased.
4. The library will not purchase:
5. Reprints of articles already in the library;
6. Textbooks; or
7. Expensive and infrequently used materials.

Multiple copies will be purchased only if heavy demand and continuous use as evidenced by circulation and verifiable patron request can be demonstrated.

Generally, library materials are acquired in those languages in which academic programs are taught. English language materials will predominate.

FACULTY PUBLICATIONS

The library acquires faculty publications according to the collection policy that determines book selection in general, i.e., those works that are appropriate for an academic library are acquired.

GIFTS

1. Murphy Library welcomes donations of books and other library related materials as a way of enhancing our collections.
2. It is important to note that the scope and size of Murphy Library's collection is due in part to the generosity of past and present donors.
3. Materials are evaluated and accepted for inclusion in our collections based on their relevance to the university curriculum and research needs of library users as determined by the library's collection policies. Murphy Library reserves the right to decline or dispose of donated materials in a manner that best benefits it.

CONDITIONS OF ACCEPTANCE

Please keep in mind that not all donations can be added to the library's collections. In such cases, gift materials are disposed of as follows:
1. Item transferred to another UW library;
2. Donations are sold in bi-annual book sale. Proceeds are used for library acquisitions, library programming, and staff enhancement; and
3. Disposed/recycled in another way as deemed appropriate.
4. All donations become the property of the University of Wisconsin-La Crosse and the State of Wisconsin, and may not be re-claimed at a later time. Murphy Library does not accept gifts on long-term loans nor can we accept gifts where the donor places restrictions or limitations on use or disposal of such gifts. Generally, library policy dictates that gift material becomes integrated into the existing collections and is subject to the same conditions of use.
5. Appraisal: Murphy Library is prohibited by law from appraising donations for tax deduction purposes. However, the Library does provide letters of acknowledgment, which include a list of the donated materials.

Contacts: If you are interested in donating materials to UW-La Crosse's Murphy Library, please contact:
(names withheld) 7/18/95 (Gift Policy revised 9/10/2002)
Acquisitions/Collection Development Department Home Page [1]

---

[11] University of Wisconsin La Crosse, Murphy Library. General Library Collection Management Policy. Retrieved Jan 24, 2010, from http://www.uwlax.edu/murphylibrary/departments/collpol.html

7

ACCESS AND PUBLIC SERVICES

Access or public services departments in academic libraries encompass several units such as reference services, circulation, reserve section, interlibrary loan, bibliographic instruction, also known as information skills, periodicals, and special collections, to name a few. According to ACRL *Standards*, academic library services must provide access to a broad range of information resources. Reference and referral services, orientation activities, and instruction sessions that teach students the critical thinking skills necessary for using library resources are basic services provided by library personnel.

Most reference departments provide additional services such as interlibrary loan (ILL) services, either separately or as part of the circulation desk services. These units may be combined under the "Access" unit or department in the library. This unit may also include the "Special Needs" and assistive technology services that include services to the blind, deaf and physically challenged, and thus shows adherence to the ADA (*Americans with Disabilities Act*), and other applicable federal and state laws for accommodating people with special needs.

The ACRL *Guidelines for University Library Services to Undergraduates* states

> Varied and innovative undergraduate teaching programs include teaching by personal contact and through the preparation and use of instructional materials in various formats, formal group instruction, and informal, unstructured contacts with students. Undergraduate library services provide a laboratory for students to acquire information literacy skills: identification of needed information, effective and ethical use of intellectual and physical resources, and knowledge of when to ask for help, as well as the confidence to do so.

The ACRL *Guidelines* also states "reference services for undergraduates often involve, not only answering specific questions, but also personalized instruction in the methods of identifying and locating library materials.

Databases, bibliographies, and other aids designed to introduce undergraduates to the materials the library provides and to guide them in finding the materials further enrich the pool of available resources. Reference services provided by undergraduate librarians introduce the wide variety of resources in the library system and beyond, connecting undergraduates with branch or specialized libraries and other campus supportive services, including academic, financial, writing, and counseling services."

Some of the functions of the reference department are:

1. Orients new users to the library;
2. Communicates with teaching faculty and students;
3. Teaches users how to use the OPAC; and databases, look up, find, and retrieve library materials
4. Reference staff explains and answers questions related to copyright;
5. The interlibrary loan is usually part of the reference department and as such, its staff helps users look up and retrieve difficult to find items; and
6. Distance education library service, located within the reference department combines the function and roles of access services with reference, information literacy, and instruction as they concentrate on serving distant education students and faculty

Orientation activities are part of the functions of the reference department. According to the ACRL *Guidelines* "orientation activities and resources may take many forms, but all acquaint undergraduates with the facilities and services of the library system for the first time. Orientation may also include public relations activities that introduce students to information resources available within the university community or any information network." To assist academic librarians in providing and evaluating access services to their students and faculty, the ACRL *Guidelines* poses the following questions regarding reference services:

1. Do the services offered meet the information needs of the undergraduate students and the faculty and staff who work with them?
2. Are user studies, statistics, and other measures of quantity and quality collected and utilized effectively?
3. What is the ratio of public services staff to the number of primary clientele? Is this an acceptable ratio in the context of the library's mission?
4. Are additional services or added availability of existing services needed?
5. Are new services, which are needed by users, anticipated and implemented?
6. Are there any services that have become obsolete and could be eliminated?

According to Brophy (2005) enquiries from users can take many forms. For example, they may be:

1. Directional, asking "where is" a particular collection, subject literature, or simply a facility?

2. Factual, asking for a discrete piece of information, such as the boiling point of a chemical;

3. Library policy or procedure, such as opening hours, reservation procedures or loan periods;

4. Skills-related, such as how to use a microfilm reader or a library's desk top computer or OPAC;

5. Known-item searching, such as how to check whether an item, bibliographic details of which are known, is in the library's holdings; and

6. Subject, such as how to find information on any particular topic.

CIRCULATION

The circulation unit is part of the access or public services department or division. Virtually every library in the U.S. has, or is about to have a computerized circulation system, probably as a module in a totally integrated library automated system. These computerized circulation systems have brought order to olde fashion manual chaotic circulation departments and files, produce accurate and timely statistics. Circulation policies and procedures have also been standardized and their efficiency increased as computer systems improved and technologies enhanced.

Circulation systems allow for most materials to be circulated out for a given period. A renewable period and number of renewals must be specified. Books can be recalled by library staff at the request of another reader. The system should specify the period for reserve checkout for books and audiovisuals and specify the levels of fines imposed on delinquent returns. These and other conditions should be spelled out in the academic library's circulation policy, which normally answers questions such as:

1. Who can borrow library materials?
2. What materials will be lent?
3. For how long may they be borrowed?
4. What will happen if they are not returned?
5. What are the rules and guidelines for reserve materials?

As the focal point for interaction with the library's public, the circulation department and counters must have cheerful and helpful staff who can handle a great deal of details politely and process borrowed materials promptly. Academic libraries are fortunate to have an abundant of student workers who can staff the circulation desk, and other areas of the library for nominal costs. The circulation staff should maintain accuracy, orderliness and meticulousness and perform work in the face of constant interruption. A good sign of efficiency is short lines, and a brief wait at the circulation counter. The circulation department also has the responsibility for the security of the library's collection and should identify materials in need of preservation, rebinding, or replacing as they are discovered or brought to the staff's attention.

A good measure of the efficiency of the circulation department is meeting the following expectations:

1. Promptness of checking out materials;
2. Maintain the efficiency of the materials supply service by keeping the stacks in good order, returning books on time, returning books to the shelves promptly;
3. Keep track of book loss; and
4. Administer the reserve materials.

RESERVE

Most reserve collections are made available online through course sites using the digitizing process by turning print articles into a web accessible PDF files. This requires: receiving a clean copy from faculty; obtaining copyright clearance, if necessary, scanning material, creating a record in a special e-reserve database, creating a quick bibliographic record in the OPAC, including an 856 field link to the items' Internet location, checking links and PDF files for accuracy and availability.

This is different from the old manual reserve which gave students limited time to read and return the reserved materials. In the traditional system the reserve unit places reserve materials arranged by course numbers behind the reserve or the circulation desk whose staff hand them out to students on request. In such a manual system, materials placed on reserve become inaccessible to the other patrons who are not in the course, unless materials are scanned and made accessible electronically. In this system reserve collections can be of two kinds: those that are in high demand, charged out for two hour periods during the day and for overnight; and those suggested for collateral reading and made available for a one-or three-day period. Fines levied against delinquent reserve readers were of sufficient magnitude to ensure the prompt return of materials so designated.

THE DIGITAL LIBRARY AND THE ACADEMY

A digital library is an assemblage of digital computers, storage, and communication machinery, together with the context and software needed to produce, emulate, and extend those services provided by conventional libraries based on paper and other material means of collecting, cataloging, finding and disseminating information. A full service digital library must accomplish all essential services of traditional libraries and also exploit the well known advantages of digital storage, searching and communication." (Fox, 1994). Other definitions describe the digital library as "that set of global inter-networked libraries" that includes the following criteria: a collection of texts, images, or data in digitized form; a set of systems for indexing and navigating or retrieving in that collection; and one or more defined community of users.

What made digital libraries possible are the following: collaboration between libraries beyond the limitations of space, time, efficiency and effectiveness; increased efficiency and effectiveness; and the convergence of academic libraries and computing centers on campuses.

Advantages and characteristics of the digital library include ease of remote access to both print and electronic materials in many different academic libraries: provision of materials not owned by the library, development of electronic delivery tools, services based on interlibrary cooperation, access to materials in digital format; and expansion of teamwork.

A major issue facing academic librarians is digitization and consolidating print collections for high density storage. Efforts are being made to expand digital collections and the acquisition of digital sources of information. Libraries are also involved in ongoing efforts to digitize their archives and special collections. An example is the Collaborative Digitization Program (CDP) at the Bibliographic Center for Research (BCR). The mission of the CDP is to help libraries, museums, and cultural heritage institutions provide digital access to collections in order to increase access. (Bibliographic Center for Research, www.bcr.org/cdp/about/index.html).

The International Digital Library Initiative (IDLI) began with the following six universities receiving support from the IDLI: Michigan; Illinois-Urbana; California at Berkley; Carnegie Mellon; Stanford; UC Santa Barbara Alexandria Project. The Committee on Institutional Cooperation (CIC) is a consortium of 12 major teaching and research universities and institutions which also supports a virtual electronic library. The CIC virtual library offers staff, faculty, and students of any member institution access to any of the information resources owned or licensed by CIC universities.

REFERENCES

American Library Association. 2004. *Guidelines for Distance Learning Library Services.* http://www.ala.org/ala/mgrps/divs/acrl/standards/guidelinesdistancelearning.cfm (accessed Dec 27, 2009)

Barclay, D. A. 2000. *Managing Public Access Computers: a How-to-do-it Manual for Librarians.* New York: Neal-Schuman Publishers.

Beagle, D. 1999. "Conceptualizing an Information Commons," *Journal of Academic Librarianship* 25, no. 2: 82-89.

Burke, John J. 2009. *Neal-Schuman Library Technology Companion: a Basic Guide for Library Staff.* 3rd ed. New York: Neal-Schuman Publishers.

Brophy, P. 2005. *The Academic Library.* 2nd ed. London: Library Association.

Budd, J. M. 2005. *The Changing Academic Library: Operations, Cultures, Environments.* Chicago: Association of College and Research Libraries.

Casado, M. 2001. "Delivering Library Services to Remote Students." *Computers in Libraries*, 21(4): 32 - 38.

Cervone, H. 2009. "Strategic Analysis for Digital Library Development." *OCLC Systems & Services* 25, no.1: 16-19.

Chowdhury, G. G. and Chowdhury, S. 2003. *Introduction to Digital Libraries.* London: Facet Pub.

Cohn, J. M., Kelsey, A. L. and Fiels, K. M. 2002. Planning for Integrated Systems and Technologies: a How-to-do-it-Manual for Librarians. 2nd ed. London: Facet Publishing.

Dhanavandan, S., S. Esmail, and V. Mani. 2008. "A Study of the Use of Information and Communication Technology (ICT) Tools by Librarians." *Library Philosophy and Practice.* http://www.webpages.uidaho.edu/~mbolin/dhanavandan-esmail-mani.htm (accessed Dec 27, 2009)

Fang, X. 2006. "Collaborative Role of the Academic Librarian in Distance Learning – Analysis on an Information Literacy Tutorial in WebCT." *Electronic Journal of Academic and Special Librarianship* 7, no. 2. http://southernlibrarianship.icaap.org/content/v07n02/fang_x01.htm (accessed Dec 27, 2009)

Fox, E. A. 1994. *Source Book on Digital libraries.* Blacksburg: University Printing Services.

Hanson-Baldauf, D., and S. Hassell. 2009. "The Information and Communication Technology Competencies of Students Enrolled in School Library Media Certification Programs." *Library & Information Science Research* 31, no. 1: 3-11.

Heller-Ross, H. 1996. "Librarian and Faculty Partnerships for Distance Education." *MC Journal: The Journal of Academic Media Librarianship* 4, no. 1 (summer) http://wings.buffalo.edu/publications/mcjrnl/v4n1/platt.html (accessed Dec 27, 2009)

Hernon, Peter. 2009. *Convergence and Collaboration of Campus Information Services.* Santa Barbara, CA: ABC-Clio.

King, D. 2009. "Building the Digital Branch: Guidelines for Transforming Your Library Website." *Library Technology Reports* 45, no. 6: 1.

Kirk, E. and Bartelstein, A. 1999. Libraries Close in on Distance Education. *Library Journal* 124, no. 6: 40-42.

Liew, C. 2009. "Digital Library Research, 1997-2007: Organizational and People Issues." *Journal of Documentation* 65, no. 2: 245-66.

Lim, S. 2007. "Do Information Technology Units have More Power than Other Units in Academic Libraries?" *Journal of the American Society for Information Science and Technology* 58, no. 9: 1242-53.

Lim, S. 2008. "Job Satisfaction of Information Technology Workers in Academic Libraries." *Library & Information Science Research* 30, no. 2: 115-121.

Lim, S. 2007. "Library Informational Technology Workers: Their Sense of Belonging, Role, Job Autonomy, and Job Satisfaction." *The Journal of Academic Librarianship* 33, no. 4: 492-500.

Long, C., and R. Applegate. 2008. "Bridging the Gap in Digital Library Continuing Education: How Librarians Who Were Not "Born Digital" are Keeping up." *Library Administration & Management* 22, no. 4: 172-82.

Lynch, B., ed. 1995. *Information Technology and the Remaking of the University Library.* San Francisco: Jossey-Bass Publishers.

Martin, H. 1999. "Lessons from the Information Commons Frontiers." *The Journal of Academic Librarianship* 25, no. 2: 90-91.

Maruskin, A. 1980. "*OCLC: Its Governance, Function, Financing and Technology.*" New York: Marcel Dekker.

Mittrowann, A. 2009. Strategic, Digital, Human: The Library of the Future. A View on International Developments by a German Library Supplier." *Public Library Quarterly* 28, no. 3: 193-203.

Morgan, E. 2008. "MyLibrary: a Digital Library Framework and Toolkit." *Information Technology and Libraries* 27, no. 3: 12-24.

Reeves, L. 2005. "Starting Small: Setting up Off-campus Library Services with Limited Resources." *Journal of Library Administration* 41, no. 3/4: 355-364.

Resnick, T., Ugaz, A., Burford, N., and Carrigan, E. 2008. "E-resources: Transforming Access Services for the Digital Age." *Library Hi Tech* 26, no. 1: 141-156.

Schiller, N. 1996. "World Wide Web Library Support for Distance Education at the State University of New York at Buffalo." *MC Journal: The Journal of Academic Media Librarianship*   4,   no.   1   (summer) http://wings.buffalo.edu/publications/mcjrnl/v4n1/schiller.html (accessed Dec 27, 2009)

Secord, A., R. Lockerby, L. Roach, and J. Simpson. 2005. "Strategic Planning for Distance Learning Services." *Journal of Library Administration* 41, no. 3/4: 407-412.

Seymour, C. 2007. "Information Technology Assessment: a Foundation for School and Academic Library Collaboration." *Knowledge Quest* 35, no. 5: 32-35.

Shearer, B., C. Klatt, and S. Nagy. 2009. "Development of a New Academic Digital Library: a Study of Usage Data of a Core Medical Electronic Journal Collection." *Journal of the Medical Library Association* 97, no. 2: 93-101

Shiri, A., and S. Chase-Kruszewski. 2009. "Knowledge Organisation Systems in North American Digital Library Collections." *Program* 43, no. 2: 121-39.

Su, M. 2008. "Beyond Circulation: The Evolution of Access Services and its Relationship to Reference Librarianship." *The Reference Librarian* 49, no. 1: 77-86.

Subramaniam, M. 2009. "Women and Information Technology." *The Library Quarterly* 79, no. 2: 275-278.

Territorial Kansas Online. http://www.territorialkansasonline.org (accessed Dec 28, 2009)

Marcum, J. W. 2003. "Visions: The Academic Library in 2012." *D-Lib Magazine*, 9 (5), http://www.dlib.org/dlib/may03/marcum/05marcum.html (accessed Dec 28, 2009)

Waller, A. 2007. "Technical Services and Open Access: A Few Challenges." *Feliciter* 53, no. 5: 241-243.

Wolpert, A. 1998. "Services to Remote Users: Marketing the Library's Role." *Library Trends* 47, no. 1: 21-41.

Wood, P. and J. Walther. 2000. "Future of Academic Libraries: Changing Formats and Changing Delivery." *The Bottom Line: Managing Library Finances* 13, no. 4: 173 – 182.

DIGITAL LIBRARY PROJECTS

Library of Congress American Memory Project - http://memory.loc.gov/
Library of Congress Thomas Project - http://thomas.loc.gov/
Project Gutenberg - http://www.gutenberg.org/wiki/Main_Page
The Internet Public Library - http://www.ipl.org/
ACM Digital Library - http://www.acm.org/dl/
The Digital Library Initiative (U of Illinois) - http://dli.grainger.uiuc.edu/
California Digital Library - http://www.cdlib.org/
International Coalition of Library Consortia -
http://www.library.yale.edu/consortia/statement.html
Ebrary - http://www.ebrary.com
The LSU Digital Library - http://www.lib.lsu.edu/epubs/
World of Escher - http://www.WorldOfEscher.com/
Bartleby.com - http://www.bartleby.com
Alex Catalogue of Electronic Texts - http://sunsite.berkeley.edu/alex/
Internet Quick Reference - http://internetquickreference.net/
The Healthy Gourmet - http://www.bizdistrict.com/food.html
The Hermitage Museum -
http://www.hermitagemuseum.org/html_En/index.html
The Nine Planets -
http://www.seds.org/nineplanets/nineplanets/nineplanets.html
The American Kennel Club - http://www.akc.org/

8

LIBRARY INSTRUCTION/INFORMATION LITERACY

Patricia Knapp is often cited as the librarian who "sparked the modern-day library instruction movement" (Grassian & Kaplowitz, 2001, p.15). Her instructional work began in the early 1960's at Monteith College Library, a branch of the Wayne State University System. Displeased with students' critical thinking skills, Knapp's instructional goal was the improvement of their ability to discern quality information. Evan Farber followed Knapp's lead, and, in 1964, created the first face-to-face fully course integrated instruction. The highly successful Farber approach is still practiced in many campuses today. In recognition of his work's longstanding contributions, the American Association of College and Research Libraries awarded Farber the 1987 "Instruction Librarian of the Year Award." Around this same time, Miriam Dudley took an asynchronous, or remote, approach to teaching students about their library. Rather than present instruction in a traditional face-to-face setting, Dudley set about creating workbooks. These self-paced modules guided students through a series of exercises requiring the use of particular library reference tools. These multiple-choice modules were then graded by library staff and returned to students with appropriate comments and coaching.

Though early approaches varied, Knapp, Farber and Dudley helped in shaping the concept of the teacher librarian. Theory surrounding bibliographic instruction grew, encouraged by the desire to help students "learn about library resources and information tools" (p.19).

THE RISE OF INFORMATION LITERACY

From these beginnings, there is now widespread support on campuses across the country for bibliographic instruction, and more recently the associated concept of information literacy. Paul Zurowski coined the term 'Information Literacy' (IL) in 1974 (Grassian & Kaplowitz, 2001, p.4). This term is now especially pertinent in what has become the 'Information Age,' a time of unprecedented information production, dispersal and access. Zurowski defined an information literate person as one who is able to responsibly utilize a wide range of sources and from that information solve life problems. The Association of College and Research Libraries (ACRL) echoed his sentiments in its 2001 "Objectives for Information Literacy Instruction: A Model Statement for Academic Librarians," which states "Information literacy encompasses more than good information-seeking behavior. It incorporates the abilities to recognize when information is needed and then to phrase questions designed to gather the needed information. It includes evaluating and then using information appropriately and ethically once it is retrieved from any media."

Academic librarians have used different jargons to refer to library instruction which has also been known as information literacy or library/bibliographic instruction. In the past decade the library profession has moved away from the terms bibliographic instruction and information literacy and toward the term information fluency, as it more accurately reflects the idea that information seekers learn and build their information seeking and research skills as part of a continuing process.

The Association of College and Research Libraries (ACRL) defines Information Literacy as "a set of abilities requiring individuals to 'recognize when information is needed and have the ability to locate, evaluate, and use effectively the needed information. "… the ability to navigate information structures and to evaluate information retrieved through these information structures. Information fluency includes library literacy, media literacy, computer literacy, Internet literacy, research literacy, and critical thinking skills." Most universities adopt the ACRL's Information Literacy Competency Standards for Higher Education which defines information literacy in five components, need, access, evaluate, use and issues:

> The information literate student determines the nature and extent of the information needed. The information literate student accesses needed information effectively and efficiently. The information literate student evaluates information and its sources critically and incorporates selected information into his or her knowledge base and value system. The information literate student, individually or as a member of a group, uses information effectively to accomplish a specific purpose. The information literate student understands many of the economic, legal, and social issues surrounding the use of information and accesses information ethically and legally (p.4).

According to the ACRL *Guidelines:*

Library instruction programs should improve the students' ability to use library collections and services, and should include instruction in the use of full range of information resources and knowledge. Instruction may be offered as part of coursework in an academic subject or interdisciplinary program, in a separate course on library skills and information literacy, in workshops, in network-delivered instruction, in term paper clinics, and through point-of-use aids in the library. Standards and guidelines for information literacy and instruction are useful tools in developing and assessing library instruction.

CREATING A SUCCESSFUL IL COURSE

A typical information literacy skills course includes an overview of how information is created and shared in different disciplines and how knowledge of this publication process cycle informs information finding methods. Theoretical and practical exploration of the various skills and critical thinking abilities needed to identify, use, and evaluate information found in traditional and emerging environments. Teaching information skills includes much preparation such as: Developing teaching modules for undergraduates, subject majors, and graduates and professional programs and customizing teaching to appropriate student levels and students' existing knowledge bases.

Creation and preparation for IF course requires creating a successful learning environment such as:

- User-friendly physical environment;
- Diverse electronic information access;
- Appropriate state-of-the art technology classrooms;
- Librarian-faculty cooperation and interaction;
- Librarians and their faculty partners work together to give students guidance and assistance at the time of need.

Most academic libraries mission statements speak directly to the idea that IF prepares students not only to execute course assignment but also in other settings, specifically, that it values and promotes information literacy by teaching users to identify, evaluate, and utilize information in their coursework, careers, and daily lives (life-long experience). These libraries offer formal or informal information fluency courses and programs that are well designed and professionally delivered. Such courses, when offered in accordance with recognized professional standards, may overcome and compensate for inadequate collections and facilities. Information fluency courses are offered for credit but this is not the common practice on college campuses. When not taught as a course, information fluency courses may be taught as part of a general education requirements course that all freshman students are required to take such as English 101, College Writing Seminar or a Social Studies course. In such cases, the course is mostly taught by library staffs who are invited by the instructor to help with the teaching of that component of the course. In this case, there should be regular contact between the library staff and faculty regarding the services a university library would like to offer to faculty. In some cases a faculty can submit a request for an IF or BI workshop. This can be accomplished by completing a request form, available online in most cases. The form asks faculty to describe the course and perceived IF/BI needs that the workshop is to address.

The majority of information fluency programs consist of incorporating information and technology literacy skills into courses that fulfill other university's core curriculum requirements. These courses are coordinated and taught by the reference librarians. In these courses, students will learn about the similarities and differences between computer and information literacy, as well as develop a working knowledge of how to use library resources effectively in their research. In order to accomplish that, they will explore the elements of print and electronic resources, especially citations, books, and periodicals. As an educational outcome, students will develop knowledge of primary, secondary, scholarly, and general resources and how they are to be used in their work. These methods and tools will be used to enhance critical-thinking skills, which will in-turn help the student develop their argumentative writing. These methods and tools are then brought together using information technology and computer applications to develop a written paper and electronic presentation.

Today's academic libraries provide information literacy that goes beyond printed matters to encompass multimedia. At the University of Minnesota, the main campus libraries assist students with their multimedia needs with the SMART Learning Commons (http://smart.umn.edu/). "We support students at all stages of learning and content mastery as they develop and refine their ability to think critically, evaluate information, propose and apply solutions, and assess results" Students can check out multimedia materials, such as music and video recordings, and production equipment, like microphones, digital cameras, web cams, and digital video recorders. One-on-one peer consultants can assist students with their writing assignments, filming and editing, creating website designs, graphic design, and with making PowerPoint presentations. The students are assisted by fellow students, who are extensively trained in the various services they provide. (University of Minnesota, 2008)

DESIRED IL COMPETENCIES

Typical desired competencies such as the ones listed below meet with the ACRL Information Literacy Competency Standards for Higher Education:
- Determine the extent of information needed

- Access the needed information effectively and efficiently
- Evaluate information and its sources critically
- Incorporate selected information into one's knowledge base
- Use information effectively to accomplish a specific purposes
- Understand the economic, legal, and social issues surrounding the use of information

Aside from the formal IF/BI instruction, users can receive individual assistance from library staff in a variety of ways. The most common form is with a visit to the reference desk. If the library is closed or if users cannot or do not wish to visit the library in person, they can contact the library via phone during open hours or make use of electronic modes of assistance.

ASSESSMENT OF IL COMPETENCY

No matter which IF program a library uses, it is extremely important to implement an assessment system within the information fluency program. Much of the literature attests to the fact that feedback from students, faculty and librarians is essential. Pre-testing knowledge has become important as ILAC has been implemented, both to help direct instruction where it is most needed and to give the teaching staff "before" data for comparison. It is important to assess students at multiple times during their IF courses. This will include a pre- test of freshmen students, to learn about their level of IF. A follow up test after the second year will help to assess how much students have learned from the program. It may also be helpful to establish some type of alumni survey, to measure whether the IF program has truly helped students become life long learners.

Faculty evaluation of the IF program should also be measured and taken into account. Through all of these assessment techniques, those involved in the IF program would be able to monitor the progress of students in the program and also see whether they have retained the material after they have taken the courses. The feedback could also help implement changes that are needed in the program.

EVALUATION OF IL COURSES

Regular and ongoing evaluation of information literacy courses can help in improving the delivery of these courses. Among the questions that need to be answered regarding instruction are:

- Are library instruction programs available and funded adequately for the support of coursework?

- Are instruction programs integrated with undergraduate coursework?
- How easily can undergraduates access instruction when they need it?
- Are library instruction programs informed by current research, principles, and knowledge?

A potential pitfall in the implementation of a for-credit course as part of a campus-wide IF program is the lack of support from faculty as a whole. A study at Oregon State University found that in a general survey, faculty perceived librarian-led for-credit courses as not relevant to the courses they taught, were not aware that such services existed, or did not recommend them to students for other reasons. Faculty who made use of the courses returned a much more favorable response. Likewise, students indicated that even though for-credit courses were their least preferred method of IF instruction, 63% would consider taking the course to receive IF education; the response rate increased to 72% if the course were relevant to the major field of study (Davidson, 2001).

OTHER FORMS OF IL INSTRUCTION

In addition to formal courses on library instruction or information fluency, college and university libraries also invite students to make an appointment for individual or small group instruction with the library's reference department. These sessions can provide a broad introduction to the resources available at or though the library or can guide students undertaking research with in-depth instruction on the sources relevant to the field of study. The online request page attempts to gather information about the level of assistance needed and in most cases presume or require existing base level of information fluency like the ability to list keywords and sources already consulted for the search.

In some university libraries there is what is referred to as "tenants." These are individuals or groups from other areas around campus who use and share space in the library building with the library proper. A good example is a writing center, a place where students can go to get help with writing their papers by students and staff. The Penrose Library at the University of Denver is using the writing center to provide reference assistance and bibliographic instruction to students doing research.

EXAMPLES OF IL COURSES AND PROGRAMS

At the University of Wisconsin-Milwaukee, the Library's Research and Instructional Support Department (RIS) is in charge of the BI programs. The Department has a head and a full time library instruction coordinator. All staff members in the RIS Department participate in these BI programs as instructors. The mission of RIS is to help users effectively utilize the Libraries' collections, services, and other resources. The goal is to provide users with the ability to identify, retrieve, and evaluate information. These users are not only UWM first-year students, but also high-school, middle and elementary school students from the Milwaukee metropolitan area. Local school teachers and community members are also served by the BI department. The advantages of academic libraries' offering services to the public, and to high school students are often cited as good community relations, and as a good recruitment tool. There are both formal and informal library instruction sessions. The Department offers formal instruction, individual consultation, group projects and help. The RIS librarians collaborate with instructors and coordinators to help students find resources for their class work, course-related instructional support, course-integrated instruction (librarians may assist the professor/instructor in class, and both work as a team), special or walk-in workshops, interactive online tutorials and innovative learning technologies (usually for community members, or teachers).

The University of Wisconsin-Madison Libraries offers students and non-students several different workshops that focus on information literacy. They are:

- Citation Manager: EndNote. This course introduces the software EndNote that helps students create sound citations for their writing. Some of the features covered in this course are organizing database records, searching and sorting records, importing records from databases, and formation of bibliographies.
- Citation Manager: RefWorks. This course helps people to manage their citations with software called RefWorks. This is similar to EndNote, as it allows people to organize and sort records, import the records electronically from the database to the program, and gives assistance with the preparation of the bibliography. This course is a hands-on course, allowing people to learn by doing.
- Grants Information Center: This course is intended for assisting non-profit organizations with their pursuit and application to grants. It is not intended for personal welfare assistance or for-profit organizations.
- Google for Research: This course teaches students how Google can be used to search for quality resources. It covers Google, Google Scholar, Google Patents, and Google Books. It also includes instruction on how to evaluate the resources found from these sources.
- Keeping Current with the literature: This course introduces the RSS feed and how to use it to stay current within a field of study. The hands-on sessions use Google Reader or Bloglines accounts that the students create themselves.

- PubMed: This course teaches people how to find and retrieve information from PubMed "using advanced search features such as Medical Subject Headings, limits, clinical queries, citation matcher", and My NCBI in order to save searches and customize accounts.
- SciFinder: This course is an overview of the SciFinder Databases. Students learn how to use search features such as structure, substructure, and ANALYZE/REFINE for improving their search strategies.
- UW-Madison Libraries: What You Really Need to Know. This is a course that gives students an overview of all that the UW Libraries have to offer to their students. Some of the things covered are the online public access catalog, how to retrieve a book, how to manage their online library account, and how to utilize the resources that the Libraries have to offer (UW Madison Libraries: Workshops, 2009).

The Virginia Commonwealth University Library (VCU) offers what is known as "University College", a first year information literacy program for incoming freshman. The library's role is to design a curriculum that can be used by any department, but classes themselves must be taught by regular subject instructors due to an overwhelming number of new students which exceed the library staff's capacity. Instruction is given via online tutorials and through special events and workshops.

Ohio State University offers the following three for-credit (1-2 credit) courses: ARTS&SCI 120D – Internet Tools & Research Techniques (Learn to use the Web browser and communication tools effectively; develop strong searching and evaluation skills); ARTS&SCI 121D – Advanced Online Research (Learn advanced searching skills and study specialized online research tools in a subject area of interest to you); and ARTS&SCI 122D – Online Research Strategies for Career Exploration (Learn effective techniques for finding career and employment information online).

It is common practice in university libraries to list names and e-mail addresses of library staff on the library's Web pages. A generic e-mail address can also be found and used by the user to submit questions to be answered by the library staff. Alternatively, a library Web page promotes a service like "Ask Live," "Chat with a Librarian," or the like. This is a virtual 24/7 service made available to library users whether they are faculty, students, alumni or community local members. The help services can point students to on-line catalogs and aide in their use, or other acts such as helping students obtain reserve materials or make a reservation for on-site AV equipment. It may also serve reference needs.

REFERENCES

ALA-ACRL. 2000. *Information Literacy Standards Competency for Higher Education*. American Library Association http://www.ala.org/ala/mgrps/divs/acrl/ standards /standards.pdf (accessed Jan 15, 2010)

Aldrich, M. 2007. "Falling in Line: Curricular Alignment in a Library Credit Course." *Georgia Library Quarterly* 44, no. 3: 7-11.

Allan, C. 2007. "Using a Wiki to Manage a Library Instruction Program: Sharing Knowledge to Better Serve Patrons." *College & Research Libraries News* 68, no. 4: 242-244.

Anderson, R., and S. Wilson. 2009. "Quantifying the Effectiveness of Interactive Tutorials in Medical Library Instruction." *Medical Reference Services Quarterly* 28, no. 1: 10-21.

Characteristics of Programs of Information Literacy that Illustrate Best Practices: A Guideline, (2003, Jun). Association of College & Research Libraries: http://www.acrl.org/ala/mgrps/divs/acrl/standards/informationliteracycompeten cy.cfm. (accessed Jan 10, 2010)

Collins, B. 2009. "Integrating Information Literacy Skills into Academic Summer Programs for Precollege Students." *Reference Services Review*, 37(2): 143-154.

Cardoza, *A. Core Curriculum Guide*, 3rd ed. Retrieved Jan 10, 2010, from: Loyola University Chicago: http://www.luc.edu/core/pdfs/core_curriculum_guide.pdf

Cordes, S., and B. Clark. 2009. "Business Process Management and the "new" Library Instruction: Navigating Technology and Collaboration." *College & Research Libraries News* 70, no. 5: 272-275.

Davidson, J. 2001. "Faculty and Student Attitudes toward Credit Courses for Library Skills." *College & Research Libraries* 62, no. 2: 155-163.

Downey, A., L. Ramin, and G. Byerly. 2008. "Simple Ways to Add Active Learning to Your Library Instruction." *Texas Library Journal* 84, no. 2: 52-4.

Ellis, E. and K. Whatley. 2008. "The Evolution of Critical Thinking Skills in Library Instruction, 1986-2006: A Selected and Annotated Bibliography and Review of Selected Programs." *College & Undergraduate Libraries* 15, no. 1/2: 5-20.

Ferrer-Vinent, I., and C. Carello. 2008. "Embedded Library Instruction in a First-Year Biology Laboratory Course." *Science & Technology Libraries* 28, no. 4: 325-351.

Ganster, L., and T. Walsh. 2008. "Enhancing library instruction to undergraduates: Incorporating online tutorials into the curriculum." *College & Undergraduate Libraries* 15, no. 3: 314-333.

Grant, M., and M. Berg. 2003. "Information Literacy Integration in a Doctoral Program." *Behavioral & Social Sciences Librarian* 22, no. 1: 115-28.

Grassian, E. S., and J. R. Kaplowitz. 2001. *Information Literacy Instruction: Theory and Practice*. New York: Neal-Schuman.

Guidelines for Instruction Programs in Academic Libraries, 2003, June. Association of College & Research Libraries: http://www.acrl.org/ala/mgrps/divs/acrl/standards/guidelinesinstruction.cfm (accessed Jan 10, 2010)

Hall, R. 2008. The "Embedded" Librarian in a Freshman Speech Class: Information
    Literacy Instruction in Action." *College & Research Libraries News* 69, no. 1:
    28-30.
Harrison, J., and L. Rourke. 2006. "The Benefits of Buy-in: Integrating Information
    Literacy into Each Year of an Academic Program." *Reference Services Review*
    34, no. 4: 599-606.
Harvey, P., and K. Goodell. 2008. "Development and Evolution of an Information
    Literacy Course for a Doctor of Chiropractic Program." *Communications in
    Information Literacy* 2, no. 1: 52-61.
Herron, P., and L. Griner. 1999. "Research Strategies and Information Sources in Latin
    American Studies: a One-credit, Web-based Course." *Research Strategies* 17,
    no. 1: 11-21.
Hopkins, E., and S. Julian. 2008. "An Evaluation of an Upper-division, General
    Education Information Literacy Program." *Communications in Information
    Literacy* 2, no. 2: 67-83.
Hrycaj, P. 2006. "An Analysis of Online Syllabi for Credit-bearing Library Skills
    Courses." *College & Research Libraries* 67, no. 6: 525-535.
Information Literacy Competency Standards for Higher Education. Association of
    College & Research Libraries:
    http://www.ala.org/ala/mgrps/divs/acrl/standards/informationliteracycompetenc
    y.cfm (Accessed Jan 10, 2010)
Ivey, R. 2003. "Information Literacy: How do Librarians and Academics Work in
    Partnership to Deliver Effective Learning Programs?" *Australian Academic &
    Research Libraries* 34, no. 2: 100-113.
Jacobs, M. 2008. "Ethics and Ethical Challenges in Library Instruction." *Journal of
    Library Administration* 47, no. 3/4: 211-32.
Jacobson, T., and Xu Lijuan. 2002. "Motivating Students in Credit-based Information
    Literacy Courses: Theories and Practice." *Portal*, 2(3): 423-441.
Jackson, S., Hansen, C., and Fowler, L. 2004. :Using Selected Assessment Data to Inform
    Information Literacy Program Planning with Campus Partners." *Research
    Strategies*, 20(1/2): 44-56.
Johnson, A., S. Jent, and L. Reynolds. 2008. "Library Instruction and Information
    Literacy, 2007." *Reference Services Review* 36, no. 4: 450-514.
Langhorne, M. J., ed. 2004. *Developing an Information Literacy Program, K-12: a How-
    to-do-it Manual and CD-ROM Package*, 2nd ed. New York: Neal-Schuman.
Leckie, G. 1996. "Desperately Seeking Citations: Uncovering Faculty Assumptions about
    the Undergraduate Research Process." *The Journal of Academic Librarianship*
    22, no. 3, 201-208.
Love, E. 2009. "A simple Step: Integrating Library Reference and Instruction into
    Previously Established Academic Programs for Minority Students." *The
    Reference Librarian* 50, no. 1: 4-13.
Macdonald, K. 2008. "ESL Library Skills: an Information Literacy Program for Adults
    with Low Levels of English Literacy." *Australian Library Journal* 57, no. 3:
    295-309.

Martin, J. 2008. "The Information Seeking Behavior of Undergraduate Education Majors: Does Library Instruction Play a Role?" *Evidence Based Library and Information Practice* 3, no. 4: 4-17.

Martin, J., and R. Ewing. 2008. "Power up! Using Digital Gaming Techniques to Enhance Library Instruction." *Internet Reference Services Quarterly* 13, no. 2/3: 209-225.

McHale, N. 2008. "Eradicating the Rogue Assignment: Intervention and Prevention." *College & Research Libraries News* 69, no. 5: 254-257.

Miller, J. 2004. "Issues Surrounding the Administration of a Credit Course for Medical Students: Survey of US Academic Health Sciences Librarians." *Journal of the Medical Library Association 92, no.* 3: 354-363.

Petersohn, B. 2008. "Classroom Performance Systems, Library Instruction, and Instructional Design: a Pilot Study." *Portal* 8, no. 3: 313-324.

Prowse, S. 2005. "Every Silver Lining has a Cloud: a Review of The British Library - Providing Services beyond the Reading Rooms." *Interlending & Document Supply* 33, no. 1: 63-65.

Robertson, M. and J .Jones. 2009. "Exploring Academic Library Users' Preferences of Delivery Methods for Library Instruction: Webpage, Digital Game, and other Modalities." *Reference & User Services Quarterly* 48, no. 3: 259-269.

Ronan, J., and M. Pappas. 2001. "Library Instruction is a Two-way Street: Students Receiving Course Credit for Peer Teaching." *Education Libraries* 25, no. 1: 19-24.

Shane, J. 2004. "Formal and Informal Structures for Collaboration on a Campus-wide Information Literacy Program." *Resource Sharing and Information Networks* 17, no. 1/2: 85-110.

Sharkey, J. 2006. "Towards Information Fluency: Applying a Different Model to an Information Literacy Credit Course." *Reference Services Review* 34, no. 1: 71-85.

Stephenson, E., and P. Caravello. 2007. "Incorporating Data Literacy into Undergraduate Information Literacy Programs in the Social Sciences: a Pilot Project." *Reference Services Review* 35, no. 4: 525-540.

Sutton, S., and Knight, L. 2006. "Beyond the Reading Room: Integrating Primary and Secondary Sources in the Library Classroom." *The Journal of Academic Librarianship*, 32(3): 320-325.

University of Minnesota 2008. *SMART Learning Commons* (website). http://smart.umn.edu/. (Accessed April 7, 2009)

Walker, B. 2008. "This is Jeopardy! An Exciting Approach to Learning in Library Instruction." *Reference Services Review* 36, no. 4: 381-388.

Wittkopf, B. 2003. "Recreating the Credit Course in an Online Environment: Issues and Concerns." *Reference & User Services Quarterly 43, no.* 1: 18-25.

York, A., and J. Vance. 2009. "Taking Library Instruction into the Online Classroom: Best Practices for Embedded Librarians." *Journal of Library Administration*, 49, no. 1/2: 197-209

Young, R. and S. Harmony. 1999. "Working with Faculty to Design Undergraduate Information Literacy Programs." New York: Neal-Schuman Publishers.

9

ACADEMIC LIBRARIES AND E-LEARNING

Academic librarians have inserted themselves into the development of distance-based education (DE) programs on their campus as these programs gained popularity among students and faculty. The American Council on Education (ACE) estimated that in 1998, 85% of traditional colleges and universities "offered or would soon be offering" distance-accessible courses and today almost every college and university in the U.S.A and overseas offer some form of DE courses and academic librarians, are learning how to adapt to that drastic shift in the delivery of higher education courses and programs.

The introduction of distant learning has created enormous challenges for academic librarians, among them: dealing with the enormous archive of previously published works now in print; continually deploying a global information technology infrastructure; and developing tools to support networked information retrieval. Additional challenges include: dealing with copyright issues; adhering to and developing standards for interoperability; including user-centered design principles; acquiring administrative commitment; continually seeking funding sources for research and development, prototype designs, testing, implementation, and evaluation of digital library projects, These are but a few of the challenges which will increase, as the number of colleges and universities offering distance learning is on the increase.

Academic librarians know that faculty and students need online catalogs, databases, electronic journals, newspapers, and library websites; these are all important assets for serving students and faculty who study and teach at a distance. Electronic resources are only part of what is involved with DE; also involved are reference instruction and consultation, as well as access to print and other non-digital collections. Document delivery, interlibrary loan, access to licensed electronic materials, and instruction, apart from basic Web searching, are also issues librarians have to deal with on campuses with DE programs.

The ACRL has approved a document on guidelines for distance learning library services in 2004. The document covers topics such as: definitions, management, finances, personnel, facilities, resources, services, documentation. According to ACRL:

- Access to adequate library services and resources is essential for the attainment of superior academic skills in post-secondary education, regardless of where students, faculty, and programs are located. Members of the distance learning community are entitled to library services and resources equivalent to those provided for students and faculty in traditional campus settings.

- The instilling of lifelong learning skills through general bibliographic and information literacy instruction in academic libraries is a primary outcome of higher education. Such preparation and measurement of its outcomes are of equal necessity for the distance learning community as for those on the traditional campus.

- Traditional on-campus library services themselves cannot be stretched to meet the library needs of distance learning students and faculty who face distinct and different challenges involving library access and information delivery. Special funding arrangements, proactive planning, and promotion are necessary to deliver equivalent library services and to achieve equivalent results in teaching and learning, and generally to maintain quality in distance learning programs. Because students and faculty in distance learning programs frequently do not have direct access to a full range of library services and materials, equitable distance learning library services are more personalized than might be expected on campus.

- The originating institution is responsible, through its chief administrative officers and governance organizations, for funding and appropriately meeting the information needs of its distance learning programs in support of their teaching, learning, and research. This support should provide ready and equivalent library service and learning resources to all of the institution's students, regardless of location. This support should be funded separately rather than drawn from the regular funding of the library. In growing and developing institutions, funding should expand as programs and enrollments grow.

- The originating institution recognizes the need for service, management, and technical linkages between the library and other complementary resource bases such as computing facilities, instructional media, and telecommunication centers.

- The originating institution is responsible for assuring that its distance learning library programs meet or exceed national and regional accreditation standards and professional association standards and guidelines.

- The originating institution is responsible for involving the library administration and other personnel in the detailed analysis of planning, developing, evaluating, and adding or changing of the distance learning program from the earliest stages onward.

- The library has primary responsibility for identifying, developing, coordinating, providing, and assessing the value and effectiveness of resources and services designed to meet both the standard and the unique informational and skills development needs of the distance learning community. The librarian-administrator either centrally located or at an appropriate site, should be responsible for ensuring and demonstrating that all requirements are met through needs and outcomes assessments, and other measures of library performance, as appropriate, and as an ongoing process in conjunction with the originating institution.

The two articles below written by the former and current distance education coordinators at the School of Information Studies (SOIS) at the University of Wisconsin-Milwaukee give an account of the evolution and growth of the distance education. Such a program required the support of the campus university library and its librarians to make it the success it has been, and to provide equitable service to distance education students. Mr. Kopycki is currently the Director of the Library of Congress Office in Cairo, Egypt. His paper was first published in a *Festschrift* in Honor of Dr. Mohammed Aman, edited by Prof. Shabaan Khalifa and published in Cairo, Egypt in 2009. Dr. Betsy Schoeller is the current Distance Education Coordinator at UWM-SOIS.

REFLECTIONS ON THE HISTORY AND DEVELOPMENT OF DISTANCE
EDUCATION PROGRAMS AT THE SCHOOL OF INFORMATION
STUDIES, UNIVERSITY OF WISCONSIN—MILWAUKEE

William J. Kopycki, MLIS

Under the vision and leadership of its Dean, Dr. Mohammed Aman, the School of Information Studies at University of Wisconsin—Milwaukee was able to realize success in developing its online graduate, and later undergraduate programs. With the use of innovative technologies supported by progressive-thinking faculty and dedicated staff, SOIS holds a distinct place on the playing field of online library science and information technology. This paper will take a look back and reminisce about the early development of these programs and some of the highlights thereabout.

When Dr. Mohammed Aman was appointed dean of what was then called the School of Library Science[2] at the University of Wisconsin-Milwaukee in 1979, he came forth with a vision to advance the School with its own unique identity to set it apart from other library schools in the state as well as the nation. When technologies to deliver educational content to students who could not otherwise attend classes in Milwaukee became available, he was the one who advanced the idea.

As has been documented elsewhere[3], the School's initial foray into the distance education began in the 1980s with instructor travel to remote UW campuses in the state of Wisconsin, particularly the campuses of Eau Claire and River Falls, in addition to other regions in the northeast. Not only did this give students from Wisconsin opportunities to study library science, it also enabled students from neighboring states, such as Minnesota and Michigan's Upper Peninsula to participate. To anyone familiar with Wisconsin and the inhospitable climate during winter in the heart of the academic year, there were often re-scheduled meetings and travel for the instructors turned into adventures in

---

[2] The School of Library Science was so called until 1981; the name was changed to School of Library & Information Science in 2000 and then to the present name School of Information Studies. Because of the chronological overlap, will simply refer to it as "the School" throughout this paper.

[3] Fong, W, Senkevitch, J., and Wolfram, D. "The Evolution of Distance Learning at the School of Information Studies, University of Wisconsin—Milwaukee". Unpublished paper, School of Information Studies (ca. 2002), p.5.

driving. For this reason and the reasons of travel, courses took on the form of condensed courses meeting during weekends under two or three consecutive days.

If, by "distance learning," it is meant that the instructor drives the distance and students learn, then it soon became clear that there had to be a more practical model for delivering education. UWM's introduction of newer media technology in the early 1990s made this possible, specifically through what was called "audiographics" through the support of a system-wide initiative called WISVIEW.[4] With this technology, courses were broadcast from SOIS to other UW sites, including Sheboygan, Wausau, Rice Lake, Marinette, Manitowoc, and Rhinelander. With 1995 came the introduction of a different technology, compressed video, broadcast over ISDN lines, provided similar learning experiences with students and instructor being able to interact with each other. To further enhance the experience, instructors would make occasional visits to one of the remote sites and broadcast to the remaining sites, giving everyone the chance for one face-to-face meeting.

In both models of delivery, students had to travel to the nearest UW campus. The costs of technology, including telecommunication fees, equipment rental, site coordination, etc. were also high. With the advent and growth of the World-Wide Web in the mid-1990s, the idea of online delivery was explored, and new opportunities became available. That distance education was considered an important future trend for SOIS is reflected in a statement from Dean Aman, when he announced: "We intend to push distance learning very vigorously. We will expand our efforts to draw students from around the state, the nation, and the world."[5]

In 1997, the School began experimenting with HTML course websites as a means of delivering instruction. When the limitations of this soon became apparent, a new courseware product called WebCT, developed by a graduate of British Columbia, was selected as the School's e-learning courseware management system. WebCT provided a suitable platform to create and administer multiple courses in a structured Web-based environment, with the addition of other utilities such as chat and course e-mail. Its low cost and ease of use made WebCT suitable for the School's purposes.

Of course, the WebCT platform did not replace that critical aspect of remote learning, namely the desire of students to see the face of the person who is

---

[4] Fong, et al., *op. cit.*, p. 7.
[5] *Update Newsletter, School of Library and Information Science* (No. 26, Fall 1996): p. 9

instructing them. To meet this need, the School introduced streaming audio and video with the implementation of a RealServer in 1998.

To support these efforts, the School made use of an instructional technology specialist to work with faculty in developing course sites and content, as well as facilitating student access, as the WebCT courseware was exclusively under the control of the School's IT unit. While this position was a part-time one, it soon became clear that a full-time position would need to be created to handle growth.

Because of the encouraging signs of success with these early efforts, the School was able to receive a research grant in 1999 from the UW System to further explore the opportunities afforded by Web-based learning.[6] The bar had been raised, and under Dean Aman, the School was going to move further in the area of distance learning.

The School began to attract an international online student presence that was truly global. Over time, students began taking (and completing) online courses and programs from as far away as Canada, Japan, Hong Kong, Germany, and elsewhere. Such students provided new challenges (coordinating live chats with extreme differences in time zones, sending books and other timely materials), but also gave the school an additional international reputation. But everyone was willing to work cooperatively and accommodate, as best as possible. Just like students from states that lacked MLIS programs, the international students wanted the opportunity to study and learn via an online program which gave them the quality of education they deserved from the School's experienced faculty.

By 2000, the "buzz" of the School's success in delivering its courses online reached other parts of the UW-System. For a system as large as Wisconsin's, the trend of distance learning led to the creation of various entities wanting to take advantage of its pioneering efforts. At the forefront was an UW-based entity called Dot.Edu, which offered to host the School's courses on Blackboard, an also-young, and rival courseware platform to that of WebCT. As an experiment, the School agreed to transfer its courses to the Blackboard site in the fall of 2000.

---

[6] The grant covered a study for the effectiveness of web-based vs. the traditional learning model. The results were subsequently published in Buchanan, E., et al., "A Systematic Study of Web-based and Traditional Instruction in and MLIS Program: Success Factors and Implications for Curriculum Design." *Journal of Education for Library and Information Science*, 42, (4): 274-288.

This experiment did not go as well as expected. There were a number of problems. First and foremost, because Blackboard was on remote servers, the ease and convenience of direct access to the School's staff was not always possible. This made troubleshooting and experimentation with new technology difficult. The centralized UWM Helpdesk, staffed by students with frequent turnaround, were unable to provide the same focused, personable level of support as was previously realized with School staff. All of this was a possible deterrent to retain the School's online students, and made difficult the prospect of attracting new ones. The pioneering field of distance education delivery to students in library and information science was largely known through word-of-mouth and experiences by current students; for Dean Aman, there could be no risk in jeopardizing the important foundation that was established in the previous years.

In January 2001, I was hired by the School to take on the role of Distance Education Coordinator. I was honored to have the chance to join the team of staff at SOIS, which also included Dean Aman's long-standing right-hand man, Assistant Dean Wilfred Fong, and recently-hired SOIS graduate Daniel Cook in the role of IT manager. With enthusiasm and dedication, we took on the efforts to create a supporting infrastructure with standards and practices that would serve the School's faculty and students with dedication and perseverance.

The first order of operation was to regain the School's autonomy; we moved back to WebCT on our own servers. Assistant Dean Fong, Dan and I spent a Saturday in early January 2001, rebuilding the server and preparing the new courses for that semester. WebCT's robust platform over that of the Blackboard's enabled us to experiment and create courses in different ways, depending on the nature of the course or its instructor. When it came to resolving technical issues that inevitably took place, diagnostics and resolution was always possible, as Dan lived only blocks away from the University. I remember his spending many a weekend or holiday trying to resolve a server issue or introduce a new enhancement. For my part, I instituted a round-the-clock system for answering e-mails and phone calls on technical and academic advisory nature for the students, and always kept prepared for whatever requests the faculty and instructors had for me. Our philosophy was to provide personalized, *human* support to our students and faculty, some of whom were very new to different concepts of Web-based technologies and learning. Dean Aman provided us with the support and encouragement we needed, and with Assistant Dean Fong, we could problem-solve and implement the vision that was set before us.

I recall the first video broadcasts that we did, using a semi-professional Sony DVX-2000 camera, and an Audio-Technica shotgun microphone which was capable of picking up the sound every rustle of paper or drop of a pencil that was within its range. The later discovery of a small mixing console enabled better control over the technical presentation, especially when a second microphone was introduced in live classroom situations. Eventually it was possible to purchase a second camera, a Sony PD-150 and additional equipment that led to more portability and professional recordings.

During that first year, the School faced new opportunities. The School had recently started an undergraduate program in Information Resources (BSIR), another important project championed by Dean Aman, to build strength and diversity in the School, and to increase the School's visibility campus wide.[7] Through a new UW initiative called the "College Connection," students at two-year UW colleges were able to transfer in to UWM to complete the remaining two years and acquire a BSci degree. This gave the School the opportunity to offer courses towards the BSIR degree using WebCT and streaming video. While some instructors tried to use compressed video similar to what had been done nearly a decade ago, the cost and lack of flexibility made this option short-lived, and by the Summer 2001 semester, the video component of courses were made exclusively through RealServer streaming.

I would like to mention a couple of other innovations that took place during this time as examples. In 2001, a special Comprehensive Exam Resource website was created, which aimed to give the School's DE students a similar experience as their onsite counterparts in preparing for this important exam. SOIS's MLIS program required its students to take a comprehensive exam, a requirement that was seen as an important "rite of passage" that students nervously asked faculty about during their first week of classes. How hard was the exam? What happens if someone fails? What is on the exam? How does one prepare for it? Seeking solace and answers to these questions ultimately materialized during the final few months of the student's matriculation. A formal onsite orientation was given by a member of faculty, and students would form "study groups" spending their off-hours in the basement of the UWM Library (where the Library Science books and journals could be found) discussing and debating all aspects of library science to prepare and support one another for the big day of the Comprehensive Exam. This process of preparation (sitting in the library, and in face-to-face discussions) was part of this whole student experience, and something that onsite students could naturally take

---

[7] Indeed the story of the BSIR program, with its development in the late 1990s to its rise to its current prominence, is one that is deserving of a separate study unto itself. The BSIR paved the way for students of diverse backgrounds to enter the IT sector and take important positions in the job market upon graduation.

advantage of. What about the online students? Hence the creation of the Comprehensive Exam Resource Website, which included online video of the orientation itself (presented live, and subsequently archived), a bulletin board plus chat room for communication among the students themselves, access to previous comprehensive exams, and other features that facilitated interaction between the online students as if they were on campus. This was met with great approval, and I spent each semester coordinating the chat sessions to make sure everyone could share their expertise, concerns, and hopes with one another with the aim of success in the exam.

It only seems like yesterday when, I remember, the first batch of distance education students came to Milwaukee on the day of the Comprehensive Exam in the Summer of 2001. Following the exam, a reception was held for the 10 or so students who came from all over Wisconsin, Nevada, Illinois, Minnesota, and elsewhere. Dean Aman gave these students a gracious and hospitable welcome; it had been a delight for us as members of staff to be able to associate faces with the names we had only known through e-mail and phone conversations[8].

Another innovation I was able to introduce was the creation of a Distance Education Technical Resource Site, serving as an additional model of support for students at all times with tutorials, demonstrations, and tips for the most common technical questions that were being asked by students. I received much praise from the students for the creation of this site, and although it saved me from having to answer some of the support-related phone calls and e-mails, each semester always brought new students with differing experiences onto the scene as the program grew.

By 2002, the School's online programs and student numbers grew. More than 30 courses or sections of courses were being offered by the School online, and nearly 150 students from all over the state, country, and indeed the world were taking these courses. In addition to providing an important source of revenue for the School, it also gave justification for new faculty positions to be opened. Again, it was only with the support of Dean Aman and a forward-looking position that this could have been achieved. Because of these efforts, *U.S. News and World Report* ranked the School's online MLIS program as one of the best in the nation in the magazine's report on distance education in 2002.

---

[8] Eventually (in 2002), distance education students were allowed to take the onsite portion of the Comprehensive Exam through a local proctor. While I missed being able to meet the students in person, it did make it feasible for the students, especially those from overseas, to complete the program.

New courses were developed especially for online delivery. For example, a course in business reference resources introduced in 2002 brought in new technologies for guided instruction of databases such as Lexis-Nexis and Dialog. Advanced and more portable digital video camera solutions, as mentioned earlier, enabled online students to take a guided tour of UWM's Golda Meir Library and other libraries in downtown Milwaukee. New staff were added: Venod Kearnes, a BSIR graduate, became an assistant to Dan Cook to help support the School's rapidly-growing IT infrastructure. Milton Wong, also a BSIR graduate, worked with me in providing multimedia support and instructional design for the courses. Because of this, new horizons to experimentation in delivering our courses were enhanced. Now, online students could "attend" some of the special lectures and events that took place on campus. Even though the physical distances were far, the amount of dedication taken by faculty and staff, with the example set by Dean Aman, brought everyone closer together.

The School's presence at statewide and neighboring library conferences brought new exposure, bringing new students (and meeting current ones) into our programs. Participation in local and statewide discussions and even a participation in a WebCT International Conference enabled us to share our institutional experiences with our colleagues in the field[9].

However, like all things in life, the winds of change eventually blew in at UW-Milwaukee and within the School—just as they do in all colleges and universities. There serves no useful purpose to go into discussion here, but by mid-2003, the core team of staff, myself included, moved on to other opportunities with the backing and support of Professor Aman. He was the one who brought us all together, encouraged us to work hard, and to keep our visions high in spite of all obstacles.

It is only fitting that I conclude this short paper with a saying attributed to the Egyptian President Anwar al-Sadat, who said: "There can be hope only for a society which acts as one big family, not as many separate ones." Under the leadership of Dean Aman, we were that big family, and only because of him that the School was able make its mark in the field of distance education for library science.

---

[9] Kopycki, William, and Cook, Daniel. "Evolution and Self-Empowerment through WebCT". 3rd Annual WebCT International Conference, Vancouver, BC, June 2001.

REFLECTIONS OF THE HISTORY AND DEVELOPMENT OF DISTANCE EDUCATION PROGRAMS AT THE SCHOOL OF INFORMATION STUDIES, UNIVERSITY OF WISCONSIN-MILWAUKEE, PART II,

Betsy A. Schoeller, Ph.D.

William J. Kopycki's essay, is a comprehensive reflection on how Distance Education evolved in 2003 at the School of Information Studies (SOIS). The following paper is a continuation of this development and to document the progress made in the SOIS Distance Education from 2003 to the present (2010).

In 2003, after William Kopycki left the school, the faculty and administration decided on a replacement to fill the position of Distance Education Coordinator that included administration and management of all media-based instructional programs and liaison activities with the larger campus technology community. WebCT was still the course management tool of choice by most instructors. The School still maintained its own computer network, its own license for WebCT (and administrative control for that program), and its own email server.

The University of Wisconsin-Milwaukee was seeing continued growth in the School of Information Studies, the School of Nursing, and other pockets on campus. Other schools and departments were showing interest in online education. The university began its own research into course management platforms and after a very short experience with Blackboard, decided on Desire 2 Learn (D2L). UWM created the Learning Technology Center on campus, its purpose being to assist any Distance Education efforts anywhere on campus. Once UWM decided on D2L, the Learning Technology Center began offering introductory courses for faculty and teaching staff who were interested in teaching online. They provided guidance for transitioning existing courses into DE courses, or creating DE courses from scratch. There were a small number of faculty who attended the D2L orientations, and decided to adopt the platform for their teaching. The majority of faculty and teaching staff continued to use WebCT and relied on SOIS' in-house help for DE.

Technology-minded faculty members were stretching the limits of what commercial course management systems could support. Jacques duPlessis, a new faculty member had research interest centered on learning technology, and had worked with a courseware system called Proteus. Proteus was written by some students at the University of Utah, and offered an open source type platform with much more flexibility than D2L. A few of the faculty members had cited limitations with both WebCT and D2L, and were looking for something that they could modify in order to present their courses and use technology in new and innovative ways. Proteus could be housed on an in-house server and allowed total freedom in administrative control and adaptability. Faculty members employed new ways to deliver content and make the student experience as close to an on-site experience as possible, and sometimes even better. There was an explosion in filming lectures and providing them online. Online 'chat' sessions, where students could ask questions using the chat functions, and see and hear the instructor answer their questions. The possibilities seemed to be endless.

SOIS students found their classes being offered on three different courseware platforms at the same time: WebCT, which was licensed and housed on SOIS servers, D2L, housed on UWM servers and administered by the Learning Technology Center, and Proteus, also housed on SOIS servers and administered by SOIS. It was not unusual in any given semester for a student to find each of their classes held on a different courseware platform. To limit the amount of confusion and allow students a single point of entry for their DE classes, Rebecca Hall created a DE portal for the SOIS web site. Students could go to the portal, click on a link for their class, and be taken to the appropriate course site, regardless of the courseware platform. D2L used the students' email information as login name and passwords, linking the email and DE courseware systems together. SOIS's IT Support wrote programs so WebCT would have the same capability. SOIS's Distance Education Support manually entered students into Proteus using their email login, and students were able to set their passwords to match their email in order to maintain continuity and reduce their confusion.

Soon, there was enough interest in distance education that UWM decided it needed to standardize what was happening in the different pockets of DE across campus. It announced that no school would be allowed to maintain its own license for courseware—the entire university would use D2L. The School lost WebCT, but retained Proteus as an alternative to D2L. 2004 – 2005 was a transitional time for the administration of the school as well. There was a new Dean, Johannes Britz, a new Assistant Dean, Chad Zahrt, a new Associate Dean, Hope Olson; IT Support for the school had been reorganized. With the change in personnel there was a change in the way the school approached technology in general, and this affected the way the school approached Distance Education as well. So as the campus began to take control of campus-wide technology, SOIS lost control of much of its technology. On the positive side, SOIS eliminated the headaches brought on by touchy servers, not enough servers to handle the growing number of DE students and online classes to accommodate them, and email downtime. The negative was that SOIS had always been one of the forerunners of technology in library science schools. Administrative control allowed SOIS to mold the technologies to fit any new initiative or new advance. Now SOIS was limited to whatever D2L and the Learning Technology Center were able to provide.

More and more of the school's classes were being offered online—so many that SOIS experienced a course shortage in the Spring semester of 2004. Within the first 48 hours of registration, every slot in every required course was full. The School had to open additional sections in order to accommodate the students. Even faculty members who were not entirely comfortable with online technology were able to teach DE classes, with help from in-house DE Support. There were enough students participating in online classes that the DE Support staff recognized the need to offer a way for those online students to communicate and develop a community outside of class; and thus, the "virtual lounge was born. All students taking online classes were 'enrolled' in the virtual lounge", which was created using a class section on Proteus. The "virtual lounge" contained all of the features students found in their classes, but faculty and teaching staff did not have access. The discussion board was used by students to offer assistance, talk about degree requirements, offer and request textbooks, and of course, gripes about instructors. DE Support staff monitored the virtual lounge, answering questions and providing information to students as needed. Announcements were posted to keep students apprised of program changes, professional association meetings, and job announcements. Along with the virtual lounge came a mentoring program. Students just beginning Distance Education were able to request a mentor online, and were matched with more experienced students who could act in an informal advisory capacity. Students could share their experiences with the online environment and create a stronger sense of community. SOIS already had an orientation program in place for students taking the comprehensive exam. DE Support videotaped the orientation and made it available for students online. This allowed distance students the same opportunity as on-site students to receive valuable orientation information. At the same time, comprehensive examination discussion threads were created in the virtual lounge. Distance students were better able to prepare for comprehensive exams, and were able to form study groups, just as on-site students did. In addition, DE Support staff created an Orientation site for Distance Education students. SOIS also had an orientation program in place for new students. All students were invited to attend, but distance students usually found it impossible to break-away from their obligations in order to travel to Wisconsin for orientation. The new site offered video clips of orientation information. DE students were able to put faces to names and feel as though they 'knew' department members better. A "Frequently Asked Questions" section helped online students get quick answers to common questions. The orientation site was linked to the virtual student lounge for easy access to both new and returning DE students. As a result, students out of the geographical area could virtually participate in the orientation program, making them feel more a part of the student community. We also began to see the phenomenon of courses being offered online in place but not on site. There was enough critical mass to be able to offer the entire MLIS degree online.

This made marketing much easier. SOIS began to stand out as a leader in Distance Education with its own niche: the ability to guarantee the MLIS degree online, along with the flexibility of no residency requirement, an asynchronous platform, and no cohort restriction. The School was able to tap into a large number of non-traditional students who were already working and could not relocate in order to obtain their MLIS. Many also had family situations that prevented a more traditional synchronous or cohort model of study. SOIS's classes were offered by the same faculty and teaching staff that taught the on-site classes. Many times, instructors were teaching both an online and an on-site section of the same class in the same semester. DE Support Staff were attending both the annual and mid-winter ALA meetings, as well as Library Association meetings in Illinois and Minnesota. Students were attending SOIS classes from Nevada, New York, Germany, Canada, Hong Kong—virtually everywhere.

Also in 2004, SOIS was invited to participate in developmental meetings of the Web-based Information Science Education (WISE) consortium. This ground-breaking collaborative distance education model would attempt to increase the quality, access, and diversity of online education opportunities in library and information science. Participation would allow UWM students pursuing an MLIS to take classes from other premier library schools via Distance Education. SOIS could offer courses with historically low enrollment to other universities' MLIS students. All participating students would have the opportunity to study with experts in a specialty which SOIS might not be able to offer.

By 2005, approximately 50% of SOIS's MLIS students were online students. Many of the traditional, on-site students also found themselves taking online classes for a number of reasons. Sometimes on-site sections were full, and there weren't enough on-site students to fill another on-site section of the class. The overages went into online classes. Sometimes there weren't enough on-site students to allow the school to run an on-site section at all, but there were enough online students to run the section; if a student wanted to take the class, they needed to join in online. Sometimes a class was developed online and only taught online. It was around this time when faculty started working with hybrid courses, which combined the on-site teaching component of courses with the convenience of courseware management systems for submitting work, providing course materials, and sometimes even discussion.

With the growth of the MLIS program, there was renewed interest in SOIS's Bachelor of Science in Information Resources (BSIR) program. More and more undergraduates were interested in online programs. SOIS was not able to guarantee the BSIR online because the BSIR required courses outside SOIS's span of control. Students, for instance, were required to take English credits. SOIS could not guarantee that the English department would be able to provide the classes needed by BSIR students online. There were, however, a number of two-year state schools that could provide these prerequisite courses to students, either closer to where the students lived or online. SOIS entered into a number of articulation agreements with these two-year schools in which students would work for two years at finishing their general education courses. Then the students were able to transfer to UWM and finish a BSIR degree online. Many of the undergraduate classes were offered online already, but the articulation agreements pressed the issue a little, and in 2005 the entire undergraduate curriculum was now offered online as well.

Use of online resources was large enough at this point, that SOIS outgrew Proteus. There were a number of disadvantages to using Proteus. It was not a commercial product, and did not have the sophistication of a commercial product. Students complained bitterly about having to work on two different platforms. DE was big enough that the SOIS servers couldn't keep up with the demand, and Proteus became more unstable. There was more turn-over in the IT workers support staff, and the newly hired student workers did not always have the technical ability to keep Proteus running. Sometimes the IT Support Staff found themselves coming in late at night, on weekends, and on holidays to solve problems that put Proteus offline. D2L had gone through an upgrade process that made it easier to work with, and fewer faculty members were interested in any new 'bells and whistles' that D2L couldn't handle. The decision was made to migrate all of the SOIS courses to D2L and shut down Proteus altogether.

In 2005 the WISE Consortium started in earnest, and UWM was there at the outset. The WISE mission was more than just a way to provide specialized courses to MLIS students. The philosophy of the WISE consortium was based on three guiding pillars: quality, pedagogy, and collaboration. Being a member of WISE indicated that SOIS was one of the world's leading library and information science schools, a school that used advanced online technology to enrich education and foster relationships among students, faculty, and universities. This meant that SOIS had already risen to the best of the best in online education.

By 2006, SOIS was seeing continued and was reaching maximum capacity, even with the hiring of a number of new faculty members and teaching academic staff. In order to maintain a quality program that did not depend on adjunct instructors, the decision was made to slow down growth by not marketing at library conferences.

In the next few years, advances continued to be made in technology, and D2L saw upgrades which allowed instructors to keep up with technological advances in the online classroom. Most instructors were moving beyond the usual PowerPoint slide presentations and recorded voice-overs to make lectures more like what students would experience in the on-site classroom. Streaming video was more user-friendly and more instructors took advantage of better quality video. There were some advances that were experimental in the UWM community that just didn't seem to fit into SOIS curriculum because they were so complex that the learning curve outweighed any benefit SOIS courses might derive. Sometimes a vague feeling of 'we must be missing something' would arise, but individual instructors were being helped by the SOIS DE support staff, the Learning Technology Center staff, and each other. Classes were becoming more sophisticated, and no one ever quite put a finger on what could be missing.

In 2008 the student orientation site was developed and placed on the D2L platform. The idea of the site was to provide a place for new DE students to find out what the courseware was like before their classes started. This reduced the learning curve of the courseware and allowed students to concentrate on course content. To do this, the site provided materials about what it was like to be a good online student in the different formats that students might find in their classes. PowerPoint lectures with audio voice-overs, short video clips made by instructors using personal video cameras, a short quiz, space on the discussion board, a glossary page of technology terms and just plain text documents all helped students learn what it took to be successful in an online environment and also assured them that their own computer systems could handle the types of technologies used in their classes.

Students began seeing a rise in the types of audio-visual resources used in their classes in 2009. It became more common to see movie clips from YouTube and other resources made outside SOIS embedded into course content. This is a reflection of the ability of SOIS faculty to embrace technology as it advances and apply it to the content they teach in their courses. The DE Support staff also created a blog for faculty—a space in which new technologies could be shared within the department. 2009 also saw a number of informal sessions where instructors could share their own best practices in DE with each other and problem solve. Growth stabilized, and now at the beginning of 2010, with a total MLIS student population at just over 750, a full two-thirds of that number are distance education Students. SOIS is still an active member of WISE, both offering classes to students in the consortium and sending its own students out to take courses from other institutions.

SOIS has definitely prospered with distance education, and has weathered the storm of horrific budget cuts and economic unrest that has damaged other departments at UWM as well as other library schools in recent years. That prosperity should be directly attributed to Dr. Mohammed Aman. It was his vision that allowed SOIS to become involved in Distance Education from the very start. It was his acceptance of technological advancement that made it possible for instructors to have the freedom to be innovative. It was his drive to make the school great that pushed the entire faculty to strive to advance even when technology was not comfortable. We are not the same faculty since Dr. Aman stepped down from his position as Dean. Indeed, there are very few people still in the department who were around when SOIS was just entering the arena of Distance Education. But his contribution to this success cannot be denied or overlooked.

REFERENCES

Bedord, Jean. 2007. "Distance Education: Choices, Choices, and More Choices." Searcher 15, no. 9: 18-22.

Cloete, Linda M.. 2005. "The Education and Training of Cataloguing Students in South Africa Through Distance Education." Cataloging & Classification Quarterly 41, no. 2: 53-69.

Fritts, Beth A.. 2006. "Distance Learning Librarianship Research Over Time: Changes and the Core Literature." Journal of Library Administration 45, no. 3/4: 397-410.

Gopakumar, V. and A. Baradol. 2009. "Assuring Quality in Distance Education for Library and Information Science: The Role of the Library." Library Philosophy and Practice 2009: 1-6.

Groeling, Jeff and Kenneth A. Boyd. 2009. "The Impact of Distance Education on Libraries." Theological Librarianship 2, no. 1: 35-44.

Hines, Samantha Schmehl. 2008. "How It's Done: Examining Distance Education Library Instruction and Assessment." Journal of Library Administration 48, no. 3/4: 467-78.

Hines, Samantha Schmehl. 2006. "What Do Distance Education Faculty Want from the Library?." Journal of Library Administration 45, no. 1/2: 215-27.

Kim, Hak Joon and James Michael Kusack. 2005. "Distance Education and the New MLS: The Employer's Perspective." Journal of Education for Library and Information Science 46, no. 1: 36-52.

Marley, Judith L.. 2007. "Gender Differences and Distance Education: Major Research Findings and Implications for LIS Education." Journal of Education for Library and Information Science 48, no. 1: 13-20.

McLean, Evadne and Stephen H. Dew. 2006. "Providing Library Instruction to Distance Learning Students in the 21st Century: Meeting the Current and Changing Needs of a Diverse Community." Journal of Library Administration 45, no. 3/4: 315-37.

Oldham, Bonnie. 2008. "Providing Library Services to Distance Education Students." Journal of Interlibrary Loan, Document Delivery & Information Supply 18, no. 2: 219-27.

Rao, Siriginidi Subba. 2006. "Distance education and the role of IT in India." The Electronic Library 24, no. 2: 225-36.

Washburn, Allyson. 2006. "Career Paths of Distance Education Librarians: A Profile of Current Practitioners Subscribed to the OFFCAMP Listserv." Journal of Library Administration 45, no. 3/4: 483-509.

Webb, Paula. 2006. "Meeting the needs of distance education students: Creating an online-only library instruction course." College & Research Libraries News 67, no. 9: 548-50.

Yang, Zheng Ye. 2005. "Distance Education Librarians in the U.S. ARL Libraries and Library Services Provided to their Distance Users." The Journal of Academic Librarianship 31, no. 2: 92-7.

10

MARKETING AND OUTREACH

Academic librarians are to be commended for lately recognizing the vital importance of marketing and outreach in support of their parent institution's stated vision and mission. As with all other types of libraries, academic librarians should be concerned about attracting, retaining, and better serving customers in a competitive environment. They should be concerned about users' attitudes towards their college libraries. They should be concerned with and ask often about:

- What do customers value when they choose the services of competing organizations;
- How do customers rate the performance of the library in relationship to its customers;
- How do the answers to both these questions affect customers perceptions of value; or
- How people choose among competitors; and
- How do the answers to these questions affect customer's choices about whether to continue using the library in the same way or perhaps in different ways?

Activities and events such as exhibits, displays, public lectures, and promotional materials are commonly and regularly used in order to attract traffic to the campus library. Displays often include aspects of collections that the library is able to highlight through public events. Most recently, many academic libraries have recently opened coffee kiosks that serve a variety of coffee and drinks and selected pastries and access to cable television, wireless access, newspapers and light reading materials nearby. This has resulted in making the library part of the social networking on campus where old fashioned policing is no longer in effect at least in these areas and similar library commons. Also with coffee and other amenities, libraries have added tables and chairs that are more comfortable as those found in major bookstores.

Some academic libraries have performed marketing audits as part of their attempts to promote library and information services on campus. A market audit allows the library to find its strengths and weaknesses in regard to its services, staff, and materials available to the public. Weingand defined a marketing audit as a "comprehensive systematic, independent, and periodic examination of the library's total environment, objectives, strategies, activities, and resources in order to determine problem areas and opportunities and to recommend a plan of action." Once an audit or survey is done, the library can improve its services and products to the public user, steps can be taken to rectify the weaknesses that have been found (Weingand, 1999, p.42).

The new phenomena of the World Wide Web, especially with the introduction of Web 2.0, has opened new doors for libraries to offer their patrons a wider range of tools and services to meet their educational, research and recreational needs. Such tools as Wikipedia, social networking sites as Facebook, MySpace, Second Lifeblogs, and YouTube, among others, have become the new phenomena in online communities. Academic libraries have built their web sites to help promote their products and services. Creating accounts on My Space and Facebook is just one way that academic libraries can market to, and reach users of these and other Web sites 24/7. Users of these and other Web sites are able to share information across the world with a click of a button and share news, ideas, videos, reviews, music, and other information.

According to Stephen Abram, "Web 2.0 is about more human aspects of interconnectivity. It is focused on content in the context of people, workplaces, markets, community and learning," Libraries have already joined the World Wide Web community by offering a website that displays what they are about, what they offer, hours of service, campus news and library events. Web 2.0 and the World Wide Web have allowed libraries in general, and academic libraries in particular to branch out from the traditional services of library work to expand their services to the virtual world. Public relations is very important in enhancing the image of your library and in attracting the community to your library and supporting it. Good publicity can raise the profile of your library among its present and prospective clients. Publicity is a long term activity.

Aside from technology and its virtues, a most important part of marketing is the creation of an environment that is positive and informative. Librarians should be friendly and courteous to users, make them feel welcome, gain their trust, able to help them with research projects, course work and assignments, and provide current sources that meet users' expectations. Speed, efficiency and competency are also key components when dealing with customers.

Philip Kotler describes what he calls the "4 Ps" of marketing as: product, place, price, and promotion. One can add a fifth P to stand for positioning which refers to the strategic competitive placement of a product or service.

- Product. The definition, features, colors, functions, options, package, and services that go with the core product or service itself.
- Price: the price charged for the product, and items like maintenance fees or costs of related products.
- Promotion; the visible form of marketing
- Place: where the product is sold and how it is delivered
- Positioning: the strategic competitive placement of your product or service

According to Hammer & Champy, in their book *Reengineering the Corporation* (1993*)*, the three forces (3Cs) that influence marketing are:

CUSTOMERS

Customers are taking charge. Sellers no longer have the upper hand—customers do. Library customers are under the impression that they are the main reason why libraries exist. Customers are the ones who check out and request print and non-print materials, attend programs such as book talks, and book signings, provide the financial support for the library to operate through tuition, in the case of academic libraries and the taxes they pay in the case of public libraries and public universities. When selecting books to purchase, a library wants to ensure the books or other library materials bought by the library are what the students and faculty want and will use in their teaching and research. Some psychologists from the "We Generation" inform us that the new generation seeks instant gratification and will not accept anything less.

COMPETITION

Traditionally, it has been hard to think of a library having competitors. But, recently, librarians have begun to look at other institutions as being competitors. There are now alternative sources for information available via personal computers on the Internet from various Web sites and data bases, bookstores, and video stores. People can go to a book or video store and buy or rent books and videos. However, most want free books and videos if they can get the choices they want at the right time. Public libraries are also in competition for funding, along with other public agencies and institutions such as the police and fire departments, sanitation, parks and recreational facilities and other city hall departments. In the case of academic libraries, the competition libraries face from other instructional, research and students' service units on campus are very strong. Hammer believes that "technology changed the nature of competition because of the availability of information" (p. 22).

CHANGE

In today's corporations, change has become both pervasive and constant. The pace of change has accelerated (p. 23). Change encompasses how the customers and the competition affect the library. Customers can cause change by their needs, and competitors can also cause change. Change is all around us— "nothing is constant. Change is continual and no sooner have we adapted to one change, then another comes along" (Evans and Ward, 2003, p. 4). Change can either be a positive or a negative event, depending on how the people involved perceive it. If the entire staff is involved in the process leading up to the change, they will be more likely to endorse it as planned change, instead of opposing it, in what can be described as imposed change. Change is what keeps the library going. Change can be an opportunity to try new programs or ideas.

In her book, *Library Marketing that Works*, Suzanne Walters describes the main elements of a marketing plan. While she was emphasizing public libraries, her plans can be adapted to academic libraries as well.

1. Strategic Planning—developing the library's mission and vision statements with a larger eye toward an ultimate marketing strategy. "It forces you to take a critical look at your library, your products and services, your customers, and community, and even your competition" (Walters, 2004, p. xv). The mission statement outlines the priorities of the library, while the vision statement describes the future.

2. S.W.O.T. analysis—determining the present strengths, weaknesses, opportunities, and threats of your library by conducting an environmental scan.

3. Goals—"precise statements of the results you hope to achieve in the next five years. Your goals should be believable, measurable and achievable by a set deadline…" (p. 25).

4. Customers—determining distinct sets of customers (segmentation), what their demands are, why they use the library, and what other competition exists to threaten your customers.

5. Marketing Goals—these differ from the goals in step #3. This set of goals takes into account the marketing mix—a combination of what Philip Kotler describes as the "4 Ps": product, mentioned above. Darlene E. Weingand adds "prelude" and "postlude" to this mix, indicating the roles of auditing and evaluating in the marketing plan, while Walters believes that "positioning" and "politics" are relevant for libraries in particular. Libraries as a whole should be concerned with their position within the community; how important is the library perceived to be? Products and services within the library can also be positioned. "For example, providing an automated circulation system in various languages, as well as online services and

services from remote locations, offers an opportunity to reposition the library" (p.103). Finally, politics plays a key role in the marketing goals of a public library in particular. Relationships with the political powers that create policy and control funding must be factored into the marketing plan.

6.   Action Plan—finally it is time to get the carefully planned marketing program rolling. An action plan includes promotional campaigns, advertising, and continual evaluation of how well your marketing plan is meeting goals and matching the mission and vision of your library.

MARKETING PLAN

Several elements make up a successful marketing plan, including analysis, setting objectives, determining strategies, planning tactics and implementation. All of the elements can be applied to a library setting. To begin, a marketing plan must start with analysis, both internal and external. A library needs to understand the environment in which it exists in order to identify both possible opportunities and threats. Besides an external analysis, a library should also determine internal strengths and weaknesses. One method for combining both external and internal analysis is the SWOT method described earlier in this book which will help frame the "big picture" for the library and provide a starting point for a marketing plan. The next step is to set marketing objectives—what should be accomplished with this marketing plan? The plan should be objective, measurable, achievable, and doable taking into account the limited resources available.

Once objectives have been determined, marketing strategies can be established. Strategies are usually begun by identifying a target market or segment and focusing upon how to insert or expand your library service into that market. The next step in a marketing plan, tactics, establishes specific actions or tasks that will need to be completed in order to achieve the strategies and objectives. One method for creating tactics is to use the four marketing P's mentioned before. For example, a library might want to market a new 24/7 reference service. The product would be the 24/7 reference service whereby campus librarian(s) answer questions to anyone with Internet access. The place to market this service could range from the library itself to providing information at local schools, universities, and technical colleges. The promotion of this service could range from strategically placed flyers (both inside the library and at other locations) to information provided on the library's web page to a massive email campaign to students and faculty. Finally, after all of these steps have been completed, implementation must occur. This should include a schedule which lists a specific order of tasks, deadlines as well as evaluate the resources necessary to complete each task (Payne, 2005). A successful marketing plan will help improve visibility of the library on campus and in the community, increase its usage and most importantly, provide needed services to patrons. Academic librarians have recognized the importance of promoting their services and the value of their libraries to college decision-makers. These academic librarians are becoming increasingly aware of the value of marketing and public relations to accomplish these goals. Their marketing campaigns are tied to university's marketing campaigns to raise money from alumni, parents, friends and corporations. These marketing campaigns can be very useful in competing for diminishing financial resources, distinguishing the library from other information services providers, increasing awareness of library resources and services, and communicating the value of the profession. Marketing is a process with a beginning, middle, but no end. Librarians should be creative and learn that we live in a culture that values advertisements and promotions.

Some innovative marketing ideas were presented in an article by Gail M. Golderman and Bruce Connolly. This case study explored the concepts that were implemented at Union College in Schenectady, New York. Here, every imaginable technology was used to reach students and connect them with the information they needed for their classes or wanted for their own enjoyment for example: iTunes file sharing, podcasting, blogs, RSS feeds, tutorials using Google Scholar, Blackboard, and on-line newsletters linked through information pushed to student's e-mails. Using this myriad of technology, and in particular Google Scholar, students came to appreciate the "difference between materials that are freely available over the Web and those that are delivered over the Web" (Golderman & Connolly, 2007, p.174) which partially accomplished the goal of informing students how the library could meet their needs whereas the Internet might not.

Planning and marketing are presented as two halves of the successful implementation of the Virtual Library Project at the University of South Florida (USF). "The Virtual Library Project was based on comprehensive planning and analysis involving the user community and the library staff" (Metz-Wiseman & Rodgers, 2007, p.19). This case study also presented the concept of a marketing culture and a shift from marketing a product to overall public relations of the academic library. Marketing is a function that focuses on promoting products to its end users, while public relations serves to create awareness of the organization's products. For USF Libraries, the next step in the progression of integrating marketing into the strategic plan of the library was to participate in public relations. With this recognition, the USF library created a new position, the Communication Manager. "The shift of the USF Libraries from exclusively a marketing focus to one that integrates both marketing and public relations supports a coordinated, balanced, and strategic approach to communication activities, including both public relations and marketing, supported by research and followed up with evaluation" (p. 28).

PROMOTION AUDIT

The following questions can guide you in learning more about your library's promotional activities and its success or failure in reaching the community and letting its constituents know about its services. Focus group interviews and user surveys will supply data on the sources the library's current audience turns to for information on library services. Some of the following questions can be paused before focus groups and used in interviews. The answers can help the library in evaluating its promotional activities. Does the library:

- Advertise services to campus and the immediate community?
- Arrange to have articles about the library published in local newspapers, magazines, and newsletters?
- Use public access radio and television to advertise your programs and services?
- Have a Friends of the Library group?
- Do direct mail promotion to let your community know about new arrivals or services?
- Have posters celebrating the library displayed prominently throughout the campus/community?
- Have librarians given talks about library services at meetings, organizations, and points of service for campus groups and the community at large?
- Does the library participate in campus foundation's telemarketing and annual alumni giving events?
- Collect testimonials to attract more users from target groups?

EXAMPLES OF MARKETING ACTIVITIES AND PROGRAMS

A variety of activities related to marketing and public relations are reported in the literature, among them annual reports, fundraising, marketing campaigns, mission statements, position descriptions, and planning documents for exhibits, public relations, promotions. There are many clever ways academic librarians are using to market their libraries. Examples are: giving temporary tattoos of the library's logo to promote the newly constructed Ames Library at Illinois Wesleyan University (IWU). Library staff wearing t-shirts with logos and the motto "Reflect Traditions, Promote Scholarship, Inspire, Excellence" was a great substitute for nametags during the move to the new building.

The University of Texas-Austin has developed a monthly program celebrating faculty publications, Focus on Faculty, where specific theme is discussed (topics have included 9/11, the Patriot Act and stalking). The cost? Food: $600, Postage: $200, Postcards: $250—marketing the library: Priceless.

The @ *Your Library* campaigns at University Library Las Vegas (UNLV) and the College of William & Mary have a yearly theme (Reeling you in) that is attached to a monthly theme: Reeling you in with banned books @ your library, December: Reeling you in with gifts of literacy @ your library, etc. UNLV has taken advantage of the bright lights of The Strip as well as sunset that bleeds like melted crayons in creating their slogan: Enlightenment@ your library. UNLV library is the primary contact with the institution's public relations office which allowed them to advertise on local cable television stations.

The University of Miami's slogan "Richter 411" relates to the Millennials— "Richter" being the name of the library "411" the new number to dial for information.

At the Ohio State University, the Library was attempting to combat the nightmarish parking situation near the facility, exacerbated by the remodeling and temporary transfer of resources to the smaller Ackerman Library, by offering a drive-thru service for certain purposes. The Web site claimed: "Use the library without leaving your car...try out the drive-thru window service at the Ackerman Library, 600 Ackerman Road.... You can also use the book drop, located near the drive-through window, when the Library or the window is closed..." (Ackerman Drive-Thru Window, 2008).

Pepperdine Law School Library offers a happy-hour at the Library once a week during which faculty, students and staff gather at the Library for a drink and have a conversation with the Library's staff.

Other marketing programs are designed to increase use of the academic library by international students on campus who may have come from cultures where use of the library was not integral to the education process at their home institutions. Mu provides marketing strategies for academic libraries to use with international students. International students encounter several challenges when entering Western universities, such as the concept of plagiarism (Mu, 2007). Mu suggests several ideas for outreach to international students. An academic library can develop web pages on the library's website to promote the libraries resources for international students. Another marketing suggestion consists of developing a partnership with the international student services on campus.

The UWM Libraries Archives Department hosts an annual lecture series on local history, and displays the Archives holdings on campus, and in the community. Special Collections also hosts a series of on-going Special

Collection Programs. These include: Ettinger Book Artist Series (annual), The Scholar and the Library (annual), UWM Authors Recognition Ceremony (biennial), Great Books Roundtable Discussions (monthly), and the Morris Fromkin Memorial Lecture (annual). The American Geographical Society Library (AGSL) hosts the annual Holzheimer Maps and America Lectures Series on American cartographic history, the UWM's Academic Adventurers Series about UWM members' work abroad, and Map Society of Wisconsin (several times a year) for map enthusiasts. The Friends of the Golda Meir Library sponsors public lectures featuring local political and business leaders to speak on timely topics. The events are hosted by the Special Collections Division.

UW Madison Libraries has a committee dedicated to marketing the library's programs. This committee is called the "Campus Library Marketing Committee" (CLMC) and has two chair persons and six other members. These eight librarians coordinate the marketing plan for the services and resources provided at all of the UW Madison Campus libraries. These marketing plans are in line with the strategic plans of each individual library, so that each of the plans is tailored to each library. The goal of the committee is to facilitate communication between the library staff and the users of the library about the special offerings including initiatives, programs, and services. The target audience is the UW Madison Campus community. By having this committee, the UW Madison libraries are assured of a unified message and assurance that the libraries stay invested in the marketing activities. This committee does not represent the entire staff that focuses on marketing, but serves as a resource for the campus libraries to stay on task with the marketing campaigns. The most recent campaign that was coordinated by the CLMC was the "creation and maintenance of Tier 1 screensavers", the coordination, administration, and analysis of "campus marketing listening sessions," the creation of the CLMC Wiki, and the groundwork set up for a future marketing toolkit and staff workshop (University of Wisconsin-Madison Libraries: Library Committees, 2009).

REFERENCES

Aamot, G. 2007. "Getting the Most out of Strategic Planning: How Libraries Can Create Strategy Ovens." *College & Research Libraries News* 68, no. 7: 418-20.

Abram, S. 2008. "Social Libraries: The Librarian 2.0 Phenomenon." *Library Resources & Technical Services 52, no.* 2: 19-22.

Ackerman Drive-Thru Window. 2008, Apr 30. The Ohio State University Libraries, University Libraries, Blogs, Library News: http://library.osu.edu/blogs/librarynews/2008/04/30/use-ackermans-drive-thru-window (accessed Jan 13, 2010)

Altman, E., and Hernon, P. 1998. "Service Quality and Customer Satisfaction do Matter." *American Libraries* 29, no. 7: 53-54.

Anderson, L. 2008. "Strategic Planning for Your District or School Library." *Indiana Libraries*, 27(2): 78-9.

Backhus, S., and Summey, T. 2003. "Collaboration: The Key to Unlocking the Dilemma of Distance Reference Services." *The Reference Librarian*, 193-202.

Bahavar, S., and Truelson, J. 2008. "Strategic Planning for Reference in a Team Environment: the Preferred Futuring Model." *Reference & User Services Quarterly* 47, no. 4: 356-363.

Barry, P. 2009. "Top 10 Marketing Tips for Communication and Outreach." *Illinois Library Association Reporter* 27, no. 1: 8.

Bernstein,J. "Merchandising the Library." www.libraryjournal.com/article/CA6312504.html (accessed Jan 13, 2010)

Block, J., and Edzan, N. 2002. "Information Marketing in Sri Lankan Academic Libraries." *Malaysian Journal of Library & Information Science* 7, no. 2: 87-100.

Bonner, M., and Hudson, D. 1993. "Using Community Outreach as a Marketing Tool." *Arkansas Libraries* 50: 28-9.

Brown, W., and Gonzalez, B. 2007. Academic Libraries: Should Strategic Planning be Renewed? *Technical Services Quarterly* 24, no. 3: 1-14.

Cox, C. 2007. "Hitting the Spot: Marketing Federated Searching Tools to Students and Faculty." *The Serials Librarian* 53, no. 3: 147-164.

Cruickshank, J., and Nowak, D. 2001. "Marketing Reference Resources and Services through a University Outreach Program." *The Reference Librarian*, 265-280.

De Saez, E. E. 2002. *Marketing Concepts for Libraries and Information Services*, 2nd ed. London: Facet Publishing.

Decker, R., and Hoppner, M. 2006. "Strategic Planning and Customer Intelligence in Academic Libraries." *Library Hi Tech* 24, no. 4: 504-514.

Dodsworth, E. 1998. "Marketing Academic Libraries: a Necessary Plan." *The Journal of Academic Librarianship* 24, no. 4: 320-322.

Evans, G. E., and Ward, P.L. 2003. *Beyond the Basics: the Management Guide for Library and Information Professionals.* New York: Neal-Schuman.

Fuller, D. 2001. "From Document Delivery to Distant Learning: an Interlibrary Loan Perspective." *Journal of Interlibrary Loan, Document Delivery & Information Supply* 11, no. 4: 51-9.

Galpin, T. 1996. *The Human Side of Change: a Practical Guide to Organization Redesign.* San Francisco: Jossey-Bass Publishers.

Gregory, G. 2008. "Planning: How to Make the Process Short and Sweet." *Information Today* 25, no. 6: 48.

Golderman, G. M. and Connolly, B. 2007. "Infiltrating NetGen Cybersulture: Strategies for Engaging and Educating Students on their Own Terms." *The Serials Librarian* 53, no. 3: 165-182.

Hallmark, E., Schwartz, L., and Roy, L. 2007. The Basics of Marketing and Outreach Plan for the UT Fine Arts Library." *Texas Library Journal* 83, no. 1: 40-43.

Hallmark, E., Schwartz, L., and Roy, L. 2007. Developing a Long-range and Outreach Plan for Your Academic Library: the Need for a marketing Outreach Plan." *College & Research Libraries News 68, no.* 2: 92-95.

Hammer, M and Champy, J. 2001. *Reengineering the Corporation: a Manifesto for Business Revolution.* New York: Harper Collins.

Harrington, D., and Li, X. 2001. "Spinning an Academic Web Community: Measuring Marketing Effectiveness." *The Journal of Academic Librarianship* 27, no. 3: 199-207.

Heller, R., and Hindle, T. 1998. *Essential Manager's Manual.* New York: DK Publishing.

Idrees, H., and Rehman, A. 2009. "Preparing a Winning Marketing Plan for Your Library." *Pakistan Library & Information Science Journal* 40, no. 2: 13-22.

Keeber, D. (2007). Process analysis and standardization: The road to strategic planning success. *Indiana Libraries*, 26(4): 37-42.

Linn, M. 2008. "Planning Strategically and Strategic Planning." *The Bottom Line* 21, no. 1: 20-23.

Little, J., and Huten, J. 2006. "Strategic Planning First Steps in Sharing Information Literacy Goals with Faculty across Disciplines." *College & Undergraduate Libraries* 13, no. 3: 113-23.

Lorenzen, M. 2006. "Strategic Planning for Academic Library Instructional Programming." *Illinois Libraries* 86, no. 2: 22-9.

MacDonald, K., VanDuinkerken, W., and Stephens, J. 2008. "It's all in the Marketing: the Impact of a Virtual Reference Marketing Campaign at Texas A&M University." *Reference & User Services Quarterly* 47, no. 4: 375-85.

Metz-Wiseman, M., and Rodgers, S. 2007. "Thinking Outside of the Library Box: the Library Communication Manager." *The Serials Librarian* 53, no. 3: 17-39.

Millet, M., and Chamberlain, C. 2007. "Word-of-Mouth Marketing Using Peer Tutors." *The Serials Librarian* 53, no. 3: 95-105.

Mu, C. 2007. "Marketing Academic Library Resources and Information Services to International Students from Asia." *Reference Services Review 35, no.* 4: 571-583.

New Mexico. State Library. "Library Marketing Plan Workbook." http://www.stlib.state.nm.us/files/Marketing_Plan_Workbook.pdf (accessed Jan 13, 2010)

Ohio Library Council. 2007. "Marketing the Library." http://www.olc.org/marketing/sampleplan.htm (accessed Jan 13, 2010)

"Public Relations vs. Marketing." http://www.topstory.ca/prvsmarketing.html (accessed Jan 13, 2010)

Reid-Smith, E. 2009. "Deriving Library Value through SWOT, Scorecard, then Six Sigma." *Australian Library Journal* 58, no. 1: 122-123.

Renaud, R. 1997. "Learning to Compete: Competition, Outsourcing, and Academic Libraries." *The Journal of Academic Librarianship* 23:85-90.

Riehle, C., and Witt, M. 2009. "Librarians in the Hall: Instructional Outreach in Campus Residences." *College & Undergraduate Libraries* 16, no. 2/3: 107-121.

Siess, J. A. 2003. *The Visible Librarian: Asserting Your Value with Marketing and Advocacy*. Chicago: American Library Association.

Singh, R. 2004. "Branding in Library and Information Context: the Role of Marketing Culture," *Information Services and Use* 24:93-98

Small, R., and Paling, S. 2002. "The Evolution of a Distance Learning Program in Library and Information Science: a Follow-up Study." *Journal of Education for Library and Information Science* 43, no. 1: 47-61.

Summey, T. 2004. "If You Build it, Will They Come? Creating a Marketing Plan for Distance Learning Library Services." *Journal of Library Administration* 41, no. 34), 459-70.

Turner, J., Sweany, D., Stockton, M., and Gaetz, I. 2009. "Collaborating to Serve Alumni with E-resources: the Regis University Experience." *Technical Services Quarterly* 26, no. 1: 1-12.

Walters, S. 2004. *Library Marketing That Works*. New York: Neal-Schuman Publishers.

Weingand, D. 1999. *Marketing/Planning Library and Information Services*, 2nd ed. Englewood, CO: Libraries Unlimited.

Wolpert, A. 1998. Services to Remote Users: Marketing the Library's Role." *Library Trends 47, no.* 1, 21-41.

11

LIBRARY BUILDINGS AND PHYSICAL MANAGEMENT

As mentioned in the historical introduction, in their early stages of development, academic libraries consisted of a few donated books. John Harvard's name was given to a university by contributing his books to it. At the time, most of the books donated or found in the Colonial libraries covered subjects like the classics, philosophy, Latin and Greek, the Bible and other books on religion. They were housed in a single room or in small rooms on campus and managed by the president of the college who was also a teaching member of the faculty.

As colleges expanded and subjects taught increased beyond religion and the classics, so did college libraries, and eventually, trained librarians were hired. The size of a college or university library collection became an indicator of the prestige of the institution. The 1960s was a period of expansion in higher education not only in the U.S., but in other countries as well, including those in Asia, Africa and the Middle East after their independence from European colonization. In the U.S., new buildings and expansion of old library buildings were designed to accommodate a growing demand for higher education. College and university administrators, faculty and alumni took pride in their libraries as cultural monuments. With the widespread of information and communication technology (ICT) and its adaptation to the needs of higher education, a new concept of libraries without walls and wireless access to information emerged.

The extreme vision envisioned more remote access to library holdings and information resources from outside the walls of the academic library. Information on demand, and gathering materials "just in case" a user asks for it was juxtaposed against the "just-in-time" concept which relies more on interlibrary cooperation, interlibrary loans, and digitized access to information. Valuable library space has been given away to allow for the addition of more computers which are now used for all purposes of communication and access to information from resources inside as well as outside the library and the campus, and social networking.

Remodeling old library buildings can be very expensive. The cost of gutting old buildings, removing asbestos and disposing of it can be a very delicate and expensive job. On average, every day wasted on removing the asbestos before the project is contracted out to a construction company could cost on average $5000 to $10,000 per day. It is advisable to include asbestos removal as part of the original contract, or just tear down the old building and start anew, unless it is a very valuable and historic old building.

The expansion of physical facilities on campuses resulted in the addition of new courses on library buildings in American library schools. Institutes and conferences on library buildings were held by the ALA and its divisions and the publication of new books on library buildings like those by Keyes Metcalf, *Planning Academic and Research Library Buildings*; Anthony Thompson's *Library Buildings of Britain and Europe; Academic Library Buildings: a Guide to Architectural Issues and Solutions*; *Reader on the Library Buildings*, by Hall B. Schell, among others. The annual April issue of *Library Journal* became a very useful tool for academic librarians and library architects to learn more about new building projects and advancements in library's physical planning. Equally important is the chapter on library buildings in the *Bowker Annual*.

Regardless of the age of the library building, the major functions of an academic library building are:

1. Protection of books and collections from the elements. In the old days air-conditioning and humidity control and fire extinguishers were either a luxury or never thought of. A visitor to old university libraries in the U.S., as well as in Europe will notice the difference between these and the new libraries being built here or anywhere else in the world.

2. Housing of books and other collections in a variety of accommodations for ease of access, and accommodation of readers and other clientele who need frequent and immediate access to the collections. As one could observe from a visit to an academic library, one would observe a variety of seating arrangements: regular tables and chairs in the reading areas, examination tables in the reference area, carrels for faculty and graduate students, seminar and group-study rooms, computer labs, rare book rooms and vaults to secure valuable books and manuscripts, special accommodations for physically-challenged readers, etc.

3. Housing of various catalogs and related bibliographic tools. It is rare now to find the old 3x5 catalog drawers in academic libraries as they have disappeared and can be found only in antique stores. The majority of libraries now provide online catalogs, known as OPACs (online public access catalogs) for their users. They are found on every floor of the library and they can be accessed remotely from home or office. In the old days, the card catalog was the heart of the library located in or near the reference

department. Now the computer terminal is our gateway to the information world and special wiring, ports and wireless access outlets are required in every corner of the library.

4. Provision for staff that select, acquire, or organize, care for, and service the collections and who aid readers in their quest for informational purposes. This means desks and chairs for staff in public areas (as in banks), and also in private areas where they can do professional work away from the public eye. The reference/information staff is always in the public eye, while the staff in the technical services department is hidden away in basements or behind closed doors. Same applies to administrative staff (like personnel/human resources, business office, data-processing, or server room, etc.)

5. Quarters for ancillary functions such as photocopy service, bibliographic instruction, audio-visual material preparation, computer support facilities, etc.

6. Other functions may be added as time and life-styles dictate. For example, in the new building of Marquette University Library, they added a student commons with a coffee bar, comfortable chairs, television sets turned on to national news, and other amenities. The same was done in the newly added library commons at the UWM Library.

When planning a new library building, steps, like those mentioned by Keyes Metcalf and other academic library building consultants should be followed:

- Definition and analysis of the problem. This is a statement written by the librarian, on his/her own or at the behest of the president or the board of trustees of a college. A wise librarian should seek the help of a consultant who has done it before for other colleges of similar size and ranking;

- Consideration of the options. To build or not to build, that is the question. Unless you have limitless sources of funding, you have to show that all options for solving the space problem have been addressed. They can include: remodeling the building (architects tell us it is cheaper to build a new building unless the old one is a historical landmark), move to another building, and using additional space for storage, among others;

- Review of the academic plan of your college. You don't wish to plan for a new library on a campus that will be moving to another location in the next twenty years;

- Preparation of the written library building proposal in terms of basic academic purpose, scope, and rationale for the specific size, and costs to construct the building;

- Consideration of the campus master plan in order to assure compatibility of the library proposal with respect to setting, traffic, utility trunk lines, and general physical mass. An urban campus may be subject to local rules and regulations for urban renewal, zoning laws, etc;

- Administrative review, negotiation, and approval, including the board of trustees or regents, and other governing authorities;
- Staff educational preparation. This includes readings, visits to other campuses where new library buildings have been completed, inviting experts to speak to the staff about their experiences and what to expect;
- Formation of a planning team. The building project team should include people from the library, faculty, students and academic staff, the local community, certain academic business and budget officers, chair of the library committee, and other consultants;
- Preparation of the formal written building program. This document, commonly known in library architecture as the building program, outlines the specification of the major requirements desired of the facility, including space needs, explanation of these needs by function, statement of purpose, relevant goals from the long-range plan; the site, and any major limitations;
- Choice of architect and the consultants to the architect. The campus business office knows best and they will consult with the president, the librarian and appropriate local and state governments. The office of legal affairs on campus will be responsible for reviewing and approving the contracts and other legal instruments associated with the building project;
- The architect prepares the schematic design. The design includes site studies and a master plan phase, as well as actual building mass, floor size, and vertical and horizontal traffic patterns;
- Design development plans. These plans carry the schematics into precise spatial plans including all walls and doors, and provide the first mechanical and other non-architectural drawings;
- Contract documents which constitute the final architectural working drawings with elevations and full drawing for structural, mechanical, plumbing, electrical, and landscaping details, as well as business conditions and performance specifications on everything from hardware to the mechanical systems. A similar level of documentation will be required for interior design elements;
- Bidding process which includes bid analysis, selection of general contractors, and signing of the base contract with the general contractor or the construction manager;
- Constructing stage during which the architect and librarian maintain a weekly, if not daily, review of progress. This phase begins with the groundbreaking or cornerstone ceremony;

- Selection and purchasing of furnishings phase which could start with the construction phase, or even earlier with the drawing phase. A selection of a consultant will be useful since it is important to have ergonomically designed furniture and effective use of space. You should get as many furnishing catalogs from companies and library equipment suppliers, visit their booths at the IFLA or the ALA annual and midwinter conferences, ask to test their furniture and furnishings in your library. They will be pleased to send you samples of ergonomically designed furniture so you and your library staff, students and faculty can test them and rate them before purchasing;
- Legal acceptance of the building and grounds from the contractor;
- Occupancy. Moving of furnishings, equipment, furniture, books, etc.;
- Dedication. Celebration of the completion of the project, inauguration of the building, occasion for celebrations, thanks to all those involved in the project, and more fund-raising. A good way to involve the community in the new library project is to establish a fundraising committee. The money raised could be used to buy furniture or other items after construction, or it can be used to upgrade the quality of the design such as in buying better building materials. Members of the fundraising committee will be goodwill ambassadors of the library construction project, drumming up support for the new library throughout the campus, among alumni, friends and the local community;
- Warranty corrections which are the last phase and involves the completion of all deficiencies against the bid contract documents.

As you can see, there are a lot of people that you will be working with and depending on when embarking on this professional and exciting undertaking. This group of people can be brought together as a planning team. The team usually consists of the chair of the library committee, the library director, an architect, a building consultant, a member of the library board or Friends of the library, perhaps an interior designer. The more informed you are about developments in your profession, the better equipped you will be to add to the discussion and acquire a valuable experience from this venture.

STEPS TO FOLLOW TO FACILITATE PLANNING

1. Familiarize yourself with the literature on academic libraries space planning;
2. Project future service requirements; your library's long range plans and needs assessment;

3.   Write a detailed building program statement which describes the overall space needs;
4.   The library should select the architect who will translate the library's expressions of needs into a plan for an expanded facility;
5.   Select a site that is in the heart of the college campus, and large enough to support expanded facility and equipped for the latest ICT;
6.   The architect develops a preliminary design that outlines the location of basic structural elements (walls, doors, windows, etc.). Campus community reviews the functional implications, and the library committee approves the final schematic;
7.   The architect expands upon the preliminary design and prepares completed working drawings for library committee's approval and submission to bidders;
8.   Contractors are then invited to bid on the project described in the working drawings, bids are opened, and after negotiations a contract is signed;
9.   The constructor(s) builds the new structure or addition as instructed by the working drawings; the architect typically monitors construction as the library's official representative, the librarians assists with monitoring; the board receives the authority to approve payouts and change the contract;
10. The dedication ceremony is the time to celebrate this great accomplishment.

PHYSICAL MANAGEMENT

Managing physical facilities is like managing human resources, budget, and library materials. If the facility is attractive and functional, library staff and users are happier and more productive. If the building is dull, ugly and not functional, staff and users are miserable and the facility is less inviting and used. Like any other piece of real estate, location is very important. In this case, where the library building is located on campus can make the difference in its use based on accessibility. The library should be in the heart of its campus, clearly visible and impressive. Location of the library is very important, for it can encourage or discourage use and staff recruitment. Both the exterior and interior are very important considerations. Furnishing, good lighting, noise control, functionality, technology, flexibility, energy conservation and other green-building elements, ventilation, visual supervision, security, etc. are very important, so are the ergonomically designed seating, wireless access, number of computer terminals, and the quality of collections, services, and programs provided.

The library should have ample space to use for the present and the foreseeable future expansion. Having the flexibility to be able to add on to the library building at a future date could well save some future building committee from having to decide to relocate in order to accommodate expanding library needs. When faced with the fortunate decision to build a new academic library building or to expand an existing one, college decision-makers may decide to hire an architect or to plan for and announce design competitions for the new library building. In the case of such competitions there should be librarians on the architectural jury. Architectural competitions can be expensive and there must be good reasons and ample funds to support that decision. Decision-makers, like college presidents, and boards of trustees should watch for cost overruns when architects indulge in grandiose buildings. Library buildings should also be functional and not built as monuments or artifacts. A good library architect is someone who has a "reputation in the construction industry as having in-depth specific criteria." A new library building needs an architect who understands the details of energy efficiency, and has had experience planning green buildings, that are durable and of low maintenance costs. Library budgets suffer periodic extreme cutbacks, and the architect must design a building that can almost maintain its appearance and ability to function in terms of electricity, public utilities and even plumbing.

In choosing an architect, make sure that s/he has prior experience in building or remodeling academic library buildings, visit these buildings and talk to librarians as well as library users there. Ideally the library building should be functional and attractive at the same time. One does not preclude the other. The library building should be aesthetically pleasing so that the college community can take pride in it and continue to provide support. The building should be welcoming, visible, functional, accessible and identifiable.

A project budget for building or remodeling a library should include discussion of funds for the project including a breakdown of fund sources. An estimated budget including the best estimates for: planning and consultation fees, architectural fees, site acquisition, site preparations, construction, furniture and equipment, in addition to contingencies should be carefully thought out and presented. When budgeting for the new library, there are two ways of looking at the budget for constructing a new college library building. The first is the initial costs of simply building the facility. The second way of looking at a building is to prorate the operational cost over the lifetime of the building. Academic library directors and their library building committees could use available computer software to estimate the costs of building a new library. One product is called LIBRIS DESIGN which is used extensively around California because funding is available to train library staff in how to use this computer tool. LIBRIS DESIGN allows a user to account for all sorts of variables like site development costs versus donated land, choice of building materials and many other factors. However, the user must remember to account for all the space within the library including walls, mechanical spaces, stairways, elevator shafts, and other such "inconsequential" architectural features. When used correctly, LIBRIS DESIGN becomes a powerful tool for a library director to estimate building costs.

Some library administrators (boards and directors) may opt for what is known as "design-build" method of constructing a new library. Design-build simply means that the architect and construction workers are partners in the same firm. One vendor both designs and constructs the library. Using one firm to both design and construct the library has many advantages over choosing separate companies for both jobs. For example, contractors are usually paid additional compensation for "errors, omissions, or ambiguities" in the architect's plans. But when architects and contractors work for the same firm, that firm must bear the costs of mistakes in the architectural plans.

Another advantage in design-build is that architects and contractors are forced to maintain good communications throughout the project since their firm bears responsibility for design and construction errors.

Designing security into the library is a very important feature in any library building. The best time to build security into a library is in the planning stage. The key is open sightlines and good lighting. The stacks must be arranged so that there are no enclosed areas where a vandal or potential criminal can hide. A strategically placed security camera should be able to see all the way to a far wall without having its view blocked. Also, all areas of the interior must be lit. A good point to remember in design is that light bulbs should be easily replaced, so light must be situated within easy reach (Woodward, 2005, p.143). It is recommended that the library hire a security consultant to plan security precautions while the library is still in the design stage. This will be money well spent when one considers how many books and possibly human lives will be saved and how many lawsuits will be avoided over the lifetime of the library. The design of the library must be checked and rechecked so that there remain no passages for criminals to exit the library. "It may not dawn on anyone that the equipment storage room is accessible through the suspended ceiling from the room next door" (Woodward, 2005, p.149). For security reasons, some library designers place restrooms outside the security gates where books must be checked out in order not to set off alarms. It is inconvenient for patrons but safe for the library's materials (Faulkner-Brown, 1992, p.77).

Some of the common features that can be observed in new or remodeled library buildings include:

1. Atriums: An atrium is a glass roof with open space beneath the glass. An atrium provides visitors to a building light and a sense of open spaces. These are very popular because an atrium brings nature inside. Unfortunately, an atrium ceiling has a tendency to leak. Also, an atrium makes it difficult to control temperature inside the library which is also

hazardous to library collections. Atria also amplify noise (Woodward, 2005, p.85). But the biggest problem is that an atrium cuts off future shelving space.

2. Opening in the floor surrounded by balconies (as in the San Francisco Public Library) also creates an inviting, airy feeling in a building, but these floor openings eliminate potential collection-growth storage.

3. Designing noise out of the library is an important feature in any library building. Therefore, the library should employ materials and a design to absorb noise. These materials include "acoustical tile ceilings, fabric-wrapped fiberglass panels on walls, acoustically-effective solutions sprayed on building materials on ceilings, and on or carpets." (Wrightson, 1999, p.352).

4. Signage for the library must be effective. "The key to a really good sign system is its ability to respond to the users'need to progress from general to specific information and to provide directional information at decision points where a choice of routes must be made." (Woodward, 2005, p.188). The library director and sign vendor must walk through the building as soon as they can anticipate the way library users might navigate the building, and then develop an idea of what signs to use. The Library should take bids from sign vendors early in the construction process because they will "need to get started designing and locating signs long before opening day." (pp. 187-188). The biggest challenge in choosing a sign vendor is finding one who will stay in business so that interior signs can be prepared and changed over time. Sign vendors go out of business very quickly.

When it comes to technology, libraries should make full use of new technology. Wireless technology is becoming common in libraries, college campuses, coffee places, and hotels, and even in whole towns and cities. Wireless Internet technology costs much less after being installed into a new building than does wire technology (Clipperton, p.179). Wireless antennas should be placed in strategic locations to maximize coverage within the library. There are some disadvantages to wireless. It is still not as fast as the fastest wire technology. Wireless is susceptible to some interference. But wireless technology evolves rapidly, and these problems will be overcome sooner than later.

Information Commons (IC's) which emerged in the late 1990s mean that libraries provide access to electronic library resources and productivity software applications in the same location. ICs emerged as a new and important way to deliver resources and services to users. They involve functional integration of technology and service delivery and incorporate changes in user needs and expectations by creating an environment that wholly supports the whole research process from beginning to end.

An old library building should be remodeled to provide easy access to individuals who are physically challenged. A new building should have that access already built in. The *Code of Ethics* of the American Library Association lists the first responsibility of libraries and librarians as "to provide the highest level of service to all library users through appropriate and usefully organized resources; equitable service policies; equitable access; and accurate, unbiased, and courteous responses to all requests." Libraries have the ethical and legal responsibility of ensuring equitable service to the disabled. The *Americans with Disabilities Act of 1990* (*ADA*), calls for the elimination of discrimination against people with disabilities. Working within the framework of ADA, the academic library can insure equitable service to disabled patrons through compliance, proper staff training and education, and the use of assistive technologies. Providing physical access to the library is the most visible compound of ADA compliance. Physical accessibility to the academic library must be achieved in accordance with ADA's *Guidelines for Buildings and Facilities*. Title II libraries also have the option of complying in accordance with the *Uniform Federal Accessibility Standards* (*UFAS*). The guidelines include, but are not limited to, accessibility routes, protruding objects, ramps, stairs, parking spaces, elevators, signage, alarms, doors, telephones, and restrooms. Compliance with ADA is not a onetime project. The academic library must continually be evaluated for accessibility. Librarians need to be familiar with ADA or UFAS as compliance will be required any time library furnishings or shelving is purchased or rearranged, new signs are hung, or any alteration of the library is undertaken. Librarians should be assessing the library daily, looking for any particular hazards or problems with accessibility.

Intellectual access can be provided through appropriate auxiliary aids and services such as qualified readers and interpreters, assistive listening systems, or telecommunication devices for deaf persons (TDDs), large print materials or Brailed materials, audio recordings, and the like. As with physical access, intellectual access to the collection must be continually evaluated so that the library may respond to changes in patron need as well as to keep current with recent technologies and developments. Adaptive Technology made it possible for many to pursue higher education with ease. Almost every university library has or soon will have an Adaptive Technology Study Room like the one at UWM, which is well equipped to meet users' various special needs. Enlarging viewers and JAWS software are located in the Accessibility area for those who may need them with help from the RIS staff. The microform area has magnification lenses and foot pedal controls. Wheelchair accessible tables are located throughout the building. A Telecommunication Device for the Deaf (TDD) pay phone is also provided. The UWM Library's Directory of Library

Services/Facilities for Library Users is available at the Reference Desk and on line at http://www.uwm.edu/Libraries/adatech.

Evaluating access to the academic library is very important way to measure user satisfaction. One of the most effective methods for evaluating physical access to the library and its collections is to solicit opinions and suggestions from disabled students and faculty. The library staff should take measures to become familiar with disabled patrons needs and requests. This may be accomplished through focus groups, general surveys, or one-on-one discussion during which patrons may voice specific needs and concerns. Hiring physically challenged librarians and library staff and student workers can also help in identifying and responding to the needs of library users with disabilities.

REFERENCES

Andre, I. 2008. "Planning the Library of the Future." *Scandinavian Public Library Quarterly* 41, no. 4: 4-5.

Axelroth, J. 1999. "The Impact of Technology on Library Space Planning and Design." *Legal Reference Services Quarterly* 17, no. 3:11-25.

Bahr, A. 2008. "Special Issue: New Library Security for Buildings, Users, and Staff." *Library & Archival Security* 21, no. 2:57-8.

Bogart, D., ed. 2004. *The Bowker Annual Library and Book Trade Almanac.* 49th ed. New York: R.R. Bowker.

Carey, J. 2008. "Library Security by Design." *Library & Archival Security* 21, no. 2: 129-140.

Clipperton, K. D. 2003. "Wireless Networking in the Library: Creating Network Connectivity Throughout the Library a Decision Making Guide for Planners." In B. MaCabe. B. and James R. Kennedy, eds., *Planning the Modern Public Library Building.* Westport, CT: Libraries Unlimited.

Cohen, A. 2009. "Learning Spaces in Public Libraries." *Public Library Quarterly 28, no.* 3: 227-33.

Decker, R., and Hermelbracht, A. 2006. "Planning and Evaluation of New Academic Library Services by Means of Web-based Conjoint Analysis." *The Journal of Academic Librarianship* 32, no. 6, 558-572.

Evans, G. E. and Ward, P. L. 2007. *Management Basics for Information Professionals,* 2nd ed. New York: Neal Schuman. Ch. 17.

Faulkner-Brown, H. 1992. "The Role of Security and Design in a Security Strategy." In Michael Chaney and Alan F. MacDougal, eds. *Security and Crime Prevention in Libraries* (pp. 70-87). Brookfield, VT: Ashgate.

Foos, D. D., and Pack, N. C. 1992. *How Libraries Must Comply with the Americans with Disabilities Act of 1990.* Phoenix, AZ: Oryx Press.

Holt, R. 1989. *Planning Library Buildings and Facilities: From Concept to Completion.* Metuchen, NJ: Scarecrow Press.

Hudson, A. 1992. "Planning for Change: Building a Library for the Twenty-first Century." *Illinois Libraries 74*: 496-500.

Kuchi, T., Mullen, L., and Tama-Bartels, S. 2004. "Librarians Without Borders: Reaching Out to Students at a Campus Center." *Reference & User Services Quarterly 43, no.* 4: 310-317.

Lashley, E. 2008. "Library Safety and Security—Campus/Community Police Collaboration." *Library & Archival Security* 21, no. 2:195-201.

Lawrence, E. 2003. "Researching Historic Library Buildings in the British Isles: Problems and Ways Forward." *Library History* 19, no. 1: 39-54.

Leeming, A. 2008. "'Our Beautiful New Library': Planning a Primary School Library." *The School Librarian* 56, no. 1:15-16.

Lunde, D., and Smith, P. 2009. "Disaster and Security: Colorado State Style." *Library & Archival Security* 22, no. 2, 99-114.

Lushington, N. 1993. "Getting it Right: Evaluating Plans in the Library Building Planning Process." *Library Administration & Management* 7: 159-163.

McGinty, J. 2008. "Enhancing Building Security: Design Considerations." *Library & Archival Security* 21, no. 2, 115-127.

McGinty, J. 2008. "Insuring Libraries Against Risk." *Library & Archival Security* 21, no. 2: 177-186.

Myree, S. 2008. "Fire Suppression and Water Mist Systems." *Library & Archival Security* 21, no. 2: 169-176.

Payton, A., and Shields, T. 2008. "Insurance and Library Facilities." *Library & Archival Security* 21, no. 2: 187-193.

Piotrowicz, L., and Osgood, S. 2009. "Building Science 101." *American Libraries* 40, no. 4: 56-58.

Stevens, N. 2006. "The Fully Electronic Academic Library." *College & Research Libraries* 67, no. 1: 5-14.

Sweeney, R. 2005. "Reinventing Library Buildings and Services for the Millennial Generation." *Library Administration & Management* 19, no. 4: 165-75.

Teper, T. 2003. "Re-establishing Key Control as a Security Measure." *Library & Archival Security* 18, no. 1: 53-61.

Trapskin, B. 2008. "A Changing of the Guard: Emerging Trends in Public Library Security." *Library & Archival Security* 21, no. 2: 69-76.

Webb, T.D., ed. 2000. *Building Libraries for the 21st Century: The Shape of Information*. Jefferson, NC: McFarland.

Westenkirchner, S. 2008. "Integrated Library Security Systems." *Library & Archival Security* 21, no. 2: 159-167.

Woodward, J. 2005. *Creating the Customer-driven Library: Building on the Bookstore Model*. Chicago: ALA.

Wrightson, D., and Wrightson, J. 1999. "Acoustical Considerations in Planning and Design of Library Facilities." *Library Hi Tech* 17, no. 4: 349-357.

12

DEVELOPMENT, GRANTS AND FUNDRAISING

With the declining library budgets, academic librarians are now adopting strategies used by other deans on campus to pursue additional financial resources to supplement their declining budgets. In today's and tomorrow's economy, money will be tight and therefore, librarians must be proactive in seeking additional opportunities to do things that otherwise will not be done in their libraries due to limited or even declining budgets. Individuals in the U.S. give more than $100 billion to charities each year. Families and corporations have established charitable foundations worth billions of dollars to give back to the community. The academic library is in a good position to get its fair share from these charitable donations—from alumni, friends, trustees, corporations and others. Because of the importance of such fundraising activities, it is customary to find a development office on every American campus whether publicly or privately supported. The common and underlying purpose of a development office is to raise additional funds through donations from friends, alumni, and corporations to support the operations of the institutions, provide additional scholarships, support faculty research and student activities and sports. Grants are usually administered by the Graduate School on campus for the purpose of supporting faculty in the pursuit of additional extramural funds to support their research.

Academic libraries are newcomers to fundraising and, unlike schools and colleges on campus, they have no alumni to call their own. A most effective way to establish a donor base to the college library is to establish links between the library and the campus president who is willing to give a high priority to the library. Another way to cultivate interest in the library is through some members of the board of trustees, who support the college financially and could suggest names of other affluent individuals or families in the community who are willing to support the library.

When done well, fundraising is a win-win situation for giver and receiver. Fundraising can be successful when the gifts contribute to the strategic vision of the library. Gifts can enable a library to achieve its goals and the gifts contribute to the strategic vision for the library. Successful fundraising depends on the leadership and participation of the library director. Not everyone is good at fundraising. It is a form of salesmanship that few can master, are not afraid of being turned down and has the ability to make convincing cases. Successful fundraising efforts are made by library directors, and are not delegated to others. But there is usually a support staff with expertise to assist the dean or director of the library with fundraising and development efforts.

Charitable contributions, grants and other fundraising activities known as development programs could provide the additional funds needed for acquisition of special materials or collections, operating different programs, or even hiring additional staff. The one philanthropist whose name has been closely associated with libraries was Andrew Carnegie. He did much for libraries by bestowing funds on communities for the construction of libraries if the community would provide annual appropriations for the operating expenses. He firmly believed in matching funds and that his gifts "were meant to prime the public pump," a philosophy taken up again in the 1990s by the Bill and Melinda Gates Foundation in their effort to bridge the digital divide by providing libraries across the U.S. with computers, software, cabling and training in order to bring the Internet and technology to every American unable to afford it in their own home. Not everyone is, or can be as generous to libraries as Carnegie or Gates. But other lesser known foundations, friends and volunteers can be as effective. Friends' groups are thriving across the U.S., with over 2,000 groups and more than 500,000 million members. Of the 700 surveys sent to these groups, 46% were returned, with 90% of those coming from public libraries. Most groups were found in small towns or small colleges, and did not have a state-wide organization with which to affiliate. More than 100 million Americans volunteered, donated to, or worked in the non-profit sector, and that does not include the millions more who went to the shelters, centers, the arts, museums, clinics, schools, marches and campaigns organized by local organizations, and the like. It is estimated that individuals in the U.S. give more than $100 billion to charities each year. Your library should get its fair share starting with your library board or friends. Each board member should give generously to the library. When board members show their personal commitment to give, others will follow suit. Expect every member, as a matter of policy, to be a donor of record every year, to have made a duly recorded contribution to your library fund. Potential board members should know this policy before they are elected to serve. During the year, the board should receive information on how much has been raised from the board and how many of its members have given to date. Active friends of the library boards expect their members to make annual financial gifts appropriate to their means. They are expected to encourage others to give as well. Try to have on the friends of the library board members whose first love is raising money for the organization they serve. The amounts are not as important as the fact of giving. This fact is helpful when submitting a grant application to an outside foundation. We will discuss this more under the subheading "Role of the Volunteers" in development.

Fundraising, like management, is both an art and a science. The science of fundraising involves important terms and concepts such as prospects, development cycle, solicitation, etc. The science of fundraising is represented by the concepts that are more complex, are highly situational, and rely on good instincts and an understanding of donor psychology. Most of fundraising activities target private foundations. A private foundation is a "non-governmental, nonprofit organization with its own funds (usually from a single source, either an individual, family or corporation), and program managed by its own trustees and directors that was established to maintain or aid educational, social, charitable, religious, or other activities serving the common welfare, primarily by making grants to other nonprofit organizations." Having said that, one has to admit the word foundation can be misleading unless it is used in its most generic sense to refer to different kinds of charitable organizations and endowments such as: Cystic Fibrosis, Lilly Endowment, Carnegie Foundation.

It is common to identify three types of foundations as: 1) independent which can have one of three structures: general purpose, specific purpose, or family supported; 2) company sponsored which might consist of donations of goods and /or services as well, or instead, of funds; and 3) community foundations which are usually focused specifically on the community in which they are founded (Wedel, 1979).

There is a difference between annual giving (a fundraising method that produces large numbers of small gifts) and major giving (a method that produces a small number of large gifts). The distinction is fundamental to the methods the library director employs when asking for a gift. Annual-giving programs use mass communication methods, namely mail and telephone. Major gifts require a face-to-face, personalized approach.

There are more than 61,000 private foundations in the U.S. More than 47,000 bestow grants. Foundations hold more than $476 billion in assets. By law, most foundations must disperse at least 5% of their assets each year.

The following information gives a snap shot of the concentration of foundations wealth;

- 0.2 % hold about 50% of assets;
- 100 largest foundations hold nearly half of total foundation assets;
- 25 largest foundations hold nearly one third of total foundation assets;
- 10 largest foundations hold one fifth of total foundation assets;
- Some of the facts that librarians should keep in mind regarding foundations:
- About 70% of foundations limit their giving to their geographic locales

- "Company-sponsored foundations tend to give to areas where the company has facilities;
- "Community" foundations generally must limit their gifts to the area they serve, e.g. California Trust;
- Even national foundations may favor local and national recipients, e.g. Bill & Melinda Gates Foundation.

A library director should know who are the potential big donors in his/her community, how and when to ask, what will make people give to his/her library, what are their interests (art, children, minorities, immigrants, women, science, business, etc.); the library director should also thank donors in innovative ways that will make them want to give more.

Donors like to satisfy their own altruistic needs and the library's needs. Donors respond to big ideas, not to operational matters (such as keeping the library's doors open, or its collection stocked). Many donors want their names on rooms and other spaces in your library. Donors also give when they believe in an organization's mission and in its leader.

Librarians should familiarize themselves with the largest foundations, among them are the following:

- Bill & Melinda Gates Foundation
- Lilly Endowment
- Ford Foundation
- J. Paul Getty Trust
- Robert Wood Johnson Foundation
- W. K. Kellogg Foundation
- William & Flora Hewlett Foundation
- David & Lucile Packard Fund
- Pew Charitable Trusts
- John D. & Catherine T. MacArthur

Librarians should also learn what areas the foundations support. Studies show that foundations support:

- Programs that relate to their areas of emphasis;
- Institutionalized programs'
- Programs that become permanent after their funding ends; and
- Programs that avoid duplication of funding when funding is provided by the government.
- Before you do the asking you should learn more about the foundation you plan to approach. The Foundation Center (there is one at Marquette University Library) has a large and most comprehensive database on private foundations. Look for Form 990-PF of desired foundations. The tax forms give you a good idea about the financial aspects, programs and the history of giving of the foundations.

FOUNDATIONS' WEALTH

- Approximately ten thousand foundations have assets of $3 million or more to endow grants of more than $200,000 per year or more.
- 5,000 foundations have assets between one and three million, and endow grants between 50,000 and 200,000 per year.
- 32,000 foundations have assets of more than $1 million and annual grants of more than $50,000

IN SEARCH OF GRANTS AND DONATIONS

- Buildings and furnishings
- Staff awards and development
- Endowment of collection
- Digitization Projects
- Internships for librarians
- Library networks

It is important for librarians to look at foundations and charitable organizations as potential sources for securing additional funds for their libraries' operations. This requires librarians to be involved in the life of their communities and not just be limited to the narrow traditional functions of a library. The idea of a librarian being passive and bookish is a thing of the past. There is value in contacts with potential donors by the librarian and the development officer—when one exists. Many librarians are adding or sharing development officers because they now realize how important development and fundraising is for the financial welfare of their library. Both the librarian and the development officer should set goals for fund-raising. There is an advantage for developing a list of projects in priority order for the time when resources may become available. It is important to understand what one is requesting. It is important to match the donor's interests and the library's needs. Armed with this understanding and other relevant information, the discussion and interaction between the librarian and the donor can be beneficial to both.

To be successful in pursuing grants, librarians must submit well conceived and well documented grants, use appropriate methodology, incorporate a method of evaluating the effectiveness of the project, include adequate funding in the budget and justify it in the narrative, show cost-sharing and direct and indirect costs as more and more funding agencies are also requiring matching funds when evaluating and considering grant proposals. The submission should state clearly the qualifications of the investigating officer(s) as well as the institutions' capabilities. It is always advisable to submit a proposal on time and according to the published criteria required by the funding agency. When rejected, ask for reviews of your grant proposal and prior submissions in the hope of avoiding the pitfalls that resulted in the rejection of your proposal as you try again until you succeed.

MATTERS TO CONSIDER IN DEVELOPMENT AND GRANT WRITING

- Assign a current member of the library staff;
- Appoint a new staff member, if the dean or director of the academic library does not have the time, interest or inclination; and
- Rely on the university development staff.

MATTERS TO CONSIDER WHEN WRITING A GRANT

- Select a research with obvious and immediate application, or one announced in the guidelines of the granting organization. Abstract and statement of need should be included in the grant's letter of intent.
- Work with underserved populations. The U.S. *Library Services and Technology Act* (*LSTA*) gives special emphasis to programs serving un-served populations;
- Select a project with high public visibility;
- Address a cause championed by the foundation;
- Address more than one priority of the foundation; and
- Provide naming opportunities for private donors.

ASKING FOR GRANTS AND GIFTS

Asking is only one part of fundraising. It is the main part, but not the only way a person can participate in the process. Before you ask you should develop a long-range plan to clarify funding needs. The plan should help formulate a persuasive case settlement. You should add names to the prospect list and assist in the evaluation of names on that list. Cultivate, write letters, notes, etc. to support a written appeal. Thank the donor for his/her contribution.

RESEARCH AND PREPARATION FOR THE ASKING

It is estimated that 90% of your effort goes in prospect identification, research, cultivation and preparation, and 10% in the asking. In order for the asking to be successful, you should know enough about the donor to make a sound judgment. Your research should enable you to answer the following questions:

- Who is the right person to approach?
- Who controls the giving in the organization?
- Who, in your community, have the capability and the interest to warrant solicitation?
- Who is the right person in your library or organization undertake the asking?
- What activity of your organization would the prospect be most interested in supporting?
- How much should you ask for?
- Where, when and how should the prospect be solicited?

For individual major donor prospects, these additional questions need to be asked:

- What are the prospect's interests?
- What relationship does the prospect have to your library?
- What are the prospect's giving habits?
- What family does the prospect have?
- Who are his/her close friends?
- What personality traits of the prospect should influence the manner of asking?

THE PROCESS OF CULTIVATION

To find out who in your community are good prospects, talk to friends, business people, members of your board and friends' group. Examine the local and national newspapers, *Who's Who, Standard and Poor's*, etc. No individual or foundation will give your library money until he/she knows about your organization. Getting people ready to give is called "cultivation." To cultivate large donors you should use creative ideas and approaches to involve them in your library. Examples of cultivation include:

- Inviting prospective donors to your library;
- Sending them materials;
- Asking them for advice;
- Giving them special treatment;
- Emphasizing personal recognition of their contributions;
- Giving them the feeling of being insiders;
- Thanking supporters for their contributions;
- Board members should send notes of thanks to donors, especially if they themselves made the solicitation; and

- Making telephone calls of appreciation.

Former board members can be important to your library. Don't forget them. They can continue to give generously and help in evaluating and making introductions to key prospects.

WHO TO ASK

- Government grants. These come in response to a written proposal-RFP. The proposal is the asking. Board members are not involved
- Foundations-make grants by responding to formal or informal proposals.
- Companies make grants by responding to formal or informal proposals.
- Companies may make a donation following a visit by board members and/or the head librarian.
- Other non-profit organizations, religious, professional, trade, and civic associations of various kinds also respond to written appeals.

Major capital gifts always call for a visit to a prospect and a direct asking.

GOVERNMENT GRANTS

The request for proposal (RFP) is the asking. Foundations endow grants by responding to formal or informal proposals. Foundation people can make an introduction where they have a contact and help to draft the proposal. A company may make a donation following a visit by a university official. Other non-profit organizations also respond to written appeals.

COMMUNICATION A PREREQUISITE FOR CULTIVATION

- Pick the most effective communication medium reasonable and proper in the circumstances;
- Direct discussion is more effective than a letter;
- Annual reports and videotapes are two most useful cultivation material
- A CD is better than a written brochure;
- Write for annual giving and membership dues;
- For big donation from an individual, nothing short of a one-on-one conversation can be considered;
- In thanking a donor, a hand written note is most effective than a signed formal typed letter;
- Expensive brochures do little for fund-raising effort.

IMPORTANCE OF PUBLIC RELATIONS

Public relations is very important in enhancing the image of your library and in attracting the community to your library and supporting it. Good publicity can raise the profile of your library among its present and prospective clients. Publicity is a long term activity.

Printed and visual materials have value in cultivation. Writing letters is a good thing for fundraising. It is a good idea to enclose an attractive brochure or a handout or flyer to introduce people to your library.

Two most useful cultivation materials are annual reports and videotapes.

A well-produced annual report can convey the information appropriate to inviting and holding the interest of prospective or loyal supporters.

A good annual report should:

- Highlight your library's programs activities and accomplishments during the year;
- Give a brief summary of the financial picture;
- Bring the library's leadership to the attention of your clients;
- Recognize principal supporters (gift recognition);
- Determine the cost of Fundraising;
- Emphasize that it takes money to raise money; and remember
- Small libraries cannot afford a development position, but they can share or outsource.

If you are going to hire a development person, you need to develop a job description. In large organizations like universities and large public libraries, there is a division of labor such as research records, and mailing lists; annual giving, memberships, and program support; foundation and corporate support; capital campaign and planned giving. In small institutions, the work is done by one person. Regardless of the size of the library, these are the kinds of activities that raising money costs: direct mail, annual giving, corporate and foundations solicitation, special events and benefits, capital campaign and planned giving. Indirect costs include: rent, administration and facilities for each program. The development office is one of the few programs of nonprofit organizations that pays for itself. Libraries with an annual budget of $300,000 need at least one person giving half time to the fundraising program. Libraries with more than $50,000 need a full time development officer. As the budget goes higher, further assistance under a development officer is needed.

THE ROLE AND QUALIFICATIONS OF THE DEVELOPMENT OFFICER

In some large institutions such as universities, large public libraries and hospitals, the top development officer will personally solicit contributions, calling on foundations and corporations.

Development officers initiate, prepare, point the way, assist, and accompany, but do not themselves do the asking. Development officers are to be heard but not seen.

A DEVELOPMENT OFFICER MUST HAVE

1. A track record in positive experience in fundraising;
2. Other qualities include: integrity, willingness, and humor;
3. Initiative a self-starter-someone with ideas, willingness to risk moving with them;
4. Communication: ability to speak and write effectively;
5. Compatibility: a capacity to get along with people especially associates, board member prospects; and
6. Humility: a willingness to let others take the front position.

WHERE TO FIND DEVELOPMET STAFF?

Development officers are hard to find and hard to keep. Their salaries have risen sharply, and additional compensations are paid in the form of tuition assistance, housing assistance, cars, club memberships and deferred income plans.

THE ROLE OF THE HEAD LIBRARIAN IN DEVELOPMENT

* Good communication with the community and donors;
* Communication should be timely, courteous and assuring;
* The head librarian should be visible in the community;
* Write a signed page in the library's annual report[
* Do his/her home/office work;
* Establish individual file folders on each major contributor and prospect;
* Folders should be classified, or color coded to indicate an individual, a foundation, a corporation, or another nonprofit organization;
* Include all information on the prospect (interests and potential). Key information include: name, address, phone number, names of potential

contacts, and a summary chronology of correspondent action and past contributions;

- Profile sheets are to be continuously updated and reproduced for sorting by category, geographic location, or other criteria; and
- Acknowledge every contribution by issuing a prompt acknowledgement.

THE HEAD LIBRARIAN SHOULD LEARN

- How to marshal and train volunteer support for the fund-raising effort;
- What do they need in terms of automation, databases, calling lists, etc;
- To develop a development strategy plan and establish goals;
- What will the fund-raising effort cost;
- How do you judge the effectiveness of the development program;
- How to work closely with board members. It is therefore essential that the chief librarian help the trustees to understand what is involved in maintaining a development office;
- How to avoid the term fundraiser when referring to a development staff person;
- That the development officer does not directly raise money. It is the responsibility of the board or friends with the help of the director of the library at the staff level; and
- That the development officer does the research (endless, systematic and thorough). The officer researches government agencies, foundations, corporations, churches, other nonprofit organizations, and individuals. The officer writes proposals, drafts correspondence, arranges cultivation events, maintains files and record systems, and generates ideas. Only occasionally does a development officer visit foundations, corporations, or other prospects, and then it is the CEO or a board member, who, in most cases does the asking.

THE ROLE OF THE FRIENDS OF THE LIBRARY

Every board member can volunteer a few hours to do what they do best and enjoy the most within the broad range of activities related to fundraising. Let individual members select one or two tasks such as host a luncheon, sell tickets to an event, and make follow-up thank you calls to donors. Most importantly the librarian should recruit a few board members willing to raise funds.

Library friends are very important in supporting fundraising programs. An effective friends' group can raise endowments, host functions, recruit members, and form part of the library's annual giving base. Positive relations and communication between the library director and friends are very important. But, while friends of libraries groups can be beneficial to libraries, some of them can also be detrimental. Friends' groups should not form an exclusive club, have their activities as buying books for the library, host unimaginative events, see the library director as playing a minor role, or comprise the only annual-giving activity.

The management of friends and volunteers constitutes another challenge to librarians. The three largest influences on volunteerism in the latter half of the 20th century were: 1) widespread public awareness of the world around them, 2) an increase in discretionary time, and 3) the need to fulfill interests and talents outside of the work environment-along with the three types of volunteers: 1) policy-making by board members, 2) management volunteers as chairpersons or leaders, and 3) service volunteers who provide the needed insight into creating a volunteerism program that will be fulfilling to volunteers as well as useful to the library with minimal discord.

ROLE OF VLUNTEERS

Giving time and often doing jobs a staff member cannot do. board members are volunteers. Other volunteers help with programs: as teachers and docents, as coaches and big brothers. Volunteers can also be valuable in fundraising. The head librarian should be concerned with what volunteers can do, how they are organized, and how they are trained.

Volunteers can help with:
- Fundraising events;
- Office work-maintaining mailing lists, records, files, envelope stuffing and general staff assistance;
- Print materials and newsletters assembling, processing;
- Addressing envelopes for friends;
- Being host or hostess at library programs;
- Delivering posters to local stores to advertise book sales;
- Helping sort books for sales;
- Sponsoring story-hours, and storytellers, book discussion groups, art appreciation groupS, chess club, craft workmanships, etc.
- Sponsor and administer book sales;
- Host authors and book luncheons;
- Organize and administer book clubs;
- Create and stimulate public support of the library's programs;
- Interpret the library to the community;
- Encourage gifts, endowments, and memorials for the library;
- Provide financial support beyond the library's budget category

- Work and gain support for library legislation and/or appropriations at local, state and national levels;
- Create and/or intensify community awareness of the library's programs and possibilities;
- Campaign for better building facilities;
- Sponsor programs designed to add to the cultural life of the community; and
- Participate in public relations activities in the community.

EMBRACING A PLAN

Once the rationale for strategic planning is clear, the head librarian should look at different models and present a proposal. The proposal should have the library's board's approval and reflect at least the following items:
- Who will lead the strategic planning process? The head librarian should have this role, assisted by an outside consultant or not;
- What is the time frame/ Six to nine months is most effective. Don't drag the process on for too long. Participants will get tired and loose interest;
- Who will be involved? Board members, staff, major donors and key "moral owners", community leaders and others;
- What is the budget? The process need not too expensive, but there are some direct expenses if it is done well;
- What are the expected outcomes; and
- Be specific about reports. How relative priorities are to be identified and whatever else the leadership expects from the process.

Every board member can volunteer a few hours to do what they do best and enjoy the most within the broad range of activities related to fund-raising. Let individual members select one or two tasks such as host a luncheon, sell tickets to an event, and make follow-up thank you calls to donors. Most importantly the librarian should recruit a few board members willing to raise funds.

ADOPTING MAJOR GOALS AS POLICY

One product of strategic planning should be a fairly short list of major goals embraced by the board. The plan your board formally adopts should consist of long-range, macro policies dealing with mission and results. It should not be a full blown plan containing staff action steps that might need to be changed from time to time. The board should expect the planning process to generate specific goals, objectives and action steps for the staff that go beyond major board-approval goals.

A formal planning process will encourage strategic thinking by the organization's leadership. The opportunity should give staff and board a chance to dream about what they would like to happen, without regard to cost, energy, or time. Develop "dream sheets" and revisit them every few years. You will be surprised to see what you have envisioned actually did happen.

Strategic plan is an attitude of thinking strategically, new ideas that may seem disparate often come together in support of the mission and major goals of the organization

WHAT SHOULD YOU SAY ABOUT EACH ELEMENT OF DEVELOPMENT PLAN

1. Objective: What would you hope to achieve with the element of the program?
2. Current situation: Where do you stand now?
3. Course of action: What steps do you plan to take?
4. Goals: What specific markers dollars or achievement points will you strive for on the way to the objective?
5. Cost: What will the plan for the element cost?

The strategic plan, not to exceed 20-25 pages can be revised annually for approval by your board.

CORE ELEMENTS FOR A DEVELOPMENT PROGRAM

- Develop a plan and a strategy for getting contributions from government, business, foundations, and other nonprofits and for soliciting individual donations including fund-raising events
- Develop a plan for seeking support of special projects such as exhibits, research projects, acquisition scholarship funds, etc.
- Develop a plan for strengthening each of the development activities such as filing systems, mailing annual report, planned giving, case statements. Etc.
- Both boards and staff should be active in fund-raising. Division of labor between the chief executive, who is usually supported by a development staff, and the board should be cleared
- Be clear on personal strengths and weaknesses when allocating responsibilities and duties
- Some executives are experienced and talented in raising money; others shy away from it. Boards ultimately responsible for success must adapt their own activities to support, oversee, or take leadership as active participants.

- A development committee of board and staff can bring focus and force to board efforts, and work with and oversee staff

The *modus operandi* of a development program can be summarized as follows:

- Idea (this is the start and the success of the grant relies on a good idea)
- Cultivation (let donors and foundations know who you are and how valuable is your organization to the welfare of the community or what they are interested in)
- Matching (matching the right idea with the right donor)
- Meet the foundation's staff (getting to know you)
- Use the right figure (don't ask for the moon; be realistic and provide matching funds and in-kind contributions from your institution)
- Follow up (keep the donor informed of progress, results and positive impact of the project as part of accountability and something for the donor to brag about)

Capital Campaigns: Endowments and Buildings. The term capital campaign refers to large endowments especially those that go towards buildings and other major projects. The term is used because people are being asked to make capital-sized gifts that will be drawing on their capital-their savings, securities, or real property.

What should a capital campaign statement include?

A summary: a brief statement about the organization's mission; a convincing description of the purpose to which the capital funds will be put together with funding needs associated with each purpose; something about ways one can give pledges, gifts of securities or gifts of real property; recognition opportunities-buildings, rooms, or scholarships to be named for donors; list of names of the board and campaign leadership.

The presentation should be attractive. Pictures help. Your case statement is your vehicle to convince people that their support is worthwhile. A compelling case statement must be formulated, an organization put in place and representatives selected to go out and ask for contribution.

PLANNED GIVING AND BEQUESTS

Planned giving is that category of gift made with a present commitment to a donation that the recipient institution may receive only after a period of time, often many years.

The greatest portion of institutional gift income today, outside capital campaigns, comes through planned giving.

MAJOR CHARACTERISTICS OF PLANNED GIVING

1. It is a deferred gift
2. Such a gift comes from the donor's capital holdings-real property, insurance, securities, not from current income
3. Donors themselves gain, from a lifetime income they currently receive as well as tax benefits. This is a very important consideration.
4. Planned giving are inextricably linked to estate planning, even as donors should have their lawyers or accountants participate in arranging planned gift, it is in the interest of the library or college to have the donors' advisors involved to assure that the transaction is in order and fully conforms to the donors wishes.
5. Planned gifts fall into the following categories
6. Bequests: designating a library or a college as a beneficiary in a will
7. Insurance: taking out policies with the purpose of making a contribution, or donating policies after their protection features are no longer needed.
8. Gift of property or other assets: contributing gifts through trust or other arrangements so that receipt of the gift is deferred to a future date-while the donor and perhaps a beneficiary either have use of the property or receive its income.
9. Gifts of income: placing assets in trust for a period of years for the income benefit of the recipient library or college, with the assets ultimately returning to the donor or a beneficiary.

LIFE INSURANCE CONTRIBUTIONS

Seeking contributions through life insurance can be an effective dimension of a development program. Such programs are not without hazard or controversy. Their ramifications are not always clear. You should be aware of a distribution between the contribution of mature policies and the taking out of new insurance for planned giving purposes.

The assignment of ownership of a mature paid-up policy by someone who no longer has need of its protective features can only be welcomed and encouraged. Making a life insurance gift is, in fact, simpler than making a residual gift through a bequest, and from the standpoint of the receiving institution, it has advantages that a bequest does not have. Paid-up policies already yield an income, have an immediate cash value, and unlike new policies, permit their donor a higher tax deduction.

DISCLOSURE

Donors, and in particular, corporate and foundation officials, expect their donations to go to charitable purposes and not to administrative or overhead costs. They may ask for figures on fund-raising costs to confirm that expectation. When asked, the development office must respond openly. The IRS has its Form 990 which all charitable organizations except churches with gross receipts of more than $25,000 must file. These forms are available to the public at Foundation Center Libraries. The library's foundation board should make available full financial statements disclosing assets, liabilities, fund balances, revenue and expenses. Expenses should be broken down to show costs of program services, general management, and administration, and fund-raising.

FUND SOLICITATION AND GRANT APPLICATION

Wedel offers advice on the right and wrong ways (do's and don'ts) of soliciting foundation support including: DO look for a partner in an endeavor, not just a benefactor; DO identify the foundation's goals and objectives; DO compare those goals and objectives against the needs and wants of the library to be certain that your proposals fits their mission; DO be creative with your proposal; DO ask for something specific. But DON'T submit an inappropriate proposal—it's a waste of your time and the foundation's—and DON'T rely on one resource to investigate the foundation. The article "Winning Money," by Emma Bradfor Berry emphasizes team approach to grant writing where the entire team shares the grant writing responsibilities. The article gives step by step directions on the processes needed to complete the grant process, and provides tips in writing grant proposals, putting the proposals together, and advice about following the specific guidelines, obtaining the appropriate signatures and meeting the proposal guidelines, as a team.

The American Library Association offers several tips for making a grant application:

1. Applications that have been thoroughly prepared stand out to reviewers;
2. Read the application carefully, and answer all questions directly and with as much details as possible;
3. Think beyond the boundaries of normal library operating procedures in completing the application;
4. Use statistics to describe your service area, your targeted audience, or any other part of the proposal;
5. Think through the answers to each question on the application;
6. Provide all signatures and attachments requested;

7. Pay close attention to your application's appearance (check spelling, run several drafts before the final copy is sent for approval); and

8. Read the original application carefully after you have completed your proposal to be sure you have answered all questions, and are submitting the attachments required, secure all signatures, and nake sure all other requirements are met.

USEFUL ORGANIZATIONS

- The National Society for Fundraising Executives (NSFRE)
- Association of Governing Boards of Universities and Colleges
- American Association of Fund-Raising Counsels (AAFRC)
- Clearinghouse for Research on Fund-Raising of the University of Maryland
- Counsel for the Advancement and Support of Education (CASE)
- National Association of Hospital Development (NAHD)
- Council of Foundations
- Friends of Libraries-USA (FOLUSA)
- *Philanthropic Monthly*
- *Foundation News*
- *Foundation Grant Index*. N.Y.: The Foundation Center (latest edition).
- *Boards*. Washington, D.C.: Association of Governing Boards of Universities and Colleges.

Good marketing, public relations and community awareness of your library and institution are essential elements that can help you with your fundraising and development plans. Therefore, the chapter on "Marketing" in this book is essential reading.

USEFUL ORGANIZATIONS WEBSITES

1. The National Society for Fundraising Executives (NSFRE)
   http://www.afpnet.org/
2. Association of Governing Boards of Universities and Colleges.
   http://agb.org/
3. American Association of Fund-Raising Counsels (AAFRC).
   http://www.aafrc.org/
4. Clearinghouse for Research on Fund-Raising of the University of Maryland
5. Counsel for the Advancement and Support of Education (CASE).
   http://www.case.org/
6. Council of Foundations. http://www.cof.org/

7.   *Finding the Sites and Resources for Fundraising & Grants*,
     http://librarysupportstaff.com/find$.html
8.   *Foundation Grants Index (annual).* N.Y.: The Foundation Center.
9.   Friends of Libraries USA <http://www.folusa.org/resources/fact-
     sheets.php>
10. Foundation News. Retrieved Jan 18, 2010,
     http://www.foundationnews.org/
11. The Foundation Center http://foundationcenter.org/findfunders/
12. Foundation Grant Index.
     http://library.dialog.com/bluesheets/html/bl0027.html
13. Friends of Libraries-USA (FOLUSA). www.folusa.org

APPENDIX A
PROPOSAL REVIEW GUIDELINES

The template below gives a good example of the type of questions proposal writers should keep in mind, and reviewers consider when evaluating research/grant proposals.

For each item, please check either the "Yes" or "?" columns, or write an explanation in the "No" column. Use "?" when you lack the information or expertise necessary to answer the question.

Question	Yes	No (explain)	
1: Proposal presentation and Technical Aspects			
Is the proposal clearly written and effective in communicating the author's intent?			
Is the proposal formatted according to the requirements?			
Is the timeline present, correctly presented, and appropriate?			
Is the budget present, correctly presented, and appropriate?			
Are all required elements of the narrative description present and correct?			
2: Research Topic and Questions			
Does the proposal clearly specify a research topic or problem?			
Does the proposal clearly define a research questions about that topic? (Note that the appropriate format for presentation of a research question will vary greatly according the methodology and disciplinary approach adopted).			
Does the proposal situate the proposed research within a well defined academic literature or body of theory?			
Does the proposal convincingly articulate the new contribution this research will make to important open questions within this literature?			

Question	Yes	No (explain)	
Is the research methodology adopted in the proposal appropriate to the questions posed in the proposal?			
Does the author show that he/she has sufficient grounding in the proposed research methodology to successfully carry out the proposed research?			
Does the proposed research fit within or built upon the applicant's current research agenda as described in the most recent annual merit review statement?			
3: Research Products and Follow up			
Does the proposal clearly define tangible products from the proposed research (book chapters, journal papers, conference presentations, etc)?			
Can the promised research products realistically be produced within the time and resource limits specified in the proposal?			
Does the proposal suggest plausible venues in which to disseminate these tangible products (association meetings, journals, book series, etc)?			
Has the author shown that the proposed activities and budgeted items will contribute directly to the production of the tangible research products?			
Has the author shown that the proposed research will serve as a foundation for subsequent work planned for the future?			
Has the author identified possible sources of external funding for future work building upon the current research proposal?			

REFERENCES

Abshire, Shirley I. 2002. "Grant Writing Made Easy," *School Library Journal,* p. 38-39.

Alexander, G. D. & Carlson, K. J. 2005. *Essential Principles for Fundraising Success: an Answer Manual for the Everyday Challenges of Raising Money.* San Francisco: Jossey-Bass.

Allen, B. 2003. "Public Opinion and the Funding of Public Libraries." *Library Trends* 51, no. 3: 414-423.

American Library Association. Public Programs Office. "Writing Grant Applications: Some Helpful Hints." http://www.ala.org (accessed Jan 10, 2010)

Bourke, C. 2007. "Public Libraries: Partnerships, Funding and Relevance." *Australasian Public Libraries and Information Services* 20, no. 3:135-9.

Burlingame, D. 1990. Library capital campaigns. *Journal of Library Administration* 12, no. 4: 89-101.

Camarena, Janet. 2000. A wealth of information on foundations and the grant seeking process, *Computers in Libraries* 20, no. 5: 26.

Canady, D. 2008. Libraries get creative, involve communities to raise funds. *Indiana Libraries 27, no.* 2: 76-77.

Carbone, R. T. 1989. *Fundraising as a profession.* College park: Clearing House for Research on Fundraising. University of Maryland.

Cassagne, S. 2005. Fund America's libraries. *Mississippi Libraries* 69, no. 2: 27.

Coffman, S. 2004. Saving ourselves: Plural funding for public libraries. *American Libraries* 35, no. 2: 37-39.

Corry, Emmett. 1981. *Grants for the smaller library: Sources of funding and proposal writing techniques for the small and medium-sized library.* Westport, Conn.: Libraries Unlimited,

Dewey, B. 2006. Fund-raising for large public university libraries: Margin for excellence. *Library Administration & Management* 20, no. 1: 5-12.

Donohue, W. 2006. For charity or profit? A case study of the friends of Ferguson library's used bookshop program. *Library Philosophy and Practice 9*, no. 1:1-30.

Dowlin, K. E. 2009. *Getting the Money: How to Succeed in Fundraising for Public and Nonprofit Libraries,* Westport, Conn.: Libraries Unlimited.

Eberhart, G., & Jordan, A. 2003. School libraries feel state funding losses. *American Libraries* 34, no. 1:17-18.

Evans, G.E. and Ward, P. L 2003. Beyond Basics: A Management Guide for Information Professionals. New York, N.Y.: Neal Schuman Publishers. Ch. 10

Foundation Grants Index 2004. (latest edition). N.Y.: The Foundation Center.

Franklin, P., & Stephens, C. 2008. Gaining skills to write winning grants. *School Library Media Activities Monthly* 25, no. 3: 43-44.

Herring, Mark Y 2004. *Raising Funds with Friends Group: A How To-Do-It for Libraries.* NY: Neal-Schuman Publishers.

Howe, Fisher 1991. *The Board Member's Guide to Fundraising.* Washington, D.C.: National Center for Non-Profit Boards.

Gerding, S. 2005. Innovative fund-raising opportunities for your library. *Public Libraries* 44, no. 4: 212-214.

Gerding, S. 2005. Library fund-raising and gift policies. *Public Libraries* 44, no. 5: 272-274.

Gerding, S. 2006. Library fund-raising success is just a wish away. *Public Libraries* 45, no. 2: 37-41.

Gerding, S. 2006. Writing successful library grant proposals. *Public Libraries* 45, no. 5: 31-33.

Gerding, S., & MacKellar, P. H. 2006. *Grants for Libraries: a How-To-Do-It Manual.* New York: Neal-Schuman Publishers.

Howe, F. 1991. *The Board Member's Guide to Fundraising.* Washington, D.C.: National Center for Non-Profit Boards.

James Swan, ed. 2002 *Fundraising for Libraries: 20 proven Ways To Get Money for Your Library.* NY: Neal Schuman.

Kerney, Carol A. 2995. "Inside the mind of a grant writer," *Technology & Learning* 25, no. 1:10536728

Kihlstedt, A. 2010. *Capital Campaigns: Strategies That Work* (3rd Ed.). Sudbury, Mass.: Jones and Bartlett Publishers.

Kivimaki, J. 1995. Denver public library--capital campaign. *Colorado Libraries*, 21:14-15.

Krummel, D. W., ed. 1980. *Organizing the Library's Support: Donors, Volunteers and Friends.* Urbana-Champaign, IL: University of Illinois, Graduate School of Library Science.

Lomax, Joanne, et all. 2000. *A Guide to Additional Sources of Funding and Revenue for Libraries and Archives,* 2nd ed. London: British Library.

Maxwell, D. Jackson. 2005. "Money, Money, Money: Taking the Pain out of grant Writing," *Teacher Librarian* 32, no. 3: 14811782

101+ Great Marketing and Fundraising Ideas for Libraries and Friends. 2004. N.Y.: Neal-Schuman.

Pearson, P., & Wilson, S. 2006. Libraries are from Venus, fund-raising is from Mars: development at the public library. *Library Administration & Management* 20, no. 1:19-25.

Perry, Emma Bradford 2000. "Winning Money," *Computers in Libraries* 20, no. 5:32

Pocock, J. W. 1989. *Fundraising Leadership: A Guide for College and University Boards.* Washington, D.C.: Association of Governing Boards of Universities and Colleges.

Price, L. 2008. Who does the library's fund-raising?. *Public Libraries* 47, no. 3: 34-37.

Reed, S. G., & Nawalinski, B. 2008. *Even More Great Ideas for Libraries and Friends,* New York: Neal-Schuman Publishers.

Rolen, R. 2009. Tips for witing grants. *Louisiana Libraries* 71, no. 3: 16-18.

Siess, J.A. 2003. *The Visible Librarian: Asserting Your Value with Marketing and Advocacy.* Chicago: ALA.

Steele, V. 2000. Becoming a Fundraiser: the Principles and Practice of Library Development, (2nd Ed.), Chicago: American Library Association.

Todaro, J. 2006. Community college library fund-raising. *Library Administration & Management* 20, no. 1: 13-18.

Zambare, A. 2004. The grant-writing process: A learning experience. *College & Research Libraries News* 65, no. 11: 673-676.

13

EVALUATION OF LIBRARY SERVICES AND PROGRAMS

The common advise "If it isn't broken, don't fix it" can be substituted with a better one that requires one not to wait for a crisis to make a change; adjustments big and small come a lot easier when not made in a pinch. Program evaluation could lead the way to evolutionary change. The simple definition of the term "evaluation" refers to the process of identifying and collecting data about specific services or activities, establishing criteria by which the success of those services or activities can be measured, and determining both the quality of the service or activity and the degree to which it accomplishes stated goals and objectives. Evaluation is different from assessment. The former focuses on a comparison with peer institutions, while the latter focuses on local improvement. However, assessment is a term commonly used in academic settings.

Evaluation is not new to librarians, as they have had a good record of collecting statistics and standardized datasets over time so that they can identify, monitor and respond to shifting patterns. Standards for library services have been published by professional associations, such as ALA, SLA, ACRL, and PLA. When evaluation was done by librarians in the past (Maurice Tauber and his contemporaries conducted many library surveys in the 1950s and 1960s; he taught a Library Surveys Seminar at Columbia University). These early surveys tended to concentrate on input measures, such as the size and quality of collections; efficiency criteria (time and motion studies), such as the number of items cataloged per day; the number of reference transactions completed per day; the cost effectiveness and advantages of conversion from DDC to LCC; and from manual to computerized systems.

Most major libraries, including university libraries have utilized a number of approaches during the last decade to assess the effectiveness of service programs for library users. Among the methods employed have been large-scale surveys of library users conducted every few years; focus groups; usability and observational studies; target surveys; comment cards; and the like. Interviews have been used to assess library programs and services as well as user needs. (Hernon & Dugan, p.131). Case studies became dominant in the seventies. The library literature contains many case reports—or "how I done it good in my library." (Mathews, 2007, p. 11). Today's libraries must consider effectiveness-related questions such as:

- Is this library performing activities and offering services that should be provided?
- Is library staff accomplishing organizational goals and objectives?
- How can staff ensure that they are providing *high quality* services and activities?

One of the traditional evaluation methods used by academic librarians is the self study report, in which several members of the administration sometime with the assistance of an experienced consultant review the library services and compare them to similar institutions and the Association of College & Research Libraries' (ACRL) *Standards*. These reports are usually a bi-product of preparation for regional and national accreditation which is a time-honored tradition that has contributed to making the American system of higher education the envy of most nations. Accreditation of colleges and universities have traditionally followed a process of evaluation that is strict and demanding to ensure quality control and continuous improvement in higher education. Onsite accreditation is usually administered about every five or six years on average and includes administrative, as well as user assessments. There are annual reports to be filed, and follow ups to be made as results of these onsite visits. By using a variety of methods and assessment tools, academic libraries are able to ascertain their strengths and weaknesses, and take active steps to remedy the weak points. Academic libraries have benefitted greatly from these accreditation processes.

Evaluation of academic libraries takes into account the ACRL *Standards for College and University Libraries*. The early ACRL *Standards* relied almost exclusively on inputs, outputs, and formulas to create what some believed were arbitrary baseline quantitative measures. The revised 2000 and subsequent standards incorporate outcomes assessment to determine the academic library effectiveness and quality. The new standards are less prescriptive; this allows for more subjective interpretation on the part of the institution and the regional associations and their review committees. Currently, when evaluating academic libraries, the ACRL looks at a number of characteristics such as: Planning, Assessment, Services, Instruction, Resources, Access, Staff, Facilities, Administration, and Budget. By examining these different aspects of the ACRL guidelines, academic libraries can compare themselves to other comparable institutions and use this information in support of the library's requests for additional support and expansion.

PURPOSE OF EVALUATION

Robbins and Zweizig (1988) point out that the purpose of evaluation "is to allow us to make better decisions about the library; to identify aspects that might be improved and functions that need to be speeded up or made less expensive." In other words, evaluation is part of the decision-making process and encourages organizational change to meet the high expectations of library users. In academic library settings, assessment seeks to document how libraries contribute to the learning process, and to the research enterprise. In academe, assessment also attempts to answer the question how does the library contribute to the research and scholarly production of the faculty? How does the library contribute to faculty teaching and to lifelong learning experience of students? Assessment objectives may differ from one type of library to the next. For example, unlike academic libraries, in special libraries, assessment will center on how the library contributes to the bottom line of the for-profit company, or for achieving the objectives of the not-for-profit organization. Comparison with other library evaluation reports can provide statements of good library practice, and they suggest ways to assess that practice in the context of the institution's priorities.

EVALUATION PROCESS

The evaluation process of today provides a method by which basic assumptions about the organization's activities and services can be assessed. The process identifies alternative strategies to improve these activities and services, and assists the organization in better meeting the information needs of its clientele. Evaluation could also lead to comparison with other libraries and that could garner headlines and attract public attention that could enhance accountability.

Both evaluation and assessment rely on planning documents and are part of strategic planning. As a process, evaluation is a systematic means that offers insights into the appropriateness, quality, or benefit of a service or activity. In this case, evaluation process becomes a catalyst for change—a tool that assists decision-makers in assessing organizational effectiveness and efficiency and in developing strategies to improve both in an organization. Higher education, just like business and government, faces rising demands for evaluation and accountability, and academic libraries are not exempt or immune from this process. With very tight academic budgets, many services and programs are no longer immune from the budget ax. Academic library users are now forming expectations based on their experiences in other competitive environments such as major bookstores chains, video rental stores, music stores, and Web search engines like Google. Evaluation has become both a research and political process for assessing programs, services, or activities. Results of evaluation should have practical consequences that lead to improvement in the delivery of services and the quality of the product provided to library users.

Accountability is important especially for publicly supported service organizations like libraries. Drucker (1973) suggests that service organizations like libraries should:

1. Answer the question, "what is our business and what should it be?"
2. Derive clear objectives and goals from their definition of function and mission;
3. Identify priorities of concentration that enable them to select targets, set deadlines and make someone accountable for results;
4. Define measurements of performance;
5. Build feedback from results into their systems;
6. Perform an audit of objectives and results to identify those objectives that no longer serve as useful purposes. (Drucker, 1973)

EVALUATION AS PART OF PLANNING

Taking the above steps into account, evaluation then becomes a part of larger organizational activities of planning and decision-making. Environmental factors and constraints, institutional missions and resource availability, and clientele information needs which influence specific library evaluation activities and procedures. Responsible librarians and information decision-makers must rely on information gained from the evaluation process to conclude which services and activities the library should support, what levels of resources support are necessary, and whether the offering of these services and activities successfully contribute to the overall effectiveness of the library.

Ongoing and regular evaluation of library services is a key and critical component for effective planning and decision-making to ensure efficiency and effectiveness of these programs and services. Understanding the relationship between planning and evaluation is essential for improving the effectiveness of a library. Planning and evaluation are two sides of the same coin.

EXPECTED OUTCOMES OF EVALUATION

"The role of evaluation is not to prove, but to improve"

As a result of the evaluation process, librarians can identify specific activities, questions, or areas appropriate for evaluation. To do so, they need to collect data that specifically assess the service or activity to be evaluated, and analyze the data in such a way that one can describe and compare the quality and performance of the service or activity against appropriate criteria. Library managers should then report and implement the results to change or improve that particular library service or activity. The evaluation of these operations and services should reflect value judgments about what the library or information center *should* be doing, *adequate* levels of performance, and criteria that describe *success* or organizational *effectiveness*. To engage in an ongoing evaluation process is to question what the library *should* be doing, develop methods to accomplish those objectives, and encourage constant change to occur. The availability of adequate staff time and organizational resources is essential for the successful completion of evaluation research.

CONSEQUENCES OF LACK OF EVALUATION

Absence of or ignoring evaluation can have consequences such as:
- Continuation of many library services and activities that are ineffective and/or inefficient;
- Failure to set priorities and improve poor services;
- Inability to support claims of services and activities that are deemed to be of high quality; and
- Limited understanding of the value of evaluation and how to achieve quality of service.

POSITIVE OUTCOMES OF EVALUATION

The following actions and products can benefit from evaluation:
- Making stronger case for library funding by demonstrating to governing bodies that the college library is not only essential, but effective;
- Possible improvement of library funding, or at least reducing the amount of budget reduction, especially in bad budget cycles;
- Knowing how things are;
- Improved customer-focused culture;
- How satisfied users are with library services and programs;
- Realizing the impact of library services on the community;
- Awareness of services, e.g. peer-to-peer library consultants, online book renewal;
- Laptops for students to use in a wireless library;
- Adding more e-resources;
- Improved access to collection;
- Implementing new services;
- Improving business hours;

- More friendly and welcoming and less policing environment and staff;
- Increased visibility and interaction with users;
- Improved knowledge of library services;
- Need to improve the marketing of library services;
- Improved access to electronic information;
- Introducing new services; and
- Promotion of "best practices" which document and highlight efficient and best practices in libraries.

SHIFTING PARADIGM OF ASSESSMENT

Part of the evaluation is to justify the amount of money academic libraries receive and provide evidence about the extent of the library's use. The shifting paradigm in assessment indicates that the amount of input does not predict quality. Furthermore, service quality is not based solely on the perception of the librarians who provide these services, but rather it is highly dependent on the perception of the users. It is increasingly important to make the case for library funding by demonstrating that academic libraries are, not only essential for teaching and research, but also effective. In this case, evaluation becomes part of accountability to determine the worth, merit, or value of the academic library. Joseph Mathews points out "attempting to determine the benefits or value of any library is a challenging position fraught with definitional problems about the type of benefits as well as trying to determine the magnitude of the economic impact (Mathews, 2007, p. 299). In academic libraries, we must reflect the trend in higher education where the emphasis has shifted from teaching to learning, including life-long learning as well as problem-based curricula. Furthermore, we must also attempt to answer the question "is the academic library—as we know it today in the form of brick and mortar essential—or could it substituted by something else, like a paperless, digital library or information depository (e-library) available to all on the Internet? Will academic governing boards continue to invest in building libraries of brick and mortar or find other alternatives?

EVALUATION AS PART OF PLANNING

Academic library managers should appreciate the relationship between planning and assessment and to appreciate the value and components of an evaluation and the different steps followed in evaluation. They should understand the importance of evaluation to library decision-making and develop an attitude that recognizes the importance of evaluation for the development of their library services, collections and programs. They should also search for good models and examples of evaluation processes that can guide them in conducting their own evaluations.

DETERMINING THE SCOPE OF EVALUATION

A first step in the evaluation process is to determine what will and will not be evaluated. Will the evaluation be internal or will an external focus be included and are customers involved in some manner? Perhaps both perspectives might be included in the evaluation. Some evaluation can be conducted by local staff, if time and expertise are available internally. If not, then national or international library consultants with expertise in evaluation and assessment can be contracted to conduct professional and expert evaluation. The American Library Association and its divisions are a good source to turn to for names of such consultants. Check with deans and directors of academic libraries who may have used such consultants recently and seek their recommendations.

Evaluation involves five key measurement concepts:

- *Extensiveness* or the amount of a service provided in relation to the population served. This criterion is generally a measure of quantity rather than quality;
- *Effectiveness* or the extent to which a service or activity accomplishes stated objectives. This criterion might also examine the extent to which a service satisfies the demands that users place on it;
- *Efficiency* or the appropriateness of resource allocation. This criterion might be judged in the context of stated objectives;
- *Cost-effectiveness*, or the accomplishment of objectives expressed in terms of costs;
- *Cost –benefit*, or the justification for the expense of providing a service or program in terms of the benefits derived from it.

Some of the activities that can be accomplished by the evaluation:

- *Appropriateness of organizational goals or program objectives*: In this case an attempt is made to answer how the library is addressing its mission or to justify why the library does what it does;
- *Objective accomplishment*: The use of evaluation is simply to determine the degree to which library services and activities accomplish the stated objectives for which either the activity or the service was established;
- *Appropriateness of resources allocation*: Typically resource categories include personnel, equipment, information resources and materials and supplies, space and time. This use of evaluation asks if resources were necessary to accomplish specific objectives, and if the library might

have used such resources elsewhere and thereby have generated a
larger impact. Such evaluation tends to be efficiency-oriented;

- *Monitoring and accountability*: This type of evaluation provides
  ongoing information about specific library program or service and can
  include both effectiveness and efficiency criteria. Such evaluation will
  determine the degree to which the service or activity can be justified to
  external funding agencies;

- *Impact assessment*: This type of evaluation reflects the extent to which
  a specific service or activity "made a difference" in terms of a
  predetermined set of criteria. For example, did the library instruction
  program increase the use of the library and its resources, improvement
  in student grades on their term papers, or other classroom
  assignments?;

- *Assess innovative programs*: This type of activity assesses unique or
  new service or activity that has not been done before or is presently
  done in an entirely new different way;

- *Fine tuning of library services and activities*: Fine tuning is necessary
  to maintain levels of performance and to make certain that the staff do
  all they can do to improve those performance levels; and

- *Program continuance or discontinuance*: This type of evaluation is
  typically summative, that is done at the end of the program with the
  expressed objective of collecting data that demonstrate whether or not
  that program should be either continued or discontinued. Either way
  data lend support to the resulting decision. Such evaluations are
  essential for activities and services that require significant resources
  and do not contribute to the accomplishment of organizational goals.

LEVELS OF EVALUATION

Evaluation research takes place at four primary levels of analysis:
- Organizational: this level of evaluation is concerned with changes that
  have occurred in a society or community as a result of regulations,
  legislation, cultural values, or economic, political or organizational
  factors;
- Programs: the evaluator is concerned about specific services and
  activities. Evaluation at this level is more straightforward than an
  evaluation on the *organizational* level. Because activities and services
  can be closely defined, variables better controlled, and the time for
  evaluation can be limited to one or two years; and
- Individuals: Evaluation of *individual performance* is better known as
  personnel evaluation. The purpose of such evaluation is to determine

the quality and quantity of work performed, offer guidance and strategies for how the individual can be more creative, productive, and effective, and assist the organization to better accomplish stated objectives in the future.

Broad questions to consider as a means of identifying areas for possible evaluation:

- Is there a problem?
- Is there existing data or other evidence that suggests performance or service problems in this particular area?
- Is existing performance decreasing or inadequate compared to previous performance in this particular area?
- Has the cost or allocation of other resources to this service or activity increased substantially in recent months, but no straightforward explanation is available?
- Have the institution, clientele, or other external factors changed and thereby necessitated a reassessment of the "appropriateness" of a service or activity?
- Can alternative approaches be considered to improve performance in a given area, and is there a need for some method or measure to compare these activities.

EVALUATION PLANNING TEAM

Well-planned evaluations can be conducted by qualified library science faculty supervising graduate students; independent library consultants; as part of accreditation visit, government, corporation or industry review. An evaluation "planning team" might take the form of a formalized group, a committee with rotating membership, or an assignment of one individual with responsibility for organizational planning and evaluation who enlists assistance from other individuals in the library as needed. Another approach is to establish "evaluation liaisons" throughout the various library departments. Inclusion of library users in the evaluation process can be also beneficial for the following reasons:

- First, users and potential users can provide a user's perspective on the service or activity;
- Second, they may be able to contribute external resources toward the evaluation that cannot be obtained within the organization;
- Third, their inclusion may provide political benefits-especially if such individuals are associated with the governance of the library, i.e. members of the campus-wide Library Committee, Alumni Organization, Friends of the Library, Board of Trustees, etc.

DEVELOPMENT OF STAFF EVALUATION SKILLS

Successful evaluation requires staff training on the evaluation process. Technical skills training refers to the ability of the staff to perform basic procedures related to evaluation (e.g. establish goals and objectives, collect and analyze data, write clear and concise reports, and demonstrate a host of interpersonal/group skills). Knowledge and understanding: refers to the ability of the staff to understand the conceptual basis of evaluation and how evaluation process relates to overall library effectiveness, to relate the various evaluation components one to another, and to modify those components as needed. Staff needs technical skills and knowledge if they are to participate successfully in the evaluation process. Staff development should be an ongoing process and occur throughout the evaluation process.

METHODS OF GATHERING INFORMATION FOR EVALUATION

There are two kinds of approaches for gathering information about library services: qualitative and quantitative analysis. The qualitative approach or evidence includes:

- Focus-group and interviews
- Exit interviews
- External interviews
- Directed conversations
- Observations
- Open letters
- Self-assessment

The quantitative methods include:

- General surveys
- Circulation figures
- Acquisition statistics
- Cost ratios
- Citation analysis
- Nationally developed surveys

Library surveys can provide information on the following:

- Who the users and potential users are;
- How and why the library is used? (or isn't used)
- What sources are used for library-related information?
- What faculty and students' library related needs are?
- How satisfied faculty and students are with the libraries?

- What are the best practices which can offer advice to libraries and information centers regarding how to develop or emulate strategies that are effective at the local level?

Evaluation relies on five components:

- Effective inquiry (identification and justification of a problem, conducting a literature search to place the problem in proper perspective, and formulation of a logical structure, objectives, hypotheses, and research questions);
- Adoption of appropriate procedures, i.e., research design and methodologies;
- Collection of data;
- Data analysis and interpretation;
- Presentation of findings, conclusions, and recommendations for future study.

LIBRARY ADAPTATION OF SERVQUAL

SERVQUAL was designed specifically for the for-profit sector where it remained an acknowledged industry standard. The SERVQUAL authors listed the following precursors of customer satisfaction:

- Past experience of the customer;
- Word of mouth from other customers;
- Personal needs of the customer; and
- National culture of the customer, which was later added for the LIS perspective since formation of expectations might be the national origins of the respondents.

From the service provider's point of view *communication* (direct and indirect) is about what the customer can be expecting. Factors related to *competitors* (other providers) can act as benchmarks. (Zeithaml & Parasurman,1990; Hernon & Altman, 1998). The 24 statements in SERVQUAL have been so thoroughly tested that their reliability and validity are well established.

LIBQUAL+ PROTOCOL

The SERVQUAL instrument was reintroduced within the research library community by the Texas A & M University Research Team to emerge as LibQUAL+ protocol. Web-based LibQUAL+ has been refined and now includes 22 survey questions providing information about three dimensions: affect of service; information control; and library as place. Eight additional questions deal with general satisfaction and information literacy, up to five local library questions, and some demographic questions, and there is an open-ended box for comments from the respondents. (Mathews, 2007, p. 265).

The goals of LibQUAL are to enable the libraries to:

- Foster a culture of excellence in providing library service to users;
- Help the libraries better understand user perceptions of the quality of library service;
- Collect and interpret library user feedback;
- Respond to user needs and expectations.

LibQual+ establishes four service quality dimensions:

- Access to information
- Affect of service
- Personal control
- Library as a place

The Web-based LibQUAL+ survey has been extensively documented in the literature as a viable well-researched and robust assessment mechanism for measuring perceived library service quality from a users' perspective. It also transcends a local campus survey. It is not expensive (less than $3,000) and saves time associated with staff time designing, developing, and printing of the survey.

LibQUAL+ attempts to identify and measure the gaps between expected service and perceived service. In this case, the customer or user is identified as the most critical voice in assessing service quality. As a consequence, we need to identify what connotes service quality in the minds of library users. LibQUAL+ represents the first national effort on the part of research libraries to focus directly on the voice of the customer; to move from the inward focus on inputs and production capability to outputs and outcomes. It has been designed and piloted in the spirit of sharing benchmarking information among cooperating libraries. LibQUAL+ also creates a new culture of cooperation by providing incentive to redefine relationships with the benchmarking partners. LibQUAL+ provides information that can lead to widespread improvement in research libraries nationally and internationally. LibQUAL+ enables us to learn from one another and share successful approaches. It also provides a connection with the combined set of customers that demonstrate a caring attitude, an expectation for feedback, a commitment to quality improvement, and a dedication to partnering in transforming the educational process.

Results from the LibQUAL+ surveys vary and could result in implementing recommendations such as making electronic resources accessible from home/office, better access to print and or electronic journal collections, longer opening hours and even 24/7 access.

GAP ANALYSIS THEORY

Disconfirmation theory, also known as gap analysis examines the difference between a customer's expectations and the customer's perceived sense of actual performance. It offers service providers a diagnostic tool to assess what is important to meet or exceed readers' expectations for quality service and a monitor of how well they do so (Nitecki, 1998, p.190). The emphasis is on customers' care.

The balanced scorecard is a new approach to strategic management. The balanced scorecard is a strategic planning and management system used in some organizations and institutions to align business activities to the vision and strategy of the organization, improve internal and external communications, and monitor organization performance against strategic goals.

BALANCED SCORECARD

The balanced scorecard is another method of evaluation which evolved from its early use as a simple performance measurement framework to a full strategic planning and management system. The "new" balanced scorecard transforms an organization's strategic plan from an attractive but passive document into the "marching orders" for the organization on a daily basis. It provides a framework that not only provides performance measurements, but helps planners identify what should be done and measured. It enables executives to truly execute their strategies. (The Balanced Scorecard Institute http://www.balancedscorecard.org).

EVIDENCE-BASED PRACTICE

The term evidence-based treatment (EBT) or empirically-supported treatment (EST) refers to preferential use of mental and behavioral health interventions for which systematic empirical research has provided evidence of statistically significant effectiveness as treatments for specific problems. In recent years, EBP has been stressed by professional organizations such as the American Psychological Association and the American Occupational Therapy Association, which have also strongly encouraged their members to carry out investigations to provide evidence supporting or rejecting the use of specific interventions. Pressure toward EBT has also come from public and private health insurance providers, which have sometimes refused coverage of practices lacking in systematic evidence of usefulness. (http://www.biomed.lib.umn.edu/learn/ebp/). Further information on the subject can be found in an article written by J. Eldredge (2000).

WHAT EVALUATION RESEARCH REVEALS

Evaluation research has revealed certain facts that can guide academic librarians in their decision-making. For example: circulation is not an accurate measure of total use, and the ratio of in-library-use to circulation varies greatly and should be studied locally (Mathews, 2007, p.138). While university administrators, governing boards and alumni have taken pride in the enormous sizes of their libraries collections and the edifices that house these millions of volumes, research has demonstrated that a small proportion of a collection receives the greatest proportion of use (Kent, 1980; Hardesty, 1988; Dinkins, 2003).

Despite the size of a library, building a "just-in-case" collection will result in a large proportion of the materials never being used. With the advent of online catalogs, online databases, e-book warehouses, giant search engines such as Google and other electronic resources, new methods of document delivery, and access to information, the role of the library as we know it today has begun to change. Automated systems installed in today's libraries allow for the easy and speedy analysis of circulation data for considerable periods of time. Library users do not have to be physically present in the library in order to access the library's resources.

With the Internet and the availability of new technologies and numerous indexes, abstracts, and databases, the range of services that academic libraries can provide has increased dramatically. Users can access the libraries' resources without stepping into the library building. They can also access other libraries' resources, such as online catalogs and unrestricted databases. The Internet has opened the resources of libraries to students and faculty worldwide.

Andaleeb and Simmonds (1998) identified several factors that influence user satisfaction—those factors included responsiveness, competence and assurance (which translated to demeanor), tangibles, and resources. The perceived quality of library resources is a key variable explaining the library usage. The findings also suggest that library usage is influenced by tangibles-a clean and visually appealing library.

As libraries and information centers begin seriously to assess how well they are anticipating, meeting and delighting their patrons, the primary focus should be on understanding customers' needs, learning quick and clean methods of data gathering and analysis, improving critical processes, and developing internal capacity to be successful in the future. To transform the work and how it is accomplished, libraries must begin listening and acting on the voices of customers, staff, work processes, and the organization for the purpose of learning new directions and partnering with customers.

When all is said and done, evaluation and assessment are the means to a desirable ending. There is no magical number of outcome measures to adopt or evidence to gather. The purpose of outcome assessments is to align the library better with its parent institution and to ensure that the library produces evidence supporting its impact on the communities it serves. Libraries should not just collect data related to inputs, outputs, and performance measures. They should document change in user behavior and in producing lifelong learners who are knowledgeable about digital and non-digital information literacy. Finally, the ultimate goal of assessment is to examine and enhance library's efficiency.

REFERENCES

ALA, ACRL. 2004, Jun 14. *Standards for College Libraries, 2000 edition.* American Library Association http://www.tamuk.edu/sacs/newsacs/pdfs/Mastdoc/other/ACRL.pdf   (accessed Jan 22, 2010)

Andaleeb, S., and Simmonds, P. 1998. "Explaining User Satisfaction with Academic Libraries: Strategic Implications." *College & Research Libraries* 59, no. 2:156-167.

Cronin, J. J. and Taylor, S. A. 1994. "SERVPERF versus SERVQUAL: Reconciling Performance-based and Perceptions Minus Exceptions of Service Quality," *Journal of Marketing,* 58(1): 125-131.

Dinkins, D. 2003. "Circulation as Assessment: Collection Development Policies Evaluated in Terms of Circulation at a Small Academic Library." *College & Research Libraries* 64, no. 1: 46-53.

Dugan, R., and Hernon, P. 2002. "Outcomes Assessment: Not Synonymous with Inputs and Outputs." *The Journal of Academic Librarianship* 28, no. 6: 376-380.

Drucker, P. 1973. "Managing the Service Institution." *The Interest* 33, (fall): 43-60.

Eldredge, J. 2000. "Evidence-based Librarianship: an Overview." *Bulletin of Medical Library Association*88, no. 4: 289-302 http://www.ncbi.nlm.nih.gov/pmc/articles/PMC35250/ (accessed Jan 22, 2010)

Griffiths, J., and King, D. 1993. *Special Libraries: Increasing the Information Edge.* Washington, DC: Special Libraries Association.

Grimes, D. J. 1998. *Academic Library Centrality: User Success through Service, Access, and Tradition.* Chicago: Association of College and Research Libraries.

Hardesty, L. 1988. "Use of Library Materials at a Small Liberal Arts College: a Replication." *Collection Management* 10, no. 3/4: 61-80.

Hernon, P., and Altman, E. 199). *Assessing Service Quality: Satisfying the Expectations of Library Customers.* Chicago: American Library Association.

Hernon, P., and Dugan, R. E. 2002. *An Action Plan for Outcomes Assessment in Your Library.* Chicago: American Library Association.

Heath, F. M., & et al., eds. 2004. *Libraries Act on Their LibQUAL Findings: from Data to Action.* Binghamton, NY: Haworth Information Press.

Hernon, P., and McLure, C. R. 1990. *Evaluation and Library Decision Making.* Norwood, NJ.: Ablex Pub.

Hernon, P., and Whitman, J. R. 2001. *Delivering Satisfaction and User Service Quality: a Customer-Based Approach for Libraries.* Chicago: American Library Association.

ISO 1998. *ISO 11620 Information and Documentation: Library Performance Indicators.* Geneva: International Organization for Standardization.

ISO 1999. *ISO 13407: Human Centered Design Processes for Interactive Systems.* Geneva: International Organization for Standardization.

Kent, A., et al. 1980. "A Commentary on 'Report on the Study of Library Use at Pitt by Professor Allen Ken, et al.' The Senate Committee, University of Pittsburgh, July 1969." *Library Acquisitions: Practice & Theory* 4, no. 1:87-99.

Kingdom of Saudi Arabia. Ministry of Higher Education. National Commission for Academic Accreditation and Assessment. 2006. *Quality benchmarks for postsecondary institutions: the National Qualifications Framework for the Kingdom of Saudi Arabia*. Riyadh, SA: Ministry of Higher Education.

————.2006. *Handbooks 1, 2 and 3 for Quality Assurance and Accreditation*. Riyadh, SA.

Mathews, J. R. 2008. *Scorecards for Results; A Guide for Developing a Library Balanced Scorecard*. Santa Barbara, CA: ABC-Clio

------------------2007. *The Evaluation and Measurement of Library Services*. Westport, CT: Libraries Unlimited.

------------------2007. *Library Assessment in Higher Education*. Westport, Conn: Libraries Unlimited.

Nelson, S. 2001. *The New Planning for Results: a Streamlined Approach*. Chicago: ALA.

Nickel, S. 2004. "An Adventure in Cooperation: The McNet Library Consortium." *Kentucky Libraries* 68, no. 1: 23-24.

Nelson, S., Altman, E., and Mayo, D. 2000. *Managing for Results: Effective Resource Allocation for Public Libraries*. Chicago: ALA.

Nitecki, D. A. 1999. Service Quality in Academic Libraries, in: *Encyclopedia of Library & Information Science*. New York: Marcel Dekker. Vol. 65, pp. 216-232.

---------------- 1998. "Assessment of Service Quality in Academic Libraries: Focus on the Applicability of the SERVQUAL," in: *Proceedings of the 2nd Northumbia International Conference on Performance Measurement in Libraries and Information Services*. New Castle-Upon-Tyne: University of Northumbia, pp. 181-196.

----------------1996. "Changing the Concept and Measure of Service Quality in Academic Libraries." *The Journal of Academic Librarianship* 22: 181-190.

Pung, C., Clarke, A., and Patten, L. 2004. "Measuring the Economic Impact of the British Library." *New Review of Academic Librarianship* 10, no. 1: 79-102.

Quinn, B. 1997. "Adapting Service Quality Concepts to Academic Libraries." *Journal of Academic Librarianship* 23, no. 5: 359-369.

Robbins, J. B., & Zweizig, D. 1988. *Are We There Yet? Evaluating Library Collections, Reference Services, Programs, and Personnel*. Madison, WI: University of Wisconsin-Madison. School of Library and Information Studies.

Robinson, S. 1999. "Measuring Service Quality: Current Thinking and Future Requirements." *Marketing Intelligence & Planning* 17, no. 1: 21-32.

Rossi, Peter, Mark Lipsey; Howard Freeman. 2004. *Evaluation: a Systematic Approach*. Thousand Oaks: Sage.

Rubin, R. J. 2006. *Demonstrating Results: Using Outcome Measurements in Your Library*. Chicago: ALA.

Southern Association of Colleges and Schools (SACS). http://www.sacs.org/ (accessed Jan 22, 2010)

Special Libraries Association. 2003. *Competencies for Information Professionals of the 21st Century*. rev. ed. New York: SLA.

Tenopir, C. 2003. "What User Studies Tell Us." *Library Journal* 128, no. 14:32.

Total Quality Management (TQM). Free Management Library http://managementhelp.org/quality/tqm/tqm.htm (accessed Jan 22, 2010)

Wall, T. 2002. "LibQUAL As a Transformative Experience." *Performance Measures and Metrics* 3, no. 2: 43-47.

Westbrook, L. 1989. *Quantitative Evaluation Methods for Reference Services: An Introductory Manual.* Washington, DC: Association for Research Libraries.

Wilson, F., and Town, J. S. 2006. "Benchmarking and Library Quality Maturity." *Performance Measurement and Metrics* 7, no. 2: 75-82.

Zenithal, V. A., Paraguayan, A. and Berry. L. L. 1990. *Delivering Quality service: Balancing Customer Perception and Expectation.* New York: Free Press.

INDEX